DARK PSYC

CW01082280

4 BOOKS IN 1

The Art of Persuasion. How to influence people. Hypnosis Techniques. NLP secrets. Analyze Body Language. Cognitive Behavioral Therapy and Emotional Intelligence 2.0

TABLE OF CONTENTS

3

5

7

11

15

including any legal fees potentially resulting from the application of any of the information provided by this book. This disclaimer applies to any loss, damages or injury caused by the use and application, whether directly or indirectly, of any advice or information presented, whether for breach of contract, tort, negligence, personal injury, criminal intent, or under any other cause of action. You agree to accept all risks of using the information presented in this book. You agree that by continuing to read this book, where appropriate and/or necessary, you shall consult a professional (including but not limited to your doctor, attorney, or financial advisor or such other advisor as needed) before using any of the suggested remedies, techniques, or information in this book.

17

Book Description

Have you been thinking of dark psychology and manipulation? Are you fed up of people manipulating you to get what they want? Do you use people? Would you like to master secret techniques to positively influence people?

Well, if this is you, then you have come to the right place.

One thing that is important to bear in mind is that dark psychology refers to the art of manipulating and controlling people's minds. Yes, psychology focuses on how we behave and it is central to our thoughts, interactions, and actions. On the other hand, however, dark psychology is about people using tactics of persuasion, motivation, coercion, and manipulation to get what they want.

Here, you will learn;

- The tenets of dark psychology
- Dark psychology triad
- Tactics used by everyday people to manipulate others
- Secret techniques of dark persuasion
- How you can positively influence people
- Mind games, hypnotism and brainwashing

There is so much to learn about the psychological nature people use to prey on others. The truth is that all of humanity has the potential to victimize others. Yes, some try to sublimate this tendency while others choose to act on their impulses. However, the most important thing for you is to understand your thoughts, perceptions, and feelings that lead to predatory behavior so that you can learn to control yourself and use it for good.

So, what are you still waiting for?

Come with me and let's discover more!

Introduction

You may be wondering what dark psychology is all about and where mind control comes from. In this book we will discuss what it is and why people can be manipulated and mentally controlled by psychopaths and narcissists. We will also shed some light on what you can do when that happens to you.

One thing that is important to note is that manipulation often happens in families with parents who have narcissistic tendencies. In cases where there is parental alienation, one of the parents may use their child as a psychological weapon to abuse the other parent. The truth is that mind control, a form of dark psychology, happens in a system where there are people – such as churches, families or workplaces.

The key ingredients of dark psychology are people, narcissistic leaders, lieutenants, scapegoats, and keeping secrets. What is not allowed in this kind of system is having a free spirit or free-thinking mentality. It is such kind of people who are banished from the community of manipulators.

Think about someone that joins a cult, what happens to them? The truth is that cult leaders prevent intelligent people from loving their friends and families in exchange for false promises. People who are manipulated tend to think that the decisions they make belong to them when, in fact, they belong to the manipulators.

It is important to note that human social interaction dynamics are powerful. Since time immemorial, people have been manipulated with false doctrines, propaganda, and social pressure. Have you read about Hitler? How did he manage to manipulate an entire country into hating specific groups of people?

It is the works of dark psychology!

If you are fighting to rescue yourself from someone else's mind control, then read on because you will learn how they do it and how you can rescue yourself from their mind games and undetected mind control.

But how can another person manipulate you?

Well, the first thing is that your manipulator will keep you in the dark so that you do not realize that you are being changed. In other words, they will try everything they can to psychologically lead you to a change of behavior just so that they can satisfy their selfish agendas. Their end goal is to have you do the bidding for them. Think about parental alienation, for instance – the end goal is to hurt the other targeted parent. In other cases, leaders manipulate masses to satisfy their personal need for control and power – and even the fulfillment of their fantasies. The second trick is that dark psychology sets out to control one's physical and social surroundings. In other words, mind control leaders offer others ample structure, assignments, and rules to keep others continually focused. The main aim is to ensure that they create a sense of powerlessness in the victims.

How do they do this?

They will make sure you are away from your social support network, and with people who are already entrenched in the group. This way, they can easily control your mind so that you lose personal autonomy, confidence, and power. They erode your intuitions, and as your powerlessness increases, your sense of understanding of the world and good judgment diminish. They attack your world view, and the outcome of which is cognitive dissonance, and you are not allowed to talk about it at all.

Dark psychology attempts to incorporate a reward and punishment system in the victim's life. In other words, they aim at promote the manipulator's agenda to undermine the autonomy and individuality of the target. The only time you get positive feedback is when you conform to the beliefs and behaviors of your leaders. Otherwise, you get negative feedback for choosing to hold on to your old beliefs and ways of life. Their aims when creating punishments, rewards, and experiences are to promote learning the ideologies of the group and their approved behaviors. In other words, this kind of leadership has a top-down pyramid structure where the leader never loses. What you must bear in mind is that people who are manipulated by users of dark psychological techniques are not valued because of their individuality. They are instead used as objects of the manipulator's productions, where the leader in the story is the author, director, producer, and playwright of their own story.

Read on to learn what dark psychology is and its benefits!

Chapter 1 What is Dark psychology?

"Dark Psychology is the study of the chasm within us all, which only a few enter, and even fewer ever exit. Without a natural predator to cause humans to rally, we prey upon one another."

– Michael Nuccitelli Psy.D.

Many people do not understand what dark psychology is all about. Well, the first thing you must note is that this is a field of study of the human condition, about the psychological nature of people that it is used to prey on others to manipulate them. Manipulators possess certain deviant drives that are characterized by a lack of purpose. That said, one thing you need to understand is that the entire human race has the potential to manipulate others into doing what they want. Some try to restrain themselves from manipulating others while most act on their impulses.

The main aim of dark psychology is to understand the feelings, thoughts, and perceptions of others, as well as the subjective systems that contribute to their predatory behaviors. According to dark psychology, the manipulator has a deviant and abusive behavior that causes them to intentionally take advantage of others to fulfill their rational and goal-oriented motivation at least 99.9 % of the time. The remainder 0.1% derives its argument from the Adlerian theory and Teleology.

In other words, dark psychology assumes that there is a region within the human mind that allows them to commit heinous acts without any reason. This theory has coined the dark singularity.

What is interesting about dark psychology is that it postulates that the entire human race has the intention to harm others in reserve. This desire to harm others goes from minimally obtrusive to pure thoughts of psychopathic behavior characterized by a lack of cohesive rationality – otherwise called the dark continuum.

The mitigating factors that serve as catalysts for the dark singularity and where one's actions are said to be heinous and fall under the dark continuum are called the dark factor. According to Michael Nuccitelli, *"Dark Psychology is not just the dark side of our moon, but the dark side of all moons combined."*

In other words, everything that makes us who we are is related to our dark side. Unfortunately, all cultures, humanity, and faith suffer from this proverbial cancer. From birth to the time of your departure – death – there is a side that lurks within each one of us – the evil side. This is the side that is deviant, criminal, and pathological.

"It is the individual who is not interested in his fellow men who has the greatest difficulties in life and provides the greatest injury to others. It is from among such individuals that all human failures spring."

– Alfred Adler

According to dark psychology, some people commit evil acts, not because of money, power, sex, retribution, or other known factors. Instead, they choose to do it because they are nasty – they have no goal. In other words, for them, ends do not justify the means. These are the kind of people who harm others just for the sake of doing it.

Within each one of us lies this potential!

You and I have the potential to harm others without any reason, purpose, or explanation. This potential is considered complex –even hard to define.

According to dark psychology, every human being has the potential for predatory behavior deep within them, a potential that has access to emotional feelings, thoughts, and perceptions. But the most important question is, do you act upon them? Think of a time when you felt like hurting someone not because they did you wrong but just because you wanted to. Did you act upon those feelings and thoughts?

If you are honest enough with yourself, then you will realize that you have had such thoughts and feelings of wanting to commit heinous acts. The only difference is whether you acted upon them or not.

Considering that each one of us consider ourselves to be benevolent, there is a belief that our thoughts and feelings would be non-existent. The truth is that we all have these thoughts but luckily we never have a chance to act on them. That said, others have similar thoughts and feelings and choose to act out on impulse or premeditation. The point is that human behavior related to their evil actions is goal-oriented and purposeful.

In short, dark psychology concerns itself with the human part that permits and drives predatory behaviors. Some of the features of this behavioral tendency include; lack of obvious rational motivation, lack of predictability, and universality. It is an extension of evolution. Well, let's look at this principle of evolution. Humans first evolved from animals and are currently the paradigm of all animal life. The frontal lobe of the brain allows us to become the apex of all creatures. However, being apex creatures does not necessarily mean that our primal instincts are to b predators.

"The greater the feeling of inferiority that has been experienced, the more powerful is the urge to conquest and the more violent the emotional agitation."

– Alfred Adler

If you subscribe to this kind of thinking, then you believe that all your behavior is based on three key instincts – aggression, sex, and instinctual drive to self-sustain. One thing you must bear in mind is that evolution follows the principles of survival of the fittest and reproduction. In other words, we live in the way that ensures our survival and to procreate. The reason we become aggressive is that we wish to mark our territories and ultimately win the right to reproduce.

It is our power of perception and thought that has contributed to our being apex creatures and of practicing brutality. Think of a nature documentary you have recently watched; you will realize that as the lion runs after the antelope, the author ensures that you feel sorry for the antelope as they are ripped into shreds. While this may be brutal and unfortunate, this model fits the idea of self-preservation. In other words, the lion kills the antelope for food – something they require for survival.

"Defiant individuals will always persecute others, yet they will always consider themselves persecuted."

– Alfred Adler

When animals are hunting, they will tend to stalk and kill their prey – mostly young, weak and female groups. While this type of behavior is psychopathic, the main reason why they choose this prey is to lower their chances of their own injury and death. All creatures act this way – brutal, violent, and bloody.

However, when we look at the human condition this tends to change, but only a little. Where are often the only creatures on earth who prey on each other and their reason is not survival or procreation? They do it for their inexplicable motivations. It is this part of the human psyche that dark psychology considers predatory behaviors. The assumption is that there is something intrapsychic that influences human actions – one that is anti-evolutionary. We are the only species that will kill each other for reasons other than food, survival, reproduction, or territory. In other words, we will harm one another with a complete lack of rational reasons because there is a part of us that fuels vicious and dark behaviors.

It is this dark side of humanity that is unpredictable and it is hard to understand why somebody acts on these evil impulses, and even carried to the extremes certain people will go on with their sense of mercy denied. This includes people who murder, rape, torture, or violate others for no reason. It is these actions that dark psychology speaks of as predators seeking out their human prey without a clearly defined purpose. Humans are incredibly dangerous to each other and themselves.

To fully grasp what dark psychology is all about, you must understand the following tenets;

Well, dark psychology is a **universal part of our human condition**. It is this construct that has exerted influence throughout history. Every creature, society, and person that resides in them maintain this human condition. Even the most benevolent of people know that they have an evil side on them, but the good thing is that they never act upon it – hence there are lower rates of violent emotional feelings, thoughts, and perceptions.

Dark psychology is a study of **the human condition in terms of their thoughts, perceptions, and emotional feelings.** All these are related to the innate human potential to inflict harm on others without a cause. Given the fact that all behaviors are goal-oriented, the truth is that the closer you get to the black hole of evil, the greater the chances that motivation will have a purpose.

The severity of dark psychology is **not considered less or more heinous through manipulation but plots a wider range of inhumanity**. Let us consider Ted Bundy and Jeffrey Dahmer – they both were severe psychopaths with heinous actions. However, the major difference between the two was that Dahmer committed his atrocious murders for the need for companionship while Ted sadistically caused others pain because of his psychopathic evil. In the range of the dark continuum, they both rank high, but Dahmer could be understood due to his desperate need for love.

There is the belief that we all have the potential to be violent. This potential is innate, and a wide range of internal and external factors increase the chance for this manifesting in volatile behaviors. The truth is that these behaviors are predatory, and sometimes they can happen for no reason. Humans are responsible for the distortion of the predator-prey dynamic. While violence and mayhem may exist in other creatures, humanity is the only species with the potential to harm without purpose.

With a better understanding of the causes and triggers of dark psychology, we are in a better position to recognize, diagnose, and reduce the risk of dangers inherent in our influence. When we all accept that there is the potential for evil in us, we are better able to reduce its chances of it occurring. Additionally, when we understand the principles of dark psychology, we will see how it fits our original evolutionary purpose for the struggle for survival.

Benefits of Knowing Your Dark Side

"I guess we're all two people. One in daylight, and the one we keep in the shade."

— Bruce Wayne

If you are honest about growing, changing, and living your life to the fullest, then you will come across parts of yourself that you will find rather disturbing – and yet you will have to accept. Aside from the bright nature, we know ourselves, there is a darker side of our nature – the ugly and frightening part. This is what we refer to in dark psychology as shadow-self.

One thing you must note is that your shadow self is always standing right behind you – just outside your view. When you stand in indirect light, you cast a shadow, right. The shadow is the part of yourself that you cannot really see. Think about it for a moment, how far do you go to just to protect your self-image from unfamiliarity and flattery?

Why is it easier to see another person's shadow but not see your own?

The truth is, when you see another person's shadow, you realize that one can show gifts in one area of life and remain unaware of their evil behaviors in other areas. Everyone is susceptible to this. Over the years, I have learned that working with my shadow has not only been a challenging process, but a rewarding one too. It is by looking at your darker side that you gain greater creativity, authenticity, personal awakening, and energy. It is this reflective process that contributes to your maturity.

You might be thinking, what is a shadow?

Well, this refers to the dark side of our personality. It is this side that involves negative emotions and impulses such as greed, rage, desire, selfishness, envy, and striving for power. Your dark side is primarily primitive.

What is it that you deny in yourself? Everything you perceive as evil, inferior, and unacceptable is what forms your shadow. If something is not compatible with your conscious attitude about yourself, this is your dark side. It is your disowned self – parts of yourself you no longer claim to be yours. These parts of ourselves do not go anywhere. Even though we try as much as we can to cast them out, the truth is that we cannot get rid of them. They remain as part of our unconscious.

Realize that you cannot eliminate your darker side. Instead, it stays with you as your darker brother or sister. When we fail to see our darker self, that is when problems arise. So, how is it born?

I want you to imagine a child – it could be yours or someone you know. Each time you look at the child playing with others, you see love, kindness, and generosity. But is that all you can see? Well, the truth is, you will also see greed, anger, and selfishness.

Just like them, we possess the light and dark side of ourselves. It is through these emotions that we all are shared humanity. However, as we grow, something else happens – traits linked with goodness are accepted, and those associated with bad are rejected.

Each one of us has basic needs – security, desire to belong, physiological, among others. These needs are either biological or instinctual. Like children, when we express one part of ourselves, you receive negative cues from your surroundings – anger and tantrums. Each time our parents reprimanded us for our outbursts, they sent us to our rooms, right? Our teachers might have shamed us for our lack of dignity in class. Whenever anything like this happened, it threatened one of your basic needs.

The truth is that when this happened, we changed our habits to meet our needs and learned to adapt to the world around us. In other words, when we are still children, the shadow self is bundled together and is swept out of view.

But what happens when you grow up? When do you finally meet your evil self?

Well, the truth is that when we ignore our shadow self, what we are simply doing is turning it against us. It is this shadow self that represents all the parts of yourself you have disowned. While our shadow self can operate on its own without our awareness – more like it is on autopilot – it causes us to do things we would not do voluntarily, and that is the reason behind regret. You find yourself saying things you wouldn't normally say. Your body language expresses emotions you would not consciously feel. In short, when you ignore your dark side, you end up damaging your relationships – with friends, spouse or family, among others. If there is anything I have learned over the years is that whatever qualities you deny in yourself, you will see them in others – a phenomenon referred to as projection. In other words, anything we deny in ourselves, we project it in others. For instance, when someone is rude to you, you get irritated. This is a good bet that you have not owned your rudeness. Well, this does not necessarily mean that the other person is not rude to you. However, if the rudeness was not on your dark side, someone being rude to you would not bother you one bit!

This is a process that does not happen consciously because we are not fully aware of our projections. Instead, our ego uses this mechanism for self-defense – defend its perception of self. Our false identities of "good" stand in the way of us connecting with our dark side. In other words, through projections, we distort reality and create a thick boundary between our perception of self and our behavior in reality. Just as Robert Johnson said, *if we don't work on ourselves, the shadow will always be projected. In other words, it is laid on another, just so that we don't take responsibility for it.*

So, what are the benefits of our dark side/shadow?

While our dark side is not something enjoyable to talk about, exploring it offers us an opportunity for growth and development, because let's face it – no one likes talking about their flaws, weaknesses, nastiness, selfishness, and hate, among others. Some of the benefits of knowing our dark side include;

Improved Relationship

As you gain insight into your darker side and come to terms with the fact that you have this dark half of you, you begin to see things with more clarity. It helps you remain grounded, whole, and human.

The truth is, when you accept the darker side of you, you make it easier for you to accept the darker sides of the people around you. This way, the behaviors and actions of others will not trigger you easily. Instead, it will make it easier for you to communicate with others effectively. As a result, you enjoy improved relationships – with friends, spouse, business partners, and family, among others.

Clearer Perception

When you see others and yourself exactly as you are, you view the world around you with a clearer lens. Integrating your shadow self into everyday activities helps you approach your true self, hence offering you a realistic evaluation of who you are. In other words, you will not perceive yourself as being too small, nor will you feel as though you have a higher moral ground than others.

Your self-awareness of the dark side greatly helps you assess your surroundings more accurately. This will allow you to see others and assess situations with more clarity, understanding, and an expression of compassion.

Enhanced Energy and Physical Health

One thing that is important to bear in mind is that dragging around the baggage of your darker side can be draining and exhausting. It is draining to constantly be working to repress some part of yourself that you do not wish to face in your adult life. When you are fatigued and lethargic, you risk poisoning your unexamined life. Mental suppression has also been shown to contribute to both disease and physical pain.

Knowing and acknowledging your dark side helps liberate the huge amount of energy you have been unconsciously investing in protecting yourself. As a result, you experience improved mental, physical, and emotional health. In other words, knowing and accepting your dark side will offer you inner strength and a sense of balance so that you are in better position to face life's challenges.

Psychological Integration and Maturity

As long as you try to deny your dark shadow or repress certain parts of yourself, unity and a sense of wholeness become elusive. There is no way you can feel whole and balanced when you have a divided mind. However, when you choose to integrate your shadow into what you do, you come one step closer to finding wholeness – and that is what helps you achieve maturity.

Greater Creativity

Knowing your dark side helps unlock your untapped creative potential. As Abraham Maslow and Carl Rogers once said, creativeness is a spontaneous occurrence that only people who are mentally healthy have.

So, how then can you engage your dark side so that you have the upper hand at approaching your shadows with ease?

Center Yourself

Perhaps this is the most important thing to do before you get into your dark side, and yet it is seldom mentioned in the literature. You might be thinking, "what will happen to me if I discover my dark side when I am not centered?"

Well, it's simple – you will not get a constructive result.

One thing you must note is that your shadow self represents various clusters of hidden parts within your psyche. It is only when you are at the center that you will get to know these parts. If one of the parts is blended with you, the process is hijacked, leaving you confused, judgmental, and critical. It will inhibit your ability to integrate your dark self. Before you get to work on your dark side, make sure that you are clear, calm, and neutral. That is what it means to be centered.

Cultivate Self-compassion

Before you get to know your dark side, you must cultivate a sense of friendship – unconditional one – with yourself, what is referred to as *Maitri* in Buddhism. Without friendship and compassion, it will be hard to look at your darkness.

Are you hard on yourself when making decisions?

If so, then realize that it will be challenging to you to face your darkness. If you are someone who easily feels guilty and ashamed, you must change these emotional feelings into self-acceptance, kindness and self-compassion. Start by acknowledging the fact that you are human. Understand that we all have a shadow.

The best way you can cultivate compassion is to start by connecting your heart. Place all your focus on your heart. Take in a deep breath and acknowledge your heart. As you breathe out, simply tell your heart, *"Thank you."*

Cultivate Self-awareness

To see your darkness, you must have a self-reflective mindset. In other words, you must have the ability to reflect on your thoughts, actions and emotions. By practicing mindfulness, you help foster non-judgmental awareness. You focus your thoughts and actions in the present moment without necessarily opening the door to the inner critic.

When you have self-awareness and -reflection, you can observe and evaluate your emotional feelings and choices without criticism.

Be Courageously Honest

The prerequisites for shadow work are integrity and honesty with yourself. It is easy to think superficially about these qualities, but what you must understand is that true honesty simply refers to a willingness to see unpleasant attributes in your behavior and personality.

Coming to terms with parts of yourself you would rather bury deep inside can be uncomfortable and that is probably the reason why the ego invests lots of energy repressing them. The ability to see all that and accept them just the way they are can be challenging. If you want to be honest with yourself, look at your dark behaviors, attitudes, emotions and thoughts – and that takes courage.

The reward of doing this plays a significant role in healing divisions in your mind. It also helps unlock untapped potential and a world of new possibilities for your growth and development.

Record Your Discoveries

It is quite fascinating to see that most of our disowned parts wish to remain out of our sight. Just the same way a dream slips out of our mind soon after we wake up, the darkness in us can be elusive.

You must keep a journal where you record every discovery about yourself. When you write down your insights and then take time to review them later, you help encode those discoverings into your consciousness.

Chapter 2 Dark Psychology Triad

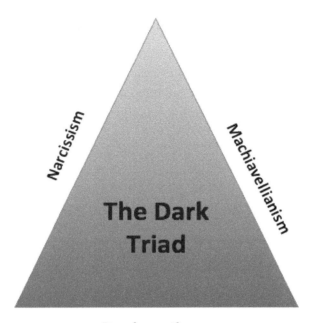

Psychopathy

So many people argue that the dark triad people are so seductive. Thus, the most critical question we must ask ourselves is why.

The truth is, the Dark triad has three personality traits; narcissism, Machiavellianism, and psychopathy. The term *Narcissism* is derived from the Greek myth of Narcissus - a hunter who fell in love with his reflections when swimming in a pool. In other words, narcissists are people who are not only selfish but also boastful, arrogant, hypersensitive to criticism, and lacks empathy.

Machiavellianism is a word that was coined from the Italian politician and diplomat Niccolo Machiavelli, 16th century. This man earned notoriety when his book *"The Prince"* was interpreted as an endorsement to dark arts – cunning and deceit in diplomacy. Some of the traits associated with this kind of personality include manipulation, duplicity, a lack of morality and emotion, and self-interest.

Psychopathy, on the other hand, includes a lack of remorse and empathy, being volatile and manipulative or others, and showing antisocial behavior. One thing you must note is that there is a difference between psychopathic qualities and being a psychopath, and this lies in the commonly held link with criminal violence.

In fact, this is one of the most researched areas in psychology. While this has contributed a great deal to a deeper understanding of the darker side of humanity, how far we differ from each other as we constantly exhibit darkness - darkness in thoughts, emotions, and behaviors in our everyday life, and the question we fail to ask ourselves is what lies on the light side of humanity.

The truth is, socially aversive people exist. But what of everyday saints? Don't get me wrong – I am not talking about the person that gives a lot and receives public applauds and awards for their giving just so that they can gain personal success. I am referring to that one person who just by *being*, they shine their light so bright that it radiates in all directions. The one person who is not strategic about their generosity but that emits unconditional love – both spontaneously and naturally – because that is what they *truly* are.

According to the study, three distinct features characterize the light triad; Kantianism, humanism, and faith in humanity. Kantianism simply refers to using people as ends for themselves and not just as mere means. Humanism, on the other hand, is valuing the worth and dignity of everyone. Faith in humanity is about believing in the fundamental goodness of human beings.

One thing you must understand is that the light and dark triads are not opposites of each other. Yes, they are negatively related to each other, but the truth is that the relationship is only moderate, which supports the idea that each person has a little bit of light and darkness in them. While some score high in the dark triad, it is best not regard them as lesser beings – after all, to have the dark side is to be human. Instead, it is important to view them as magnified and unleashed versions of the potential that lies within them.

According to a research study, the dark triad is associated with being younger, male, motivated by power, achievement, affiliation, and instrumental sex. They are the kind of people who have self-improvement values, conspicuous consumption, immature defense styles, selfishness, and perceive creative work and immortality as a path to transcend death. The dark triad is negatively correlated to such traits as kindness, life satisfaction, compassion, a quiet ego, empathy, conscientiousness and a strong belief that human beings are good.

Let us bring this closer home – think of an employee at your workplace who seems to derive pleasure from bothering others or even sabotaging the company. This kind of person does not feel remorse. They tell blatant lies when caught doing something unacceptable. These are the kind of people who can be called the "Dark Triad." When someone shows evil behavior, it is highly likely that you will see these three traits – narcissism, Machiavellianism, and psychopathy.

Let us dig deeper into each of these features. When do you say that someone is narcissistic, Machiavellian, or psychopathic?

Well, Narcissism is about having a complete focus on yourself. It is about believing that you are special and that you should follow a different set of societal rules than others. You are also known for your inability to show empathy. While these kinds of people may show cognitive empathy – empathy only through words – the truth is that empathy lacks in their actions and emotional feelings. When they tell you "I am sorry ABC happened," what they mean to say is that they don't feel any sadness, remorse, or real feelings to show of it. They tend to do things just to look good and not because they feel like it is the right thing to do.

Machiavellianism is about someone using exploitation and manipulations of others to gain control or to maintain power over others. The thing with Machiavellian people is that they have a rather cynical perception of what morality is. They think that the reason people follow morals is that they are not smart enough to figure out how to circumvent them. They are so focused on what is in it for them and how to con others so that they can make the most of the situation.

When you think of a psychopath, the first thing that comes to mind is selfishness, impulsive behavior, lack of remorse, and breaking the law. While there are people who cannot seem to decipher social norms, rules, and regulations, a psychopath knows the difference between right and wrong, but does not seem to care at all.

Interestingly, all these three dark triad qualities are genetic. Yes, the surroundings play a significant role in the development of these personality traits, but the truth is that they are more likely that you inherited them from your genes, making you more predisposed. That said, this does not mean that genetics is destiny. The truth is you can have a genotype for a certain trait, but that does not translate into a phenotype. For instance, you may have a gene for blue and brown eyes, but the phenotype is brown eyes.

Additionally, everyone has certain features of Machiavellianism, narcissism, and psychopathy at some point in their lives. The good thing is that most people can recognize these behaviors and realize that they do not work well in their professional and personal lives.

When you are not aware that these traits are negatively impacting your life and that they are pervasive, only then it can be consider a disorder!

It is important to note that these three Dark Triad factors produce different outcomes in the workplace and in personal life – depending on how low or high you are on each one. High Machiavellianism and psychopathy indicate a high likelihood of low performance at the workplace. Yes, a lack of quality in work performance means that you are not achieving a certain baseline, being counterproductive might mean that you are overachieving but in the wrong way.

The truth is you are using hard tactics one way or the other when manipulating others – common among Machiavellians and psychopaths. Narcissists, on the other hand, tend to employ soft tactics to exploit others so that they can eventually get what they want. The difference between hard and soft tactics is that hard tactics include threatening others or sabotaging work. Soft tactics, on the contrary, are about giving compliments and gifts to influence people into giving you what you want.

Take a step back in your life and think about these three Dark triad factors – are you possibly encouraging one or more of these traits without realizing it? Or are you doing them knowingly just so you can get what you want?

What can you do to ensure that your dark side does not take control of your light side?

Chapter 3 Manipulation

The art of manipulation is not really about influencing people into doing what you want them to. Instead, it is about getting them to want to do what you want them to do. The most important question here is, "how do you get people to want to do what you want them to do?"

Well, the first trick is to learn their true desires and then reverse engineer it towards the goal you wish to accomplish. One thing you must bear in mind is that the closer you are to a person, the easier it is for you to manipulate them. If you want to test your manipulation skills, the first person to do this with is your romantic partner.

Think of manipulation as persuasion.

The truth is, you must be willing to persuade people and make them feel like it was their choice all along. Generally, men seek perfectionism while women see wholeness. You may be thinking, "what does this mean?" the truth is that men are easily persuaded by dominance and an ego linked to improvement. When you display uncertainty on whether or not he can improve, you are simply teasing his ego in such a gentle way it that contributes to progress.

On the other hand, women seek balance in various areas of life – especially in relationships with family and friends. Therefore, when you suffocate time, you stir up a burning desire to balance. The truth is, we all need balance, sacrifice, and focus in life. According to statistics, women tend to lean more towards balance, while men lead more towards perfectionism.

Amid persuasion tactics, you must not disobey the law of cognitive bias – otherwise referred to as the liking and loving tendency. For instance, if Adolf Hitler says that 1+1=2 and Steve Harvey says 1+1=3, even though we hate Hitler so much, we have to accept that he is right and Harvey – loved by many – is wrong. That said, however, most people will tend to believe Steve Harvey because of association bias. In other words, most people associate him with positive things.

You must be careful about what others feel and how you make them feel because remember Maya Angelou's saying, *"I've learned that people will forget what you said, people will forget what you did, but people will never forget how you made them feel."*

Interestingly, most people would like to manipulate others for a short time. What they fail to realize is that the true art of manipulation is in the long run. Take into account that patience is a virtue you must exercise when you try to persuade others, so that it feels and flows effortlessly. The truth is that it takes time to specifically overcome your mental barriers and get into the right mindset.

I have learned over the years that one thing that mentally hurts manipulators is a failure to understand the process and then going with nature. Think of a rock rolling down the hill – is there someone forcing it down? No! Because it is the force of gravity that is pulling it down. Instead of trying to go against the force of nature, let it go down.

When it rains the only way we adapt is by putting on a jacket and getting an umbrella. When it is hot you wear light clothing and shield your eyes with sunglasses. The point is - try as much as you can not to be delusional, and allow yourself to adjust to what it is. There are two major ways you can test delusion – doing things in the wrong order still means the wrong thing (also referred to as mis-prioritization.) or setting expectations of the outcome by putting in the wrong input. With people, you must learn their personality type, how they react to different surroundings, and their boundaries.

Here's the point – the mental frameworks are out of the way. ???One way you are going to get them to do the things you want is to lead with a reward. People love it when they feel like it is their choice, and that triggers the release of dopamine – otherwise known as the reward. They want to know how the thing you are telling them to do is going to benefit them.

The trick is not to tell them to do it directly. According to research, at least 90% of the time people hate being told what to do. The best thing to do is to help them arrive to the same conclusion following their own path. The most rewarding thing is them knowing that it was their idea – when, in fact, it was yours. Therefore, you must let them own the idea. The toughest part is attaching that reward to the thing because if they don't understand how something benefits them, there is a high likelihood that they will never do it.

Once you manage to successfully manipulate others, you must not expose yourself because this goes against the tendency to like and love, causing people to cut you off –and that is the last thing you want. You must be aware of how you make them feel and try to persuade them for better and not for worse.

Techniques Used By Manipulators to Gain Control

Psychopaths are not the villains we watch in movies or read about in morality tales – they are real and they walk among us at home and offices looking like normal colleagues. According to one study, at least 3-4% of business leaders are psychopaths. The same thing applies to narcissists. Science has shown some evidence that a little bit of narcissism goes a long way to having business success.

As you go about your daily business, there is a chance that you will meet a few truly toxic narcissists and psychopaths who will try to manipulate you in one way of another. You must understand how such people can manipulate others. Here are a few techniques;

Gaslighting

This is a manipulative technique that can be described in various ways. These include three key phrases;

- That did not just happen
- You imagined it
- Are you insane?

Well, gaslighting is one of the most common and insidious manipulation tactics, because its aim is to distort and erode people's sense of reality. In other words, it eats away your ability to trust yourself, inevitably preventing you from seeing the justification for calling out your abuser.

How can you then fight back?

The best thing you can do is to ground yourself to reality. One of the ways you can do this is to take the time and write down exactly what happened, talk to a friend, or reiterate your experience to a support system that can help you counter the effects of gas lighters.

Projection

Think about it – have you ever met someone so toxic that claims that all the mess that surrounds them is totally your fault and not theirs?

Well, that tactic is referred to as projection.

Well, the truth is that we have all done this to somebody at some point in our lives. But the difference between us and narcissists or psychopaths is that they do it a lot. They simply use projection as a defense mechanism to displace the responsibility of their negative behaviors and qualities, by ensuring that they attribute all of it to another person.

What is then the solution?

Well, it is very simple – try as much as you can not to project your empathy or sense of compassion onto a toxic individual. Also, you must not own any of the projections of the toxic person. When you project your conscience and value system onto others, this has a potential result of being met with more exploitation.

Generalizations

Let us consider the case when you tell a coworker that they sometimes fail to consider long-term ramifications of their financial decisions. Then they go ahead and they tell everyone that you called them "a loose cannon." You realize that this might blow up on you if several conditions come in to play. Your psychopath of a colleague goes to the boss and tells them that you said the deal is a "wreck."

 What is going on?

Well, the truth is that your nemesis not only did not understand you, but they also had no interest in understanding you.

One thing you must note is that malignant narcissists are not intellectual masterminds. Most of them are intellectually lazy. Instead of taking the time to consider the point of view of other people they choose to generalize everything you say by making a blanket statement that does not consider the nuances of your argument. They choose not to consider your different perspectives.

To counter this, you must hold onto your truth and resist the urge to generalize things. They realize than they are instead a form of black and white illogical thinking.

Moving Goalposts

This is a logical fallacy that abusive psychopaths and narcissists use to make sure they have every reason to be perpetually dissatisfied with you. Even though you offer them all the needed evidence to validate your argument or meet their requests, they will set up another expectation and demand proof.

You must avoid playing such a game. You are the only one that needs to validate and approve yourself. You are enough, and the last thing you want is to let someone make you constantly feel small, deficient, and unworthy.

Changing the Subject

When you are discussing something, and someone keeps changing the subject, it sounds innocent enough. However, in the hands of a manipulator changing the subject is one way to avoid responsibility. A narcissist does not want you to stay on the topic because the last thing they want is you holding them accountable for something. In that case, they will find ways to divert the discussion to benefit them.

If you are not careful, this sort of thing can go on forever. It can make it impossible to engage in a relevant issue. The best way to counter this is to the user the "broken record technique" when fighting back. In other words, you must keep stating the facts without allowing yourself to give in to distractions.

Every time they redirect the conversation, you must redirect their redirection by saying something like "That is not what I am talking about – and you know it. Let is stay focused on the real issue here. If you are not interested in this, then you can choose to disengage and spend your time and energy on something a little more constructive."

Name-calling

Each one of us has been called names at some point in our lives. We have been dealing with this long enough, but that does not make it any less destructive. Trust me, this might have started from the time you were in kindergarten, but it goes all the way to presidential politics!

Even if you have encountered bullies since childhood, you must not tolerate it. End any interaction that involves name-calling and tell your manipulator that you will not tolerate this. Don't even try to take it all in – as most people do. Realize that the reason they resort to name-calling is that they are lacking and are trying to distract you from what matters.

Smear Campaigns

When a toxic person cannot control the way you perceive yourself, they choose to control how others see you. In other words, they resort to playing the martyr, so that everyone around you labels you the toxic one. This is a smear campaign that only looks to ensure them that your reputation is tarnished and your name is smeared.

Note that at times true evil geniuses will choose to divide and conquer – by pitting two or more people against each other.

The last thing you want is to allow them to succeed. You must record all forms of harassment and ensure that you don't take the bait. Do not allow their evilness to lower yourself to their level and behave just like them.

Devaluation

Consider the case where you have been just appointed the unit manager in your organization. Suddenly, one of your colleagues starts aggressively denigrating the former manager who held your position. Have you experienced this kind of manipulation?

If not, then you know the kind of person you need to beware of. Narcissists do this kind of things all the time. They will devalue your former boss to you (the new boss). They will devalue their ex to their new partner. Eventually, you start to get the same kind of mistreatment as the narcissist's ex-partner or boss. This is not just for those in the professional fields; it also applies to our personal lives.

The very first step to countering this is by raising your awareness of this phenomenon. Keep in mind that the way someone treats or speaks of another is potentially the same way they treat or speak about you in private or in the future. Be cautious!

Aggressive Jokers

The issue is not your sense of humor but the hidden intention of that joke. You will hear a covert narcissist make malicious remarks at your expense. These remarks come in the form of jokes so that they get away with saying bad things to you, maintain their innocent and cool demeanor. When you raise eyebrows at the kind of insensitivity they have, they accuse you of having no sense of humor.

They will try to convince everyone around that they were just making innocent jokes – even when they know damn right they were not!

Triangulation

One smart way toxic people manipulate you and distract you from their nastiness is to focus your attention on someone else's supposed threat. This is what we refer to as triangulation. In other words, they report back false information about what another person said. To resist this kind of tactic, you must realize that the third-party in all this drama is being manipulated.

The best trick is to reverse that triangulation or gain support from the other person who is not under the influence of the narcissist.

But does manipulation always have to be negative?

Of course not!

The truth is that manipulation can also be used in a good way. For instance, you can persuade someone to take a vacation or do something that will help them get that promotion they have always worked hard for. These are some of the manipulation techniques you can use to benefit you more;

Using Body Language to Your Advantage

It is important to note that how the brain uses physical movements and reactions each day is almost uncontrollable. It is this kind of movement that can make several people around you to think about what it means. In other words, people can read your body language to try and understand things you couldn't possibly say with words. It is the best way to influence people with more than just words.

According to research, 90% of communication is nonverbal. This simply means that this much of our interactions can just be lost because we sought for promotion with our arms crossed and looking at the floor.

Mastering the art of body language goes a long way in helping one to correctly convey the desired message. If you take time to read another's body language, you will be in a better position to know whether they really agree with you, actively engage in the conversation, or are just taking you for a complete idiot.

When you persistently perceive the body language of those around you, you stand a chance of improving your abilities as well as identifying opportunities and dead ends in every interaction. Doing things such as gestures, mimicking postures and movements can help someone to like you, or to agree with what you have to say.

Often, we see people nodding their heads not because they agree with what it is being said, but when they disagree and cannot understand why the person is speaking or even thinking this way. That said, when you nod your head when you mean to disagree, then you are setting yourself up. When someone is questioning you, they will regularly pay attention to your body language to determine if you are guilty.

The truth is that we are all animals, and we all behave this way when we are completely stripped of our sophisticated means of communication. The trick is when someone is trying to manipulate you, you can use this subconscious interaction to your advantage. For instance, you can speak with your arms open to create a sense of trust. You can also shake hands palms down to communicate dominance and up to communicate submission. If you are laughing in a group of people, the very first person you make eye contact with is the person you trust most – use that to your advantage.

Change Your Perspective

You must cover the reality of your manipulators with the type of reality you have created. In other words, to change their points of view, go to the matrix on their minds. It is all about tact, cunning abilities, and, importantly, being rhetorical.

For instance, you can say something like, "this home is a real fixer-upper – imagine the potential!"

The point is for you to turn the half-empty glass to the side of your manipulator. The truth is, perspective can make a whole difference in how someone looks at something. Your description can influence the perspective itself. Being rhetorical, in a way, underlies this notion because it encompasses several aspects beyond what was said and how

DARK PSYCHOLOGY 4 IN

it was said in the first place. It is the content, tone, and appeal to emotion, character, and reason. You can be rhetorical when you want to persuade. You can also use exaggeration when trying to be practical, or a shift of focus where you deem it necessary.

The point is for you to put thought into every argument you make – its structure and presentation. It does not matter whether it appeals to the other person's emotion or reason; the point is that you think twice about it. Ask yourself whether you sound like you know what you are talking about – even when you don't have an idea. If you cannot convince someone to stop cutting down trees for environmental reasons, can you do it with a logical argument on how more trees mean more life?

Think outside the box and use that to reframe your perspective on a given situation. This will serve you better and build efficacy of how your argument comes forward. Think about it, when you convince yourself that you had a good night's sleep, you trick the mind into thinking it too. Use the Dunning Kruger effect where smart people underestimate themselves while ignorant people think that they are brilliant.

Leverage Your Knowledge of Others

One thing you must note is that you can depend on others psychological needs and use them as your pressure points. It might come as a need for conformity, acceptance, or inclusion – or it might just be the complete opposite – to stand out and swim against the current. If you are a risky decision maker, then you might end up making a poor choice. If you are a quiet crowd dweller, there is a chance that you will be discouraged from going after anything that might lead you astray.

What you must bear in mind is that other people's weaknesses are your strengths. All you need is to figure out how you can use all that to your advantage. Look at these people carefully, study them. Are they overconfident? Can that cause them to stumble? Do you think they feel insecure about something? Can you use that to make a convincing point?

The truth is, each one of us has kryptonite!

The more you study about psychological tendencies, thinking, and traits of others, the more you are at an advantage of gaining control over their thoughts. The key here is knowledge. Just like any other point we have made, it is also important that you gain an in-depth understanding and mastery of your pressure points. Your strong defense comes from acknowledging your insecurities and vulnerabilities.

Always bear in mind that their vision is the product of an emotional foundation. That no matter how they try to justify their position, they hold it for emotional reasons. If you want people to move in your direction, you must discover the emotional value driving their vision – their G-spot. Once you know this sweet spot, only then can you design an approach that matches their needs with yours so that at the end of the day everyone can feel successful.

Beware of Good Timing and Opportunity

Think of the jaguar – effective and calculated, right? The biological ability of great timing gives them their ancestral legacy of success and failure. The jaguar knows precisely when to strike, jump or abort its chase altogether.

My point is, you need to know when to make your moves. From a young age we have learned that timing is everything – you know when to ask your dad and mom for a gift they should get you on your birthday or Christmas. The most important thing is for you to stay aware of these things and keep your eyes open for opportunities round the clock. When someone is worried and tired, that might just be the time to ask them for certain favors. This way, they will put in the energy to refuse or disagree with you.

That said, try not to force opportunities. Instead, it is better if you welcome them with open arms and eyes. If you have been laying low for the right time to throw a pitch at your boss, don't force the conversation too early. You may have to wait several weeks before you have a good chance, and once you do, don't blow it. When you meet someone with a proposal, their mood will determine whether the battle has already been won or lost – at least in half.

The truth is the wonders of psychology are endless. With manipulation, you are just scratching the surface. If you don't mind picking up on other people's impulses, put the situation in your favor. An awareness of body language you exercise and what others are sending you will help open your eyes to maximize your exchanges in life.

Chapter 4 Undetected Mind Control

Much of an individual's communication is not based solely on what they actively trying to say. A much larger and much more active chunk of our communication is based on what we don't realize that we are saying to the world. Our bodies can reveal our deepest emotions and feelings without us realizing pretty much, twenty-four seven. This does not happen randomly, of course. The way that our mind communicates without us realizing is based on two main theories of thought – referred to as the unconscious mind and the limbic brain.

Unconscious Mind

The unconscious mind comes from Freud's Psychoanalytic Theory of Personality. They usually include feelings of pain, anxiety, or conflict. It is because of these negative feelings and emotions that our unconscious minds remain outside of our conscious awareness. Since on a subconscious level we do not want to remember or feel those feelings, we then try to ignore them and push them into our unconscious mind.

Despite this attempt at ignoring and hiding these feelings, our unconscious mind still influences our behavior even though we do not know that it is there. Many individuals compare the unconscious mind to an iceberg. The part above the water represents our conscious brain and all of the communication of ideas and feelings that we actively put out into the world.

Our unconscious mind is represented by the iceberg below and not seen. Following this iceberg analogy, it is important to remember how large an iceberg below the water truly is. This represents just how deep our unconscious mind goes and just how much tends to be hidden below the surface. The amount of information that is hidden just below the surface - within our unconscious mind - is massive. It is like the hidden part of the iceberg in the sense that we have to consider the parts of our body language that connect to our unconscious mind as a huge part of nonverbal communication.

Freud also believed and stated that our basic instincts and animal drives are contained within the unconscious mind. This includes instincts under actions of life and death as well as sexual instincts. He believed urges such as these were hidden from or pushed out of our present consciousness because our minds view them as unacceptable, irrational, or uncivilized. Freud suggested that individuals often use several different defense mechanisms to stop these hidden urges from rising above the water into our conscious mind.

Freud also goes on to explain the different ways that the information from the unconscious mind can be brought into consciousness. One of the techniques that Freud explained can be used to bring these feelings into consciousness is known as free association. Free association is a rather simple and seemingly silly form of psychotherapy. In free association, Freud asked patients to lay back and relax and say to him whatever came to their minds without any sort of filter. He wanted them to say anything that they could think of without stopping to think of it was trivial, irrelevant, or embarrassing. Later on, Freud followed the streams of thoughts until he believed that he could uncover the contents of the unconscious mind. He often used this method to try to find repressed childhood traumas or hidden desires.

Freud also believed that dream interpretation could be used to better understand the unconscious mind. Many people think of dreams as a route to the unconscious mind and believe that the information from the unconscious mind could appear randomly in dreams but typically in a disguised format. Because of this, he often asked patients to keep dream diaries and tried to read and interpret these dreams to try and understand their hidden meanings.

Freud also believed that dreams tended to serve as a form of secret fulfillment of long-indulged wishes. He believed that the fact that these unconscious urges were not expressed in real life meant they could be expressed in the individual's dreams.

The Freudian theory of the unconscious mind did not come across without controversy. Many researchers have criticized the idea of the unconscious mind and firmly dispute that there is no unconscious mind at all. Recently, in the field of cognitive psychology, researchers and psychologists have begun to focus on the automatic and intuitive functions that describe things that were previously being attributed to the unconscious mind. The idea behind this approach is a belief that a series of cognitive functions happen outside of our conscious awareness.

Meanwhile, they do not entirely support the conceptualization of the voice of the unconscious mind. However, it offers some evidence that actions that we are not aware of still influence our automatic behaviors. Unlike Freud's psychoanalytic approaches to the unconscious mind, research in the modern field of cognitive psychology is almost exclusively driven by scientific investigation and quantitative data. This idea of the unconscious mind continues to have a great effect on modern psychology and is still used in some modern practices today.

Limbic Brain System

The limbic system within an individual's brain is responsible for a variety of very important brain functions. The biggest responsibility of the limbic system is our instincts for survival and memory access and storage. The limbic system is made up of many different brain structures—two of the biggest and most important parts of the limbic system are the amygdala and the hippocampus. Amygdala is the deciding structure that chooses where each memory should be placed in the brain, while the hippocampus transports that memory to its final location. It is often believed that the amount of emotional response determines the placement that it receives from the person.

The limbic system is also very responsible for hormone levels, body temperature, and motor functions. The limbic brain system is composed of the amygdala, cingulate gyrus, hippocampus, and hypothalamus. These individual structures are very important parts of a person's brain. The limbic system, as a whole, is located on top of the brainstem and underneath the frontal cortex. The limbic system is often connected to survival-based emotions such as fear, anger, and pleasure. The limbic system is also known to influence both the peripheral nervous system and the endocrine system.

The part of the limbic system that is important to this text, in particular, is its connection with memory. Because of the perceived importance of the limbic system in the decisions about where memories go and how they are remembered, it is often connected to Freud's ideas about the unconscious mind. Freud's ideas of the unconscious mind are based on the theory that certain memories and feelings are hidden far away from our consciousness. It is easy to understand how the limbic system can play a role in that, considering that it is the deciding factor of where memories are stored.

You might think, "What does any of this have to do with our body language and understanding the body language of those around us?"

The answer lies in the fact that the unconscious mind is very powerful and controls a huge portion of our true feelings and emotions. By reading body language, we can often unlock these feelings of the unconscious mind without even realizing that they are hidden from the person we are reading. This is a very powerful skill, and it is important to understand the basis behind it. The limbic system and the unconscious mind create this foundation for the deeper readings of people.

The Process of Mind Control

A mind controller approaches the victim with the sole intent of cloning themselves, making the other person to think like them. This is a complicated thing to do, so, to achieve it, one has to possess an inflated ego, lack any self-doubt and have a high sense of entitlement. All of us are susceptible to manipulation, and what matters is how much effect the mind control will have on us.

Psychologists studying mind control have found out that the entire process seems to adhere to a common structure. This conclusion was made after a study was conducted on multiple marketing and networking companies which used mind control to persuade clients to purchase their products.

One of the outstanding similarities is that all new members joining the companies underwent a pre-planned training on how to recruit more people and convince potential customers to buy their products. The training sessions are meant to make the employees think like the company wants and use a form of mind twist to convince people.

Let us now look at the mind control process in detail.

Step 1 – Understanding the Target

Before anything else, the manipulator will seek to establish a bond or connection with their potential victim. Good intention, or friendship, will be the first step because it makes the victim lower all their social and psychological defenses. Once the controller gains the trust of the target, they now start reading them to devise the most effective method to invade them. The reading aims to tell whether their victim is susceptible to their manipulation. Just like any project manager, they do not like wasting time on a subject they suspect might outsmart them and lead to failure.

Multiple clues are used to scan the victim. They include verbal style, body language, social status, gender, emotional stability, and so on. A person's traits can be used to decode the strength of their defenses.

All this time, the manipulator will be asking themselves questions like, "Are you introvert or extrovert?" "Are you weak?" "Are you emotional?" "Are you self-confident?"

Humans give a lot of information about themselves when interacting with each other, and this is something that the controller knows all too well. From these signs, they can easily tell if the person is cooperating. They will look at body posture and immediately analyze the victim. Excess blinking might mention that a person is lying. Arms folded across the chest might show a lack of interest or insecurity. Taking large strides while walking might portray fear. As you can see, the body releases so much data at any given time that it is important to be aware of the signs that you are giving out (this will be covered in detail later in this book).

When the attacker has collected enough data from the target, they now understand their interests, strengths, weaknesses, routines, and so on. Using this information, they can decide on an entry point, which will allow for easy and accurate manipulation. They also decide whether the target is worth the effort. If they see one as a favorable target, they move to the next step in the mind control process- unfreezing solid beliefs and values.

Step 2- Unfreezing Solid Beliefs and Values

Each one of us has some beliefs and values engraved deep within. Most of them are the principles that were instilled in us since childhood, and others have been acquired from experiences are we grow older. We rarely let go of them but revise them as we proceed. Most of them are what make up our identities, so we do not like them being interfered with. If, at any point in time, these principles are threatened, contradicted, or questioned, our natural reaction is to defend them through all means possible. However, if a good-enough reason is given to us, we voluntarily question them ourselves; we undergo a process known as "unfreezing."

Tons of reasons can lead us to unfreeze: a breakup, the death of a loved one, religious interference, getting evicted from our houses, to mention but a few. These situations force us to start seeking answers to complex situations, and this goes as deep as questioning our unique beliefs and values. Take this, for example:

When I was a teenager, we had some family friends who were solid Christians. It so happened that my best friend, who was my exact age, came from this family. His name was Matthew. Matthew used to tell me about the Bible and its teachings, trying to convince me to accept salvation and live according to its teachings.

I remember asking him why he was so insistent on this issue, and he would answer that with salvation all problems could be solved and that life was much easier and happier. Fast-forward about fifteen years, Matthew's mother was diagnosed with breast cancer. They tried all forms of treatment available at the time, but cancer would grow back. One day, while talking to him about the issue, he looked at me with a pale face and said, "I think what they say about Christianity is not real!" Unsure about what he had just said, I asked him why he thought so. He responded that they had met tens of spiritual leaders for prayers, but his mother's cancer was only getting worse. What's worse, she would not live for more than a year.

Sad as this story is, it makes us realize that some situations in life might force us to question the strong principles that we grow up with. In this case, my best friend had come to doubt the very same religion that he once felt had automatic solutions to all of life's problems. In the very same manner, a manipulator will dig deep into their victim's life to understand their vulnerabilities and fully exploit them. These people will say anything they think their targets would love to hear. Once the victim swallows the manipulator's comfort, there is a shift in power dynamics, and the target is now ready for manipulation.

Step 3 – Reprogramming the Mind

The mind control process seeks to separate the target from their initial beliefs and begin reprogramming their mind. Reprogramming is meant to install the manipulator's beliefs and values into the victim's mind. Apart from distancing the initial principles, the controller also tries their best to make them look wrong or bad, or the cause of past mishaps in the victim's life. If the victim absorbs this reprogramming, their defenses are reduced to zero. They end up as robots that are ready to accept any operating system that is offered.

During the reprogramming phase, the attacker will try to ensure the victim has minimal contact with the outside world. They make everyone else seem insignificant to the victim because this raises their opportunity to deposit their malicious principles into them. This behavior is common in cults, which are mostly crafted to divert their followers from mainstream human life.

Some cults go as far as controlling the food intake of their followers as a way to weaken them. The psychology behind this idea is that a weak person will always turn to the person they feel has the power to protect them or alleviate their suffering. The same happens in relationships, where one partner plays the controlling role, and the victimized one has no choice but to adhere to the other.

You might wonder why some people put up with violent partners, but so far, from reading this book, you must already understand that the problem is deeper than it looks like. If you control a person's mind, you can control their lives.

Once the victim has been re-programmed, the manipulator moves into the final phase of the mind control process known as "freezing."

Step 4 – Freezing the New Beliefs and Values

Do you remember the "unfreezing" process we discussed earlier? So, once the victim has been fed with contrasting principles by the offender, the offender applies tactics aimed at cementing these new beliefs into their brains. This is what psychologists call "freezing." The freezing is necessary because the controller is aware that the person's new beliefs that might clash with their initial ones. As such, they need to force the victim to choose their malicious principles over their previous ones. To do this, they might apply any of the following methods.

One of the methods is using the reward/punishment approach. When the victim acts according to the manipulator's demands, they are rewarded. Hopefully, you see the similarity between the freezing process and dog training. The dog is given treats when it follows the trainer's instructions.

The trainer aims at solidifying the new skill in the dog by rewarding it. In the future, if the dog is instructed to do the same thing, it will not hesitate since it has been made to think that obeying the command is good and attracts a reward. The same applies to mind control; when the victim obeys, they are made to feel that what they did was right and deserves a reward.

Punishments are the second most-applied approach in the freezing process. If the victim deviates from the controller's commands, they are punished. If we go back to the scenario of a cult, they usually have defined punishments for violations of terms.

During the Holocaust, for instance, any Germans who failed to hail Hitler were punished with imprisonment or even death. In the same way, any German who was suspected of protecting the Jews was shot.

Hitler understood that by punishing anyone who went against his rules, he would force every German to help him attain his objective of ethnic cleansing. The psychological trick used in these situations is that the victim is made to see punishment as justice being served for breaking the rules.

The final method used by mind controllers to solidify their manipulation is to transform their victims into their agents. Better put, once the controller feels that the victim's pseudo personality has materialized, they use them to distribute their visions of the world.

Once the controlling process is complete, the victim begins to live like the attacker without realizing it. Depending on the nature of the manipulation, the victim might also be used to recruit more victims into the oppressor's way of thinking and living. This is especially true in the context of marketing and networking, which we shall discuss under the topic of deception.

All this explains why a wife is likely to be violent towards the kids if the husband is violent. The kids are also likely to be violent towards each other or their friends. The process of mind control is slow, but once it solidifies, it can result in devastating effects.

The Relationship Between Mind Control and Emotional Influence

The interaction between mind control and emotional influence is clear. Mind control is general in the sense that the oppressor controls the victim's freedom of choice and actions. When it comes to emotional influence, the attack is more specific as it focuses on the feelings. All the same, the consequences of both interferences are that they eventually snatch independence from the victim and place them at the oppressor's mercy. Therefore, we can conclude that emotional influence and mind controls are the same; only that one is specific while the other is broader.

Types of Mind Control

Just to reiterate, mind control is an umbrella term that houses different forms of control. In short, different types of controls might be applied to the victim. The oppressor determines the choice of control. In the definitions of the types of mind control, you will see clear pillars, as we have discussed in this chapter. There are five major forms of mind control studied under dark psychology.

They include:

Hypnosis: The process of malicious interaction where the controller used mind tricks to make the victim accept their recommendations or change the way they react to their surroundings.

Manipulation: A type of social influence through which a person can influence someone else's perception or behavior using dishonest tactics.

Deception: The Process of propagating beliefs in things and events using partial or complete lies.

Persuasion: A form of control that aims at influencing the beliefs, attitudes, motivations, and behaviors of the victim.

Brainwashing: The process of consciously convincing a person to abandon beliefs they have long held and to manipulate them to take up new ones.

Since this is a vast topic that we cannot cover in a single book, we shall focus on only two of these types of mind control: manipulation and deception. In the following chapters, you will understand what is deception and manipulation, as well as the techniques used to promote them. As you gain insight into the way these forms of mind control work, you will also learn how to spot manipulators and overcome their actions.

One of the driving forces is that out of the five types of mind control, deception, and manipulation are the ones that can be applied in everyday scenarios. These scenarios can range from relationships to normal conversations, advertisements, and religious beliefs. You need to acknowledge that mind control does not have to force a person to change major aspects of their lives, such as their personality.

Control can be used in minimal scenarios, such as being persuaded to buy a pair of shoes at the local store or to vote for someone who would ideally not be your favorite candidate.

Also, these two forms of mind control can be applied by the people that are closest to you. Therefore, it is important to understand the most basic level where you can get manipulated and keep yourself safe. If this has convinced you, though I promise it is not mind control, let us move ahead and discuss deception.

Chapter 5 Hypnotism

"Brains aren't designed to get results; they go in directions. If you know how the brain works, you can set your directions. If you don't, then someone else will."

-Richard Bandler

Hypnosis is pretty easy to understand if you know how it works. Of course, it takes practice to master hypnotizing others; however, simply understanding how it works is very useful in being able to observe dark psychology and manipulation in practice.

Hypnosis tends to be misunderstood as a parlor trick that requires someone to be asleep or in a nearly asleep state to become hypnotized. Then, when they are under the spell of hypnosis, they can be made to cluck like a chicken or bark like a dog or repeat any number of embarrassing phrases for a cheap laugh. Hypnosis happens every day because all hypnosis means is that someone has entered into an altered state or a trance state.

Every day we enter into trance. All it takes to enter a trance state is to affix your attention on one thing so intently that some or all of your peripheral consciousness can be shut out. Most people, for instance, enter a hypnotic state every day at work or zoning out while on the subway.

Hypnosis can be a potent tool to get people to compromise their critical faculties, and it ties into what we have been talking about so far in terms of polarization and eliciting the desired response from someone.

Stages of Hypnosis

Stage 1: Absorb Attention

The first step into altering someone's conscious state (hypnosis) is grabbing hold of their full attention. Believe it or not, there are verbal and non-verbal forms of this first stage of hypnosis. Take, for example, the situation mentioned above in which a person can be so zoned in at work that everything around them sort of just fades away.

This is a prime example of the way that our psychological states are changed when we are intently focused on something and of non-verbal hypnosis.

Of course, gaining someone's complete attention can be a bit easier if you are using words. People tend to cling more fully to someone's words when they are describing images or telling a story. It is a lot like how some people prefer visual learning over textual learning. The human mind can follow along better when pictures and mental images are involved because their visual sense is engaged.

You can practice this first stage of absorbing attention in everyday speech. Go out with a friend or coworker and see how much more they pay attention to you when you say you have a story for them. Tell them a story, either true or made up, and be sure to include a lot of details. Paint the picture with your words, use a lot of adjectives to describe the scene. The more senses you can engage, the better. Give their mind and imagination something to engage with.

When you have them wrapped up in your story, you have successfully absorbed their attention, leading to the second stage of hypnosis:

Stage 2: Bypass the Critical Faculty

The conscious mind is a rather limited entity. It takes in the data that you get every day, and processes it rationally. The unconscious mind, on the other hand, is a lot more unpredictable. It does not get bogged down with matters of reality. Consider, for example, that your unconscious mind is active when you dream. You may have never seen a purple flying turtle in real life, but your unconscious mind is free to consider such things as completely real and viable.

The conscious mind deals with what is feasible. In hypnosis, this is what is known as the critical faculty. Think of the critical faculty as a gate keeper to the subconscious mind. The critical faculty is what alerts your mind to things that are impossible, unreasonable, and unlikely. If you are attempting to hypnotize someone, the critical faculty is the enemy of hypnosis. The point of hypnosis is transferring a person's mind from a fully conscious state to an unconscious or at least an altered state, and critical faculties make it impossible for this change to occur, so it must be bypassed.

Bypassing critical faculties can be achieved by first absorbing the full attention of a person using simple techniques such as maintaining intent eye-contact with the subject and speaking a little slower and in a low tone than you normal.

Speaking in a hypnotic tone can go a long way in inciting a trance state and bypassing the critical faculty. If you are hypnotizing someone, you want to watch out for signs that your subject is in a trance state. Most importantly, do not give any hypnotic suggestions until you are certain you are past the critical faculty, and your subject is in a trance state. Otherwise, your suggestion will be rejected by the critical faculty.

Step 3: Activate an Unconscious Response

Triggering an unconscious response does not have to be as extreme as getting a person to cluck like a chicken. It can be as subtle as provoking a laugh or making someone clap their hands to their mouth in shock. An unconscious response is an action carried out that a person is not aware of or is only aware of after the action has been made. In other words, it is a response that has not been regulated by the conscious mind.

Prompting an unconscious response is very easy when a person has entered a hypnotic state. Look for dilated pupils, a change in breathing rate or flushing of the skin. These are all signs that your subject has let their critical faculty guard down and have been taken into a hypnotic state.

Once you see this, try getting an unconscious response; maybe describe in vivid detail a delicious steak dinner so that their stomachs growl in hunger or a swarm of bugs overtaking someone's body so that their skin crawls with goosebumps.

Stage 4: Lead to Your Desired Outcome

This is the point where you, the hypnotist, can lead the subject towards the desired outcome through hypnotic suggestion or associated metaphors. This stage of hypnotism is all about speaking directly to the unconscious mind and taking advantage of the altered state to either help the person or to lead them to a conclusion, result or decision that is favorable for you.

One example of this stage is called priming. Say, for example, that you want to go swimming and you want the subject to go swimming with you. Try telling them a story involving cool, cascading, and refreshing water that beats an oppressive heat. This could lead to a post-hypnotic reaction that has been geared towards your desired outcome.

Pattern Interrupts & Rapid Induction Techniques

The concept of pattern interrupts very simply. Consider each word individually: the first word in the phrase being "pattern." A pattern can be anything you do mindlessly or routinely. Getting up in the morning, brushing your teeth and taking a shower is likely something you do every day that you don't even really think about. This is an example of a pattern. A pattern can also be called a routine. Getting in your car and driving to work can be considered a routine.

Now consider the second word in the phrase: "interrupt." An interrupt in this context is anything that breaks your normal routines or patterns. Interrupts are conscious efforts to change the way you do things, the way you think or the way you act.

The major difference between the two words – the two concepts of "pattern" and "interrupt" – is that one involves an unconscious or passive state of mind, and the other involves a very conscious and active state of mind.

Pattern interrupts are often used in behavioral psychology and NLP to help people break harmful habits and routines in their lives. Routines often give us a sense of drive and purpose. Still, they can be detrimental when we get so used to them that we switch off our brains while doing them, thereby becoming vulnerable to hypnotic suggestion and manipulation.

The average human has about 50,000 thoughts per day, but the majority of these are repeat thoughts. Pattern interrupts are very effective ways to induce new thoughts, which helps the brain develop their ability to think critically. It is the difference between letting your brain atrophy and exercising it.

To get back to basics, consider pattern interrupts as a way to alter yours or someone else's mental state from a conscious to an unconscious mode. This is precisely why patterns can be used for hypnosis and NLP.

In particular, the pattern can be very useful for rapid hypnotic induction or to get someone very quickly into a hypnotic state. This may be because of a slight disconnect in a person's mind when a pattern interrupt is used on them. The switch from passive to active brain function isn't seamless. There is a lapse in which the unconscious and conscious mind blend for a brief time, and it is then that a person enters a hypnotic state and is susceptible to suggestion.

Consider it a state of confusion that a person enters for a brief time when one of their patterns or thought processes is abruptly interrupted. Confusion tactics are very common and potent methods of rapid hypnotic induction.

Remember the example of polarization we went over in the first chapter? Pattern interrupts and confusion are akin to polarization in the sense that both are used to get someone into a frame of mind where their reactions can be predicted and manipulated.

Getting someone angry about a certain subject is similar to putting someone into a confused state when their routine has suddenly been broken. It is in this state that a skilled hypnotist can implant unconscious suggestions and therefore predict a certain outcome.

Pattern interrupt techniques have become very popular in hypnosis and manipulation because they are fairly simple to perform and they can be done in virtually any setting, and sometimes without the person even realizing it. It happens in an instant and you get the desired results in an instant, which is why it has become such a widely used tool to hypnotize and manipulate people.

The most popular method of pattern interrupts hypnotic induction is the handshake technique. In this technique the hypnotist will go in for the very mundane act of shaking someone's hand. At the last second, before the hand's touch, one person abruptly disengages from the handshake and grabs the other person by the wrist.

Getting up and getting ready for work is a routine that could take hours, and shaking hands with someone only takes a few seconds, but both are patterns and both can be broken, and when they are, the mind enters an altered state.

This altered state is the goal of pattern interrupts and why they are such a powerful tool for inducing hypnotic trances.

Using Pattern Interrupt to Induce Hypnosis

Going back again to a concept discussed in the previous chapter, attention absorbing is akin to pattern interrupts for inducing hypnosis. Pattern interrupts are just another means of grabbing someone's full attention, and it can be argued that hypnosis is nothing but getting someone to be fully present in the moment.

The goal of the hypnotist is not to knock someone out or make someone unconscious. It is to heighten their sense of consciousness through the full absorption of attention. The reason pattern interrupts are so useful in getting an individual's full attention (therefore leaving them vulnerable to hypnotic suggestion) is that when someone's train of thoughts is instantly broken, the mind is frantically looking for a logical explanation for the interrupt.

It can be as easy as interrupting someone mid-sentence. Let's say you get your friend telling you a story about a run-in they had at a grocery store or a confrontation they had with someone that bumped into them on the street. Try interrupting them in the middle of the story with an unrelated phrase, "I have always wondered what makes the moon so silvery."

Your friend was fully engaged in his or her story, and they may have even been on auto-pilot if it was a story they have told multiple times before. When you interrupted them with your statement about the moon, you broke their thought process. Now, you have their undivided attention.

This leaves them in a vulnerable state of hypnotic suggestion because they are now hanging on your every word in a desperate attempt to get answers. And where will these answers come from? You, of course. It is at this very moment that hypnotists can implant their hypnotic suggestions that can have nothing to do with what the person was talking or thinking about.

This works because when the brain is engaged in a pattern, it is fully engaged in carrying out the pattern to its logical conclusion. When the pattern is skillfully broken, the brain immediately recoils and either is looking for a new pattern or trying to fulfill the old pattern.

Imagine a person walking through a winding hallway and imagine that you can turn the lights out in the corridor and make it completely dark. When you turn the lights out, the person can't see a thing and has no reliable way to navigate this winding hall. They are looking to turn the lights back on and be on their way again. Then, you turn the lights back on, and they can see.

The vulnerable state of a person is when they are in the dark in search of light. They are similar to what the brain experiences when its thought process is disrupted. It is looking to turn the lights back on so that it can get back on track with the pattern.

Now let's say you don't turn the lights on until you have noticed that the person traversing this corridor has completely turned themselves around in a frantic search for a light switch. They do not notice that they are now facing the opposite direction that they were walking in and start walking in the wrong direction.

This is essentially the concept of implanting a hypnotic suggestion when you have successfully broken the mental pattern of an individual. You get their minds going in a different direction than it was before, just like you confused the person in the corridor with darkness to the point that they start walking the wrong way. The path the person was walking was the pattern, and the darkness in this example is the pattern interrupt.

This is how a skilled hypnotist can control the way a person speaks after they have been inducted with a pattern interrupt.

Hypnotists use pattern interruptions to get minds going in a certain direction. Let's say, for example, your spouse asks you, "Can you hand me the frying pan?" and you answer "Yes" but don't hand it to them. You have simply broken the path their mind was headed, and they are wondering about the unusual response to a mundane question.

You have your spouse's undivided attention now and suppose you continue by saying, "Settle. You don't have to fry anything for what we are eating tonight."

The first word in that phrase, "settle," was a hypnotic command similar to the cliché "sleep" or "relax," and it set the tone for the rest of the hypnotic suggestion. This is just one of the hundreds ways that hypnotists can induce a hypnotic state through pattern interrupts.

Not only can pattern interrupts be deployed virtually anywhere and in any situation, but they can be used for psychological manipulation. You have probably been the subject or at least seen a psychological manipulation in action using pattern interrupts. They occur all the time without anyone realizing it.

There is an extremely simple way to manipulate people that pretty much anyone can do, but even this base tactic is an example of successful psychological manipulation through pattern interruption. Picture a situation in which your wife is deep in thought about what to make for dinner. You want chicken but you have no idea what she has in mind. Suddenly showing her a coupon in the paper or a particularly enticing video online for a chicken recipe can break her concentration on whatever type of food she was thinking of cooking and gets a new train of thought going on chicken. You have successfully used a pattern interrupt to manipulate the situation and heightened your chances of having chicken for dinner.

The other technique here is overload, which aims at manipulating a person's thought process or emotions pushing them past a threshold of tolerance. The way you can push a person past this threshold is by feeding them images or vivid explanations of something and going way over the top with it. Once the imagery becomes too much, the person cannot complete whatever pattern they were on.

Let us consider an instance where you have a friend who doesn't like asparagus. Imagine telling your friend about this awesome dinner you had – which had featured asparagus. You give details of smell, texture, taste, and the feel of the asparagus in your mouth as your teeth shredded through the thick greenery and the roughage of the vegetable. Your friend will be trying to block the imagery, but once it gets to be too much for them, they will be pushed beyond their tolerance threshold and be unable to ignore this new path that their thoughts are taking. Imagine that you were so descriptive of the asparagus that your friend has lost their appetite or even become uneasy. This is yet another example of psychological manipulation through pattern interruption.

Another very simple method for psychological manipulation through pattern interrupt is confusion. Confusion is a tactic that is commonly used in hypnotherapy because it has a way of disarming an individual. It is used to help people overcome irrational fears or to allow them to modify things about their character, like becoming more assertive or more vocal.

Confusion can be used to get the person's mind off any anxiety, anger, fear, or whatever emotions they have associated with a certain concept. Fear of flying is commonly mentioned in hypnotherapist offices. One tactic that is commonly used to help clients get over their fears is by getting them to think intently about the act of flying. What is it about flying that makes them fearful? What makes them have a vision in their minds of the worst possible scenario? Maybe a fiery plane crash. When they start to envision these things, their mind gets going on a pattern of fear and anxiety as they imagine their worst nightmares coming true.

The hypnotist will interrupt their thought process with a very confusing string of words like, "If a person answers a question with a question, wouldn't that be an answer to the initial question, or would the question be a question on itself and therefore need to answer to the question?"

This confusing diction will completely break the distressing thoughts of plane crashes in the client's mind and replace it with a puzzle that is light and, at the very least, not life-endangering.

This plants a seed in the client's mind and, when done successfully, realigns the association that the client makes when they think about flying. Instead of fear and anxiety, the thought of flying is associated with a sense of ease coming from the pattern interrupt - a confusing question that broke the pattern of fearful thoughts.

Not only is the client disarmed, and some of the itches of the concept of flying has been taken away, but a good hypnotist will have completely replaced what the client associated with flying from fear to ease.

Hypnotherapists can also use the overload tactic of pattern interrupt for the benefit of their clients. For example, weight loss is another common problem that patients come to hypnotherapists with. The therapist will then use an image or sensory overload to turn the client off of a certain fatty food that they have a hard time resisting. They can use an abundance of imagery related to potato chips, for example, to push the client past their threshold of tolerance so that they associate potato chips with an unpleasant experience and therefore become more and more opposed to them.

How to Use Pattern Interrupts for Influence

Pattern interrupts are powerful tools for influence as well because they can send a person's mind into a flexible state that you can use to your advantage or for the benefit of the individual. For instance, let's say that you want to get a dog, but your spouse or roommate is afraid of dogs and don't want to have one in the house.

By trivializing the logic by which a person associates a certain fear or emotion, you force the person to question the validity of the association. This is called the spin-out technique of pattern interrupt because it sends the person's way of thinking about a certain association into a spin. The person will then realize regarding their fear of dogs or abandon their line of reasoning altogether as you have set them on a new pattern through the spin-out interrupt.

Everything we have discussed in this chapter can be used to get a person into a hypnotic trance. The pattern interrupt method for inducing trance is an easy way to achieve a mild hypnotic state, but even these mild states can be a fertile field for hypnotic suggestion.

Make no mistake about it: getting a person off of their initial train of thought and onto another is a form of hypnosis and psychological manipulation. It may seem simple, but just like an instrument, it is easy to pick up but very difficult to master.

Once you have practiced and become adept at using the pattern interrupt method for inducing hypnotic trances, you are going to need to know what to do once you have a person in a trance, which we will see in the next chapter.

Chapter 6 Dark Persuasion

Persuasion is used all the time around us. If you have ever watched an advertisement on TV or online, or seen a billboard, you are used to this form of persuasion. But here we are going to look at persuasion on a more local level, rather than how big businesses try and persuade you to look at their products and make a purchase. This is something that we all recognize, so it is not a trick or dark manipulation. We are going to take a look at some of the ways that a manipulator and others close to us can use the power of persuasion to get what they want, without us even realizing it.

Elements of Persuasion

Like other types of control, some components are to be observed when it comes to persuasion. These components help identify precisely which persuasion clears it up. The ability to convince others is one salient feature that distinguishes persuasion from all other themes of dark psychology. In most cases, the victim is allowed to make choices at will. Eventually, the persuasion tactics lead them to change their will to that of the persuader. The subject can choose how they want to believe, whether or not they want to buy a product, or whether they believe the proof behind the persuasion is powerful enough to change their minds. There are a few components to persuasion that help describe in detail what it is, while also giving us a deeper understanding of this enigmatic topic.

The first element of this theme is that persuasion is often symbolic. This means persuasion utilizes words, sounds and images to get the message across to the target victim. The logic behind this is quite simple. For one individual to be able to persuade another into acting in a particular way, they will need to show them why they should act in a said way and not the other way around. This is best achieved by using word sounds or various images. You can use sentences to start a debate or argument to prove your point. Pictures are a great way to show the evidence needed to persuade someone to go one way or the other. Some nonverbal signs are possible, but they are not as effective as using words and images

The second key is that persuasion will be used deliberately to affect how others act or think. This one is quite obvious; you don't use persuasion to get them to change if you don't deliberately try to affect others. To get the subject to believe the same way they do, the persuader will try different strategies. This could be as easy as having a discussion with them or presenting proof supporting their point of view. On the other hand, to change the mind of the subject, it could involve much more and include more deceptive ways.

The distinctive thing about persuasion is that it allows some type of free will to the subject. In this way they are allowed to make their own decisions. For the most part, they don't have to go for it, no matter how hard somebody tries to persuade them of something. The subject might hear a thousand commercials about the best car to buy, but if they don't like that brand or don't need a new vehicle at that time, they won't go out and buy it.

Think about it for a moment - if the subject is against abortion and no matter how many people come out saying how great abortion is, it's not likely that the subject will change their minds. This enables much more freedom of choice than it is found in the other types of mind control, which could explain why, when questioned, many individuals do not see this as a kind of mind control. Persuasion is a type of mind control that can take place in many ways. While brainwashing, hypnosis and manipulation must take place face-to-face, and in some instances in full isolation, persuasion can occur otherwise.

Subliminal Persuasion

The word "subliminal" means under our consciousness. Subliminal persuasion means an advertising message that is displayed below the threshold of consumer awareness to persuade or make people change their minds without making them aware of what is going on. This is about affecting individuals with more than words. Some of the subliminal methods of persuasion impact our stimuli with smell, eyesight, sound, touch, and taste. There are mainly three subliminal methods of persuasion to affect anyone.

They include;

- Building a relationship - building relationship makes the other person feel comfortable. This will open up the other individual more. This can be accomplished through a healthy observation force that matches their mood or state. This helps build trust.
- Power of discussion – the power of a powerful, convincing person is much connected to an advertiser's conversion. The correct words and inflections help you to be downright simple.
- Suggestive power - associating useful and desirable things in a discussion or interaction allows a person to become more open to new thoughts.

Basic Persuasion Techniques

Some techniques can be utilized to make persuasion more successful. Different forms of persuasion are daily presented to all victims. A food manufacturing plant will work on getting their victims to purchase a new product. At the same time, a movie company will focus on persuading their victims to watch their latest film. Three main techniques of persuasion have been prevalent since the birth of this theme.

Create a Need

This is one of the techniques that are often deployed by the manipulator to be able to get the victim to change their way of thinking. This creates a need or rather appeals to a need that is already pre-existing on the victim. If it is done the proper way, in no time the victim will be eating out of the persuaders palm. This means the manipulator will need to tap into the fundamental needs of its victims, like the need for self-actualization.

Food, for example, is usually something that we as humans need to survive, and prolonged lack will be a very big problem.

If the agent can convince the subject that their store is the best, or if they can get more food or shelter by changing their beliefs, there is a higher chance of success.

Utilizing Illustrative and Words

The choice of words one chooses comes a long way in the success of using persuasion. There are many ways in which you can phrase sentences when talking about one thing. Saying the right words in the right way is what it will make all the difference when attempting to use persuasion.

Tricks Used by Mass Media and Advertising

The media use two main methods to persuade masses. First is through the use of images, as well as the use of sounds.

Images

Our brain's sight and visual processing areas are very powerful. Just think about it for a minute, have you ever thought of a person without ending up picturing how they look? It is because of this that makes imagery and visual manipulation a preferred method by the media. Companies will often include split-second images of their product or individuals inserted into an advertisement that seems quite innocent on face value. This is usually a form of subliminal persuasion. These split-second images that are usually assumed for the most part, usually end up taking some form of control of the victim, which persuades them to get that particular service.

Sound

Sound is yet another trick that is used by media in the persuasion of unsuspecting victims. Some people usually underestimate the powers that exist in the sounds. But answer this, how many times have you heard somewhere a song only to have it sounding continuously on your mind? Songs usually influence us even though we are not aware of it, even knowing you are listening to it. This is what the media tend to exploit in their quest for persuasion of the masses.

There will often be several phrases skillfully hidden, and repeated in an advertisement song that will most likely convince you to be inclined to prefer one company over the other. An example of this is seen at McDonald's. The melody 'I love it 'is often repeated in a manner that persuades the victims to constantly buy their meals.

Dark Persuasion Techniques to Be on the Lookout For

After looking at the different types of persuasion and what they all mean, you may be able to see why dark persuasion is such a bad thing and can be harmful to the victim. Being able to recognize the different techniques that the manipulator may, use can make it easier to understand when it is used on you.

So, how exactly is a dark persuader able to use this idea to carry out their wishes? There are a few different types of tactics that a dark manipulator is going to use, but some of the most common options include:

The Long Con

The first method we are going to look at is the Long Con. This method is kind of slow and drawn out, but it can be effective because it takes so long, and it is hard to recognize or even pinpoint when something went wrong. One of the main reasons that some people can resist persuasion is because they feel that the other person is pressuring them, and this can make them back off. If they feel that there is a lack of rapport or trust with the person who is trying to persuade them, they will steer clear as well. The Long Con is so effective because they can overcome these main problems and give the persuader exactly what they want.

The Long Con is going to have the dark persuader to take their time, working to earn the trust of their victim. They are going to take some time to befriend the victim and make sure that they trust and like them. This is going to be achieved by the persuader with artificial rapport building, which sometimes seems excessive, and other techniques that will help to increase the comfort levels between the persuader and their victim.

As soon as the persuader sees the victim is psychologically prepared, then they start their attempts. It starts convincing the individual in slow successions; after that the victim manages to do as the persuader wants. This is going to serve the persuader in two ways. First, the victim starts to become used to persuasion by that persuader. The second is that the victim is going to start making that mental association between a positive outcome and the persuasion.

The Long Con is going to take a long period to complete because the persuader doesn't want to make it too obvious what they are doing. For instance, a recently widowed lady is deemed vulnerable because of her age and grief. After her loss a man starts to befriend her. This man is maybe someone she knows from church or even a relative. He starts to spend more time with her, showing immense kindness and patience, and it doesn't take too long for her guard to drop when he comes around.

Then this man starts to carry out some smaller acts of positive persuasion that we talked about before. He may advise her of a better bank account to use or a better way to reduce her monthly bills. The victim appreciates these efforts she is getting from her persuader and starts taking his advice.

Over some time, the man tries to use some dark persuasion. He may try to persuade her to let him invest some of her money. She obliges because of the positive persuasion that was used in the past. Of course the man is going to work to take everything he can get from her. If the manipulator is skilled enough, she may feel that he tried to help her, but the money was lost because he just ran into some bad luck with the investment. This is how far dark persuasion can go.

Graduality

Often when we hear about acts of dark persuasion, it seems impossible and unbelievable. What they fail to realize is that this dark persuasion is not ever going to be a big or a sudden request that comes out of nowhere. Dark persuasion is more like a staircase. The dark persuader is never going to ask the victim to do something big and dramatic the first time they meet. Instead, they will have the victim take one step at a time.

When the manipulator has the target of only going one step at a time, the whole process seems less of a big deal. Before the victim knows it they have already gone a long way down, and the persuader is not likely to let them leave or come back up again.

Let's take an example of how this process is going to look in real life. Let's say that there is a criminal who wanted to make it so that someone else committed the crimes for them. Gang bosses, cult leaders, and even Charles Manson did this same thing.

This criminal wouldn't dream of beginning the process by asking their victim to murder for them. This would send out a red flag, and no one in their right minds would willingly go out and kill for someone they barely know. Instead, the criminal would start by having the victim do something small, like a petty crime, or simply hiding a weapon for them. Something that isn't that big of a deal for the victim, at least in comparison.

Over time, the acts that the manipulator can persuade their victim to do will become more severe. And since they did the smaller crimes, the persuader passes such actions to the victim (blackmailing). Before the victim knows it, they are going to feel like they are in too deep. They will then be persuaded to carry out some of the most shocking crimes. And often, at this point, they will do it because they feel like they have no other choice.

Dark persuaders are going to be experts at using this graduality to help increase the severity of their persuasion over time. They know that no victim would be willing to jump the canyon or do the big crime or misdeed right away. So, the persuader works to build a bridge to get there. By the time the victim sees how far in they are, it is too late to turn back.

Masking the True Intentions

There are different methods a persuader can use dark psychology to get what they want. Disguising their true desires is very important for them to be successful. The best persuaders can use this approach in a series of ways, but the method they choose is often going to depend on the victim and the situation.

One principle that is used by a persuader is the idea that many people are going to have a difficult time refusing two requests when they happen in a row. Let's say that the persuader wants to get $200 from the victim, but they do not intend to repay the money. To start, the persuader may begin by saying that they need a loan for the amount of $1000. They may go into some details about the consequences to themselves if the persuader doesn't come up with that kind of money sometime soon.

The victim may feel some kind of guilt or compassion to the persuader, and they want to help. But $1000 is a lot of money, more than the victim can afford to lend. From here, the persuader lowers their request from $1000 to $200. Of course, there is some kind of emotional reason for needing the money, and the victim feels like it is impossible to refuse this second request. They want to help out the persuader, and they feel bad for not giving in to the initial request when they were asked. In the end, the persuader gets the $200 they originally wanted, and the victim is not going to know what has taken place.

Another type of technique that the persuader can use is known as reverse psychology. This can also help to mask true intentions during the persuasion. Some people have a personality that is known as a boomerang. This means that they will refuse to go in the direction that they are thrown and instead will veer off into different directions.

If the persuader knows someone more of a boomerang type, then they can identify a key weakness of that person. For example, let's say that a persuader has a friend who is attempting to win over some girl they like. The persuader knows that the friend will use and then hurt that girl. The girl is currently torn between a malicious friend and an innocent third party. The persuader may try to steer the girl in the direction of the guy who is a good choice, knowing that she is going to go against this, and end up going with the harmful friend.

Leading Questions

Another method of dark persuasion that can be used is known as leading questions. If you have ever had an encounter with a skilled salesman, verbal persuasion can be impactful when it is deployed in careful and calibrated ways. One of the most powerful techniques that can be used verbally is leading questions.

These leading questions are intended to trigger a specific response out of the victim. The persuader may ask the target something like, "how bad do you think those people are?" This question is going to imply that the people the persuader is asking about are to some extent bad. They could have otherwise chosen to ask a non-leading question, such as "how do you feel about those people?"

Dark persuaders are masters at using leading questions in a way that is hard to catch. If the victim ever begins to feel that they are being led, then they are going to resist, and it is hard to lead them or persuade them. If a persuader ever senses that their victim starts to catch what is happening, they will quit using that one and switch over to another one. They may come back to that tactic, but only when the victim has quieted down a bit and is more influenceable again.

The Law of State Transference

The state is a concept that is going to take a look at the general mood someone is in. If someone is aligned with their deeds, words, and thoughts, then this is an example of a strong and harmonious state. The law of state transference is going to involve the concept of someone who holds the balance of power in a situation, and can then transfer their emotional state to the person they are interacting with. This can be a very powerful tool for the dark persuader to use against their victim.

Initially, the influencer is going to force their state to match the state that their target naturally has. If the target is sad, and they talk slowly, the influencer is going to make their state follow this format. The point of this is to create a deep rapport with the target.

After we get to this state match, the influencer is then going to subtly change their state and see if they have some compliance for the victim. Perhaps they will choose to speed up their voice to see if the victim will speed up as well. Once the victim starts to show these signs of compliance, then this is an indication that the influencer is at the hook point.

When this hook point is reached - however long it takes - the influencer will change their state to that of their victim. This could be an emotional state that the influencer wants. It could be positive, angry, happy, or indignant. It often depends on what the persuader wants to help reach their goals. This technique is an important one for a dark persuader because it is going to show the impact of subconscious cues on the failure or the success of any type of persuasion.

Chapter 7 Tips to Read and Analyze People

Take a moment to imagine a time when the sight of someone sent a chill down your spine. You may not have known why, but you were simply uncomfortable around that person you were facing. Despite your best attempts to identify the reason behind your problem, you found that there was no particular reason that you could think of. The only thing you knew was that you were the only thing afraid of the person in front of you and had no idea how to overcome them.

There was a very good reason for this gut reaction—your instincts were telling you that something about the other person was not right. You didn't need to know specifics, and all that mattered to you was that your reactions were accurate. This is because all these gut reactions kept you alive. So long as that is managed your instincts did their job.

When you first look at someone, your unconscious mind goes through all sorts of information to come up with what it assumes is a valid reading of the person. Of course all this happens below your consciousness. This means that you are not fully aware of what is happening, and yet you can respond to it without effort. Of course, reacting without second thoughts is a useful trait in a survival setting. You are not trying to rationalize what and why when in a survival setting. You simply react on impulse without wasting valuable time that could be the difference between life and death.

However, if you are not in a life-or-death situation, do you want to act on impulses? Will your impulses help you discern whether the person at the interview is lying or is simply uncomfortable about something? Or to determine how your partner is feeling during an argument?

There are limitless reasons why being able to rationally understand what is going on in someone else's mind is critical, even if you already have a decent gut reaction. Ultimately, when you can calmly analyze someone and be consciously aware of why you are uncomfortable or what is putting you nervous, you are better prepared to cope with the problem at hand. This is because you can act rationally. You can strategize how best to react in the most conducive manner that will allow you to succeed in the situation.

This means that in the modern world, when situations very rarely are life or death, making an effort to change to responding rationally and consciously is almost always the best option. You will be able to tell when someone is sounding your alarm because they seem threatening or because they seem deceptive. You will be able to find out what the problem is to respond appropriately.

Why Analyze People

Analyzing people is something that is utilized by various people in different capacities. The most basic reason you may decide that you wish to analyze someone is to simply understand them. When you have an in-built technique of understanding others, you will discover that having a cognitive instead of an emotional connection is critical to establishing a true connection with someone else's mind.

Consider for a moment that you are trying to land a deal with a very important client. You know that the deal is critical if you hope to keep your job and possibly even get a promotion, but you also know that it is going to be a difficult task to manage. If you can read someone else, you can effectively allow yourself the ability to truly know what is going on in their mind.

Think about it—you will be able to tell if the client is uncomfortable and respond accordingly. You will be able to tell if the client is being deceptive or withholding something—and respond accordingly. You can tell if the client is uninterested, feeling threatened, or even just annoyed with your attempts to influence him or her, and you can then figure out how to reply.

When you can understand someone else's mindset, you can regulate yourself. You can fine-tune your behavior to guarantee that you will be persuasive. You can make sure that your client feels comfortable by being able to adjust your behavior to find out what was causing the discomfort in the first place.

Beyond just being able to self-regulate, being able to read other people is critical in several other situations as well. If you can read someone else, you can protect yourself from any threats that may arise. If you can read someone else, you can simply understand their position better. You can find out how to persuade or manipulate the other person. You can get people to do things that they would otherwise avoid.

Ultimately, being able to analyze other people has so many critical benefits that it is worthwhile to be able to do so. Developing this skill set means that you will be more in touch with the feelings of those around you, allowing you to claim that you have a higher emotional intelligence simply because you come to understand what emotions look like. You will be able to identify your own emotions through self-reflection and to learn to pay attention to the movements of your body. The ability to analyze people can be invaluable in almost any setting.

How to Analyze People

Though it may sound frightening, learning to analyze other people is not nearly as difficult as it may initially seem. There are no complicated rules that you need to memorize or any skills that you need to learn—all you have to do is learn the pattern of behaviors and what they mean. This is because once you identify the behaviors, you can usually start to piece together the intent behind them.

You can begin to find out exactly what it is that someone's eyes narrowing means, and then begin to identify it with the context of several other actions or behaviors as well. You can find out what is intended when someone's speech and their body language do not match up. Body language rarely lies when people are unaware of how it works, so you can often turn to it for crucial information if you are interacting with other people.

The reason this works to understand people is because it is commonly accepted that there is a cycle between thoughts, feelings, and behaviors. Your thoughts create feelings, and the feelings you have automatically influence your behavior, as you can see through body language.

Most of the time this is an entirely unconscious cycle. You are unaware of it happening. However, several schools of therapy, such as cognitive-behavioral psychology, have chosen to identify and use this cycle. When you can recognize that this cycle exists, you can take advantage of it—you can begin to use your understanding of the cycle to follow it in reverse.

In effect, you will be looking at behaviors that people display and then tracing them back to the feelings behind them. This is why body language is so important to understand. When you can understand what is going on with someone's behavior, you can understand their feelings. When you understand their feelings you can begin to find out the underlying thoughts that they have. This is about the closest thing to mind reading that you can ever truly achieve.

To analyze other people, you have a simple process to get through—you must first find out the neutral baseline of behavior. This is the default behavior of the person. You must then begin to look for deviations in that neutral behavior. From there, you try to put clusters of behaviors together to find out what is going on in the mid of someone else, and then you analyze. This process is not difficult, and if you can learn how to do it, while also learning how to interpret the various types of body language, you will find that understanding other people could never be easier.

Establish a Neutral Baseline Behavior Set

The most important aspect of being able to analyze someone else is through learning how to identify their baseline behavior. If you can do this, you can effectively allow yourself to identify how that person behaves in a neutral setting. Effectively, you will learn what that person's peculiarities may be.

For example, someone who happens to be reserved or particularly shy is likely to show several common signs of discomfort, even by default. They may cross their arms to shield their body, or stand defensively and refuse to make eye contact. As you will learn later through reading, this is a common body language that is regularly exhibited by those who are lying and do not know how to cover their tracks. However, a shy person is probably not lying if their default behavior involves crossing arms and refusing to make eye contact.

Because people's baseline personality types and peculiarities vary so drastically from person to person, this becomes a critical first step, and you must make it a point to never skip it. Otherwise, you would assume that any shy person must be trying to deceive you. Getting that picture of the baseline personality and nonverbal communication traits are crucial.

Identify Deviations From Neutral Behaviors

Once your baseline has been established, you can begin to identify any deviations from it. This means that you can find out which of the behaviors that you are seeing do not match up with what you have come to expect via your initial observations. This stage can occur during all sorts of interactions. You may ask a question and then observe to see what the response will be to determine whether that person is answering truthfully. You can probe and look for signs of discomfort. You can effectively test to see how convincing you are being when you are trying to persuade someone to do something.

Identify Clusters of Deviations

Of course, it is not always enough just to identify those individual deviations. You must also make it a point to recognize clusters of deviations to get the whole picture. When you master the art of reading body language, you will see that much of human body language can be interpreted in different ways depending on the context. You often need to get that context from looking at other behaviors that are taking place together with the behaviors you are analyzing. For example, there are several behaviors in deception that could have several meanings. Still, as soon as they occur together you can usually infer that there is some level of deception occurring, which means that you need to proceed with caution.

Analyze

Finally, as you identify those clusters of deviations from the original, neutral behavioral baseline, you can start to find out what they mean. You can start to trace it back to find out whether or not the persons are honest or how they are feeling. When you begin to analyze, that is when you truly get the real snapshot of the thoughts inside the persons' minds. You will be able to piece together whether they have a problem in certain settings based upon seeing general repeated responses. You will be able to tell what is intimidating to them, or what seems to consistently motivate them to keep working toward their goals. In going through this stage, you can start to find out exactly what is needed to influence or manipulate them, if you should choose to do so.

When to Analyze People

Analyzing people is one of those skills that can be used in almost any context. You can use it at work, in personal relationships, in politics, religion, and even just in day-to-day life. Because of this versatility, you may find that you are constantly analyzing people, and that is okay. Remember, your unconscious mind already makes snapshot judgments about other people and their intentions, so to begin with you were already analyzing people. Now, you are simply making an effort to ensure that those analyses are made in your conscious mind so you can be aware of them.

Now, let's take a look at several different compelling situations in which being able to consciously analyze someone is a critical skill to know:

In parenting: When you can analyze other people, you can begin to use those skills toward your children. Now, you may be thinking that a children's mind are not sophisticated enough to get a reliable read on, but remember, children's feelings are usually entirely genuine. In essence, they have their feelings that they have, and though the reason behind those may be less than convincing to you as a parent, that does not in any way dismiss their feelings. By being able to recognize the child's emotions, you can begin to understand what is going on in your child's mind, and that will allow you to parent calmly and more effectively.

In relationships: When you live with someone else, it can be incredibly easy to step on someone else's toes without realizing it. Of course, constantly stepping on someone else's toes is likely to lead to some degree of resentment if it is never addressed. Yet, some people have a hard time discussing when they are uncomfortable or unhappy. This is where being able to analyze someone else comes in—you will be able to tell what your partner's base emotions are when you interact, allowing you to play the role of support.

In the workplace: Especially if you interact with other people, you need to be able to analyze other people. You will be able to see how your coworkers view you, allowing you to change your behaviors to get the company image that you desire. Beyond just that, you may also work in a field that requires you to be able to get good readings on someone in the first place.

Perhaps you are a doctor, to begin with you may need to be able to tell how someone is feeling and whether they are honest with you. Maybe you are a lawyer, and you need to be able to analyze the integrity of your client and of those that you are cross-examining. Maybe you are a salesperson who needs to be able to tell if you are convincing in your attempt to close a deal.

In public: When you are interacting with people in public, you need to be able to protect yourself. When you can read other people, you can find out whether you are safe or whether someone is threatening or suspicious. This means that you can prepare yourself no matter what the situation is, to ensure that you are always ready to respond.

In an interview, you may find that reading an interviewer's body language can give you a clue on when to change tactics or move on to something else. You will be able to tell how you are being taken, simply by watching for body language and other nonverbal cues.

When watching presentations: When you are watching a presentation, speech, or address, you may fall into the habit of simply taking everything at face value. After all, why would anyone ever make it a point to tell you something that is not true? This is because you are falling for one of the principles of persuasion—an appeal to authority.

In other words, you believe in the person's speaking authority and therefore consider them to be trustworthy. Instead, make an effort to see the other party as what they truly are by learning to read their body language. You can tell if the politician on television is uncomfortable or lying, simply by learning to analyze their behaviors.

In arguments: When you are arguing with someone else, usually emotions are running high on both ends. No one is thinking clearly and things that were not meant can be said. However, when you can analyze people, you can start to find out when someone else is getting emotional to disengage altogether. You will be able to identify the signs that you should disengage and try again later to ensure that you are not stepping on toes or making things worse.

In self-reflection: When you can analyze other people, you can start to analyze yourself as well. This means that you can stop and look at your body language to sort of check-in with yourself and find out what is going on in your mind. Sometimes, it can be difficult to identify exactly how you are feeling, but this is the perfect way to do so in a pinch. If you can stop and self-reflect, you can identify your emotions.

In self-regulation: Identifying your emotions then lends itself to the ability to self-regulate. When you are, for example, in a heated argument and feel yourself tensing up and getting annoyed, you may be able to key into the fact that you are getting annoyed and respond accordingly. Conversely, when you can analyze other people, you can look at them and see how they are feeling. This means that if you can see that you are intimidating or making someone uncomfortable, you can make the necessary changes to your actions.

How to Defend From Manipulators

We are true human. It's precisely because of this that we have to consider the views of others in everything we do. We always want and love validation from others so we can subconsciously decide whether or not we will be depressed. In this millennial age, the norm has been just bragging about your wealth in social media.

Many of these bragging is often real. In the end, this leads to a weak connection with reality. This kind of self-deception can go deep into the human interest, and one day a victim of this may wake up and realize that their perfect world exists only in their servers. Depression will then follow suit.

The first step towards protecting yourself against persuasion and manipulation is to confront the scene and to take the position to break any illusions. You won't be able to go through your lives as usual. You must be careful that you regulate your own decisions. Then choose consciously to see things for what they are. This agreement, which seems too good to be true, could be. The other thing you should do is trust your instincts without a doubt.

Sometimes you have been told a lie most competently you can believe. But by a specific instinctive rhythm, you may feel an imbalance between what it should, what it is, and what it is projected on you. There might be no physical signs that something is wrong, but you think that something is.

The next significant thing when you ask questions is to hear the answers. This may seem unbelievable because you're going to hear the answers. The truth is that we can deceive ourselves by choosing the responses we receive. We say that we look, but we only care about the reactions that we want to hear and not about the answers we receive.

You may have broken your illusions, but some of you still hold on to the comfort of those illusions. You would not listen to the real answers to your questions because of the pain of dealing with the scenario. Real hearing needs a certain feeling of detachment, but not reality this time.

You must get rid of your feelings. Your detachment from our emotions would lead you to the next step in the logical processing of new data. To behave irrationally it can make situations more complicated than they have to. It makes it so hard for your exit strategy to allow all feelings to cool down and spring.

The irrational part of you may want to let everything go to hell when you face reality. Your justified anger can encourage you to take short-term measures to calm your feelings. But in the long term you may come to regret these actions. I'm not saying that you should deny your emotions. I'm not saying that you do not act on them. First, deal with the situations and later deal with your emotions.

Act Fast

It's lovely that you have got to grips with the truth of things. But it is so much more to defend ourselves against these dark, manipulative strategies. While you try to protect yourself against the claws of these manipulators, it is often intense and exciting at first. The intensity of these feelings can slowly lead to negation.

The longer you take some action, the quicker the denial will begin, and if it occurs, there is a strong likelihood that you may fall back and end up being trapped on the same internet. You can avoid this by taking action as soon as you know someone is attempting to manipulate you. This can be done in the most natural possible way, as when informing a close friend about some facts of the specific scenario, all the events that will eventually lead you to freedom can be so started.

You should understand that after choosing to behave, the fabric is made of sturdier material than glass. The illusion can work its way back to your core by using fragmented parts of your feelings to solve it. When a liar is caught in a lie, it may try to hire others to implement that lying if they think they no longer hold you.

A disappointing partner with whom you broke up lately would attempt to use the other shared links in your lives to change your mind. You are going to need both your logic and instincts if you want to get out of this unharmed. While the reality is that when you find that you have always been lied to you get emotionally scarred, so you are still left untouched by the scenario.

However, priority should be provided to follow the path that enables you to go to this toxic condition without further harm. You're mentally all over the location. Rage, rage, hurt, and disappointment are the tip of the iceberg. But you must logically believe. Keep your head above the water and warn yourself.

Get Assistance Quickly

When you are trapped in the manipulations of others, confusion is one of the feelings you will encounter. This enables you to obscure your rational thinking and makes you feel helpless. You could even question the truth of what you're currently facing. If you continue to have those doubts, it will lead to denial.

You will likely want to say that the whole scenario is wrong. You misunderstood specific stuff and came to the incorrect conclusions. Such thinking would lead back to the weapons of the manipulator. Resist the desire to accept a second opinion. In a health crisis, people go to another physician to get a second view. This clears any doubts concerning your diagnosis and a confirmation of what the best course of therapy is for you.

Similarly, receiving an opinion from another person can assist you in discerning reality and your next steps. Just remember, it's better to go to someone who has proven many times to be interested in your best. The next step is to confront the perpetrator if you have the assistance that you need. I recommend you choose the scene or place for this.

Select a location that gives you the upper hand. That would involve some cautious planning on your part. If the offender exists in the cyber world, especially if the person has victimized you, you must engage the police and the authorities. Do some of your research to find out the truth. After you face the offender and take the measures you need to get out of the scenario, the healing method will quickly begin. The extent and severity you have been harmed, manipulated or abused does not matter. You must go through it and wait for your wounds to heal, instead of ruminating about the past.

Time would offer you sufficient distance from your experience, but it would seldom be healing for emotional scars, if you learned something about this book. If you don't do anything, an unhealthy scab might form over the wound that makes you vulnerable, if not more than you have experienced. Speak to a consultant, take part in the treatment, and actively help the healing process, regardless of what you choose. It will not occur overnight, but for sure you will get nearer each day and after every phase of your treatment.

Have Confidence in Your Instincts

While your brain interprets signals based on facts, logic, and experience, it operates in the opposite direction by filtering data through an emotional filter. The only thing that takes vibrations is your gut that cannot pick up either your heart or your brain. If you can prepare yourself to the point where you recognize your inner voice and are trained to do so, you will reduce your likelihood of been seduced by people who try to manipulate you. It's difficult to recognize this voice at first.

The reason this happens is that we have allowed doubt, self-discrimination and our inner critic to take over. This voice or instinct depends on your survival. So, trust that your brain cells will still be able to process stuff in your immediate area when you start.

Some people call it intuition, some call it instinct, and they do the same thing, particularly when it comes to relationships. You must recognize that starting to trust your instincts may not always make logical sense. If you've ever been doing something and felt like you were suddenly watched, then you understand what I mean.

You have no eyes at the rear of your head, nobody else has, but you have this small shiver running down the back of your neck, and you're looking at the "sudden understanding." That is what I am talking about. I am talking about that.

The first step in connecting with your instinct is to decode your mind with your voices. You can do this with meditation. Forget chatting. Focus on your environment. You are the voice that you understand. Next, pay attention to your ideas. Don't just throw away your head's eclectic monologue. Instead, go with your stream of thoughts.

Why do you believe in somebody somehow? How do you feel so deeply, even though you knew each other for only a few days? What's your nagging feeling about this other individual? You become more sensitive to your intuition as you explore your ideas and know when your instincts start and respond to them.

You may have to learn to stop and believe if you are the individual who, at present, wants to make challenging decisions. This break provides you the chance to reflect and evaluate your options. The next part is hard, and many people couldn't follow it. You can't sail or navigate this step, unfortunately. You need to be open to the concept of self-confidence and of trusting others to believe in your instinct.

Your lack of confidence would only make you paranoid, and when you are paranoid, it's not your instincts that kick in. It's your fear. Every molehill with fear becomes a mountain. You have to let go of your concern, embrace trust, and make your fresh relationships lead. You can hear the voice better without the roadblocks of fear in your mind. Finally, your priorities must be reevaluated.

You may not see the past if your mind is at the forefront of money and material property. Any contact you have with people would be seen as people trying to use you, and it will quickly become true if you live so often. You understand that you attract into your lives what you believe in. If you always think about material wealth, you will only attract people like yourself.

Look at your interactions with this new view with this guide; the old, the new, and the perspectives. Don't enter into a partnership you expect to play. Be accessible to them, whether it is a company relationship, a romantic relationship, or even a regular knowledge. You can receive the correct feedback from your intuition. Do not think this, too, that if you encounter suspects, your gut will tell you to go in the opposite direction.

Chapter 8 One last word

There is so much to learn about the psychological nature of people that prey on others. The truth is that all of humanity has the potential to victimize others. Yes, some try to sublimate this tendency while others choose to act upon their impulses. However, the most important thing for you is to understand your thoughts, perceptions, and feelings that lead to predatory behavior, so that you can learn to control yourself and use it for good.

One thing that is important to note is that manipulation often happens in families with parents who have narcissistic tendencies. In the case where there is parental alienation, a parent may use their child as a psychological weapon to abuse the other parent. The truth is that mind control, a form of dark psychology, happens in a system where people are – such as churches, families, and workplaces.

The key ingredients of dark psychology are people, narcissistic leaders, lieutenants, scapegoats, and keeping secrets. What is not allowed in this kind of system is having a free spirit or free-thinking mentality. It is such kind of people who are banished from the community of manipulators.

According to dark psychology, some people commit evil acts, not because of money, power, sex, retribution, or other known factors. Instead, they choose to do it because they are nasty – have no goals. In other words, for them it is not that ends justify the means. These are the kind of people who injure others just for the sake of doing it.

Within each one of us lies this potential!

You and I have the potential to harm others without any reason, purpose, or explanation. This potential is considered complex – one that is even hard to define.

One thing you must note is that your shadow self is always standing right behind you – just outside your view. When you stand in direct light, you cast a shadow, right. The shadow is the part of yourself that you cannot really see. Think about it for a moment, what lengths do you go just to protect your self-image from unfamiliarity and flattery?

The truth is, when you see other person's shadow, you realize that one can show gifts in one area of life and remain unaware of evil behaviors in other areas. Everyone is susceptible to this. Over the years I have learned that working with my shadow has not only been a challenging but rewarding process too. It is by looking at your darker side that you gain greater creativity, authenticity, personal awakening, and energy. It is this subjective process that contributes to your maturity.

Realize that you cannot eliminate your darker side. Instead, it stays with you as your darker brother or sister. When we fail to see our darker self, that is when trouble follows.

While our shadow self can operate on its own without our awareness – more like it is on autopilot – it causes us to do things we would not do voluntarily, and that is the reason behind regret. You find yourself saying things you wouldn't normally say. Your body language expresses emotions you would consciously not feel. In short, when you ignore your dark side, you end up hurting your relationships – your friends, spouse or family, among others.

When you see others and yourself exactly as you are, you view the world around you with a clearer lens. Integrating your shadow self into everyday activities helps you approach your true self, hence offering you a realistic evaluation of who you are. In other words, you will not perceive yourself as being too small; neither will you feel as though you have a high moral ground than others.

The reward for doing this plays a significant role in healing the divisions in your mind. It also helps unleash untapped potential and a world of new possibilities for your growth and development.

So, what are you still waiting for?

It is time to embrace your dark side to allow the light inside you to shine without fear of hurting others of being all that you are meant to be. Your dark side will help you overcome manipulation so that you can shine brighter!

Good Luck!

© **Written by:** JOSEPH GRIFFITH

EMOTIONAL INTELLIGENCE 2.0

TO LIVE A BETTER LIFE, FIND SUCCESS AT WORK
AND CREATE HAPPIER RELATIONSHIPS, IMPROVE
YOUR SOCIAL SKILLS, EMOTIONAL AGILITY, AND
LEARN TO MANAGE AND INFLUENCE PEOPLE

JOSEPH GRIFFITH

Book Description

Do you feel like you have been stuck in the same place for so long without making progress? Do you feel like the decisions you have been making lately are all over the place? Do you want to build stronger relationships, succeed at work and in school? Do you wish to achieve your career and personal growth? Do you consider yourself with emotional intelligence? If not, then rest assured that you have come to the right place!

One thing that is important to bear in mind is that Emotional Intelligence plays a significant role in helping you recognize, manage, and understand your emotions and how they influence those of others. It is through emotional intelligence that you can boost your performance – whether in your personal life, at home, or in the workplace.

Think of a place where your confidence, optimism, empathy, self-control, and social skills all work hand in hand to accelerate success in all areas of your life. Don't you want that?

In this book, you will learn:

- What Emotional Intelligence is
- The keys to Emotional intelligence
- How you can identify your emotions and those of others
- How to use your feelings to guide your thinking and reasoning
- To understand how feelings change and develop with the unfolding of events
- To manage to open your arms to feeling data and using that to make informed choices for success

So, what are you still waiting for?

It is time to sharpen your intuitions and position yourself for success and a better life.

Come with me!

Introduction

You have probably heard of emotional intelligence at home, school, or in the workplace. This concept continues to grow in popularity, especially in a brain-dead world where people strive to achieve success but don't know how to connect with their emotional feelings to realize their goals.

You may be thinking, "Why is emotional intelligence growing in importance among peers in an evolving workplace or in life in general?"

One thing that is important to bear in mind is that emotional intelligence is not a trend! It is here to stay. According to reports and statistics compiled by major companies across the world, it is evident that no doubt people with emotional intelligence affect their bottom line. For instance, if an employee has a high level of emotional intelligence, they will not only be productive and generate revenue for the company, but they will also achieve their personal and career goals.

Look around you – are there people you know – whether at home or the workplace – with high emotional intelligence? Do you know people who are really good listeners? Irrespective of the circumstances, they can communicate well. It is almost like they know exactly what to say, when to say it, and how to say it, so that others are not offended. These people are caring, considerate, and can find solutions for problems. When you approach them for guidance, they leave you feeling optimistic and more hopeful in life.

You probably know other people who have mastered the art of managing their emotions. Instead of getting angry when provoked by a stressful situation, they choose to look at the problem from a different perspective to calmly find a solution. These people are excellent decision-makers and have mastered the art of listening to their gut feeling. Irrespective of their strengths, they have the willingness to look at themselves with an honest eye. They take criticism positively and use it to improve their performance.

It is such kind of people that we wish that we can be like them.

What sets them apart is nothing other than a high degree of emotional intelligence. You can have that too. You can learn how to manage your emotions in every situation, while ensuring that you take care of the emotional needs of the people around you.

You may be thinking, "I can never be like this. I don't have what it takes to be like these people."

Well, I am here to tell you that you can be just like these people. As you begin to accept emotional intelligence into every area of your life, you will begin to see an improvement in your technical abilities, interrelationships, and overall success. It is through emotional intelligence that you can improve your performance. It impacts your confidence, optimism, self-control, empathy and social skills, so that you can understand and manage your emotions and accelerate success in every area of your life.

It does not matter what your profession is, whether you work for a small or a large organization, whether you are a senior or junior in your company. What matters is that realizing how effective you are at controlling your emotional energies is the beginning of a successful adventure. Yes, emotional intelligence may not be something taught and tested in an educational curriculum, but the truth is that it is really important.

The good news is that it is something you and I can learn, so that is the reason why we have compiled a book with all the tips that will help you improve your emotional intelligence skills and implement them in everyday life. Our clients have given us positive feedback on how these skills have not only helped them advance in life, but have also helped them motivate and inspire others to be better.

In summary, emotional intelligence is what helps you identify your emotions, manage them effectively, and constructively react to others' emotions. When you understand how those emotions shape your thoughts and actions, you gain better control of your behavior and establish a new skill set that will help you to effectively manage your emotions. When you are emotionally conscious, you position yourself for growth and a deeper understanding of who you truly are. This way, you can communicate better with people around you and can strengthen your relationships.

To get you started, you must discover the foundation of your emotional intelligence. The best way to do that is to;

Practice Observing Your Feelings

Take a look at your life – the chances are that you will notice how hectic and busy your lifestyle is. It is this kind of life that makes it easy for you to lose touch with yourself and with your emotional feelings. You must try to reconnect with your feelings by setting a timer for various points throughout the day. As soon as the timer goes off, you stop what you are doing, stand on your two feet, and take in a deep breath. Then bring your thoughts to what you are feeling in that moment, where the emotions are coming from, and where you feel the sensation in your body and what it feels like. Realize that the more you practice this, the more you make it your second nature.

Pay Attention to How You Act

As you practice self-awareness, you must pay attention to how you act and behave in different situations. When you experience a certain emotion, observe what your actions are like and how they affect your daily activities. Soon, you will realize that managing your emotional feelings comes easily, and your reactions become more conscious.

Question Your Opinion

We all live in a hyper-connected world that makes it easy to fall into a "bubble of opinions." In other words, you find yourself in a state of existence where your opinions are reinforced by others all the time. The last thing you want is for your voice to be completely lost because you are always flowing with the urges of life and what others decide for you.

You must take time to evaluate both sides of the story and bring your views forward with confidence. It does not matter what people think of you and your opinions. What matters most is that you are willing to get your opinions challenged even when you feel that you are right. This way, you gain a better understanding of others and become more receptive to their ideas.

Be responsible for Your Emotional Feelings

The first thing about responsibility is accepting the fact that your emotions and actions come from you. It does not matter what the situation or circumstances are like, because no one tells you to react the way you do. No one tells you to feel what you feel. When you accept the responsibility for your feelings and actions, you begin to have a positive impact in your life.

Celebrate the Positives in Your Life

The key to emotional intelligence is to celebrate and reflect on all the positives in your life. No one has a perfect life – we all go through ups and downs. It does not matter whether you have more positives or negatives in your life. The trick to celebrate every victory – big or small. When you accept the positives in your life, you allow yourself to

115

develop more resilience and you increase your chances of enjoying fulfilling relationships so that you can successfully move past adversity.

Don't Ignore the Negatives

Just because you have chosen to embrace and celebrate the positives in your life does not mean that you ignore the negatives. You must take time to reflect on all the negative feelings you might have, just as you would the positive feelings. This will help you understand the root cause of these negative feelings so that you can master how to control them and become an all-rounded individual.

Breathe

No matter what life throws your way, you must not forget to take time to just breathe. Taking time to take deep breaths will not only help you master how to manage your emotions but also will help you avoid outbursts. Just walk out the door and wash your face with cold water, take a walk, or just take in fresh air – anything to calm your nerves. This goes a long way in helping you get a hold of what is happening so that you can effectively respond to the situation.

That said, emotional intelligence is a lifetime process! It is not something you develop overnight. The truth is that to grow your emotional intelligence you have to train your mind to accept continual improvements along the way – so that you can be better with each passing day.

Chapter 1 What is Emotional Intelligence, and Why is it Important?

Most people don't know what emotional intelligence is, even if it is something we should have in our lives. Well, emotional intelligence simply refers to the ability to identify our emotional feelings and manage them, and that of people around us.

Emotional intelligence generally involves three key skills;

- Emotional awareness – the ability to identify your emotional feelings and name them
- Ability to connect with our emotional feelings and apply them into problem-solving, thinking and reasoning
- Ability to manage our emotional feelings, which includes regulating them where necessary and helping people around us to do the same

Unlike the general intelligence that has a psychometric test or scale, emotional intelligence does not have one. This is the reason several people think of emotional intelligence not as an actual construct but instead as an interpersonal skill. However, despite all the criticism, emotional intelligence is sometimes referred to the as emotional quotient.

Today, several companies have included emotional intelligence tests into their application and interview processes, mainly because they think a high emotional intelligence makes one a good coworker or leader.

While there are research studies that have demonstrated a link between emotional intelligence and job performance, there are others that show no correlation. The lack of a scientifically valid scale to measure emotional intelligence makes is challenging for one to accurately measure or predict one's emotional intelligence, whether at home or in the workplace.

So, what does it mean to be emotionally intelligent?

Well, someone who is emotionally intelligent is one who is highly conscious of their emotional states, whether negative – sad, frustrated – or positive – happy and subtle. If you can identify your emotional feelings and manage them effectively irrespective of the situation you are in, then chances are that you have emotional intelligence. For you to be called emotionally intelligent, you must demonstrate that you are tuned to the emotions other people are experiencing. When you can sense and understand what other people are going through, you become a better friend, parent, partner, or leader. And the good thing is that you can hone these skills easily with the tips we will give you in this book.

That said, when emotional intelligence was first introduced, it played a role in uniquely filling the missing link: people with average IQ outperform those with a high IQ. It is because of this anomaly that a massive change was thrown into what most people assumed that IQ was the only source of success.

Now, lots of research studies point to emotional intelligence as a central factor in differentiating between high performers and the rest of the pack. This correlation is so strong that over 90% of the top performers are said to have high emotional intelligence.

In other words, emotional intelligence is the intangible thing each one of us has and influences how we behave, handle social complexities, and make decisions to achieve success.

Despite the significance EQ has on our lives, the truth is that its intangible nature makes it hard for us to know how much of it we have and what it is that we can do to improve it if we lack it.

So, how then can you tell when you have emotional intelligence?

Robust Emotional Vocabulary

We all experience emotional feelings of different kinds, but the truth is that we don't handle them the same way. There are only a few people who can accurately identify their emotions as they happen. Research demonstrates that at least 36% of people can identify their emotions as soon as they occur. This is such a huge problem because it means a large number of individuals are unable to label their emotional feelings – hence contributing to misunderstandings. This explains why people end up making irrational decisions and counterproductive behaviors.

When you have a high EQ, you will not only master your emotions but also understand them and use a vast vocabulary of feelings to do that. While there are times when someone says that they feel "bad," the truth is that emotional intelligence allows one to specifically pinpoint their emotions as either irritable, demoralized, frustrated, or anxious. In other words, when your word choice is specific, you gain a deeper insight into precisely what you are feeling, its origin, and what you must do to overcome them.

Curiosity About People

It does not matter whether you are an introvert or an extrovert because if you are emotionally intelligent, you will demonstrate curiosity about people around you. It is through this kind of curiosity that you can demonstrate empathy – a significant gateway to a high EQ. The more you show someone that you care about them and what they are experiencing, the more you will be curious about them.

You Embrace Change

If you are emotionally intelligent, then you have the flexibility and ability to constantly adapt to change. You will know that fear of change is the reason why you will remain paralyzed and it is a major threat to your happiness and success in life. You must look for the change that is going around you and then form a plan of action in case these changes happen.

You Know Your Strengths and Weaknesses

When you are emotionally intelligent, you will not only understand emotions but also know what you are good at and what you are terrible at. You will know who and what pushes your buttons within your surroundings so that you can position yourself better to achieve success. Having a high emotional intelligence simply means that you can lean on your strengths and leverage them to realize your potential, while raising your awareness of your weak points so that they don't hold you back from reaching your fullest potential.

You Are a Good Judge of Character

Did you know that much of emotional intelligence builds down to social awareness? This is simply your ability to read people, know what they are all about, and gain a deeper insight into what they are going through. With time this skill goes a long way in helping you become an exceptional judge of character, so that others don't become a mystery to you. It allows you to know what makes them tick, understand the things that motivate them, and the things they try to hide beneath the surface.

You Are Hard to Offend

Having a strong grasp of who you are, makes it hard for others to get under your skin. If you are emotionally intelligent you are simply self-confident and have an open mind – the two factors that help you develop a pretty thick skin. The truth is you can even poke fun on yourself or let other people make jokes about you, because you can draw a mental line between humor and degradation.

Letting Go of Mistakes

If you are emotionally intelligent, then you know better than to ruminate on your past mistakes. You can distance yourself from your undoing without necessarily forgetting them. When you keep your mistakes at a safe distance but handy enough to refer to them when the need arises, you position yourself to future challenges and achieve success.

Well, no one said that this was going to be a walk in the park. The truth is that to walk this tightrope between remembering and ruminating, you must have a refined self-awareness. When you ruminate on your past mistakes you set yourself up for anxiety and becoming gun shy. On the other hand forgetting all about your past mistakes makes it easy for you to repeat them again in the future.

The key to balancing these is to learn how to transform your failures into nuggets of improvement. This way, you create a tendency to bounce back up each time you fall.

Don't Hold Grudge

Did you know that when you hold a grudge, you activate negative emotions in response to stress? Well, every time you think of an unpleasant past event, the body goes into a fight-or-flight mode as a way to survive. This forces you to get up to either fight or run away for the hills when you are faced with a threat.

The truth is, when the threat is imminent, this reaction is critical to your survival. However, when the threat is something that lies in ancient history, holding on to it will only wreak havoc on your body and in time it will negatively affect your health. According to research studies at Emory University holding a grudge tends to raise our blood pressure and causes heart disease.

In short, when you hold a grudge, you are choosing to hold on to stress. And if you are emotionally intelligent, then you know you must stay away from this at all costs. When you let go a grudge, it is not a sign of weakness. Instead, it makes you feel better and sets you up for improved health and overall wellbeing.

Neutralizes Toxic People

Dealing with difficult people is not only frustrating but also energy draining. With high emotional intelligence you are in a better position to control your interactions with toxic people by ensuring that you can keep your emotions in check. When you must deal with a toxic person, you know the importance of approaching them rationally.

In other words, you can identify your emotions and ensure that your anger over frustrations does not get the best of you fuel chaos. You also know that the other person has a point of view and that if you can hear where they are coming from, you will agree on a common ground and find a lasting solution. Even when things get completely derailed, people with high emotional intelligence can take toxic people with a grain of salt to ensure that they don't let themselves be brought down.

Don't Seek Perfection

Emotionally intelligent people don't set perfection as a goal because they know well that perfection does not exist. The truth is we are all human, and that fact alone makes us fallible. When you make perfection a goal, then the truth is that you are setting yourself up for a nagging feeling of failure that only makes you will only make you want to give up or lower your efforts.

In other words, you end up spending much of your time complaining about your failures and what you could have done differently instead of moving on. Emotional intelligence allows you to view failure as a lesson to improve yourself without forgetting to celebrate every small achievement you have accomplished, so that you can stay motivated to achieve more in your future.

You Disconnect

When you can take regular breaks off the grid, this indicates high emotional intelligence. This is mainly because taking time off to reflect on yourself is one of the best ways to avoid stress and make sure you have things under control, so that you can live in the moment. Making yourself available 24/7 sets you up for constant baggage of stressors.

You must force yourself to go offline from time to time to just breathe and do nothing! When you turn off your gadgets and just focus on yourself, you allow your mind and body to take a break. According to research, taking a break from technology – something as simple as reading emails – can reduce stress levels. Through technology, we can constantly communicate and expect to be available 24 hours a day. This makes it difficult for you to enjoy a stress-free moment away from the busyness in everyday life. When you take breaks, you allow yourself to have a change in your train of thought and relax without worrying about when is that you will have work dropping on your phone.

Limit Caffeine Intake

When you are constantly drinking caffeine, you trigger the release of adrenaline – a source of the fight-or-flight response. It is this mechanism that makes it easy to avoid rational thinking in favor of something fast for survival.

Well, one thing you must understand is that this kind of survival mechanism is brilliant if a bear is chasing you. However, this is not something you need when responding to emails. Taking too much caffeine throughout the day keeps your body in a constant hyper-aroused state of stress, so that your emotions begin to overrun your actions. With high emotional intelligence you know that caffeine is not good for you and avoid allowing it to get the best of you.

Get Enough Sleep

It is hard to overemphasize the importance of sleep in boosting your emotional intelligence and helping you manage your stress levels. Getting enough sleep every day plays a significant role in ensuring that you give the brain the time it needs to recharge, shuffle through the day's memories, store them, and discard anything that is not good for you. This ensures that once you get up, your brain is not only alert but ready to go!

People with high emotional intelligence understand that their self-control, memory and attention are reduced when they are sleep-deprived. Therefore, ensure that from now on you make sleep your top priority!

Stop Negative Self-talk in Its Tracks

Are you allowing negative self-talk to hold you back from reaching your fullest potential? One thing you must bear in mind is that when you ruminate on negative thoughts, you are giving away your power to them. The trick is whenever negative thoughts come to your mind, ask yourself if they are facts or not.

When you feel like something always happens or never happens, realize that this is the brain's way of perceiving a threat. Emotionally intelligent people can separate their thoughts from facts to escape the cycle of negativity, gain a new perspective on life, and move on with optimism and positivity.

Won't Allow Anyone Limits Your Joy

Do you let other people's opinions deprive you of your sense of pleasure and satisfaction? If you do, then you must realize that you are no longer the master of your happiness. Being emotionally intelligent means that whenever you feel good about something you have done, you will not let anyone's opinions or comments take away that good feeling.

Yes, it may be hard to switch off your reactions to what they say or think of you. However, you don't have to compare yourself to them. The trick is to take their opinions with a grain of salt. This way, no matter what others think, do or say about you, you allow your self-worth to rise from within you and take control of your thought process and actions.

That said, unlike IQ, you must note that emotional intelligence is malleable. As you train your mind to repeatedly practice new emotionally intelligent behaviors, you are promoting the growth of new pathways that turn them into habits. Your brain will start reinforcing the use of these behaviors and to make die off their connections to the old and destructive behaviors. Before you know it, you start responding to your environment with emotional intelligence without even thinking about it.

Importance of Emotional Intelligence

There are several benefits that emotional intelligence has to offer – most of which we will discuss in detail in the coming chapters. That said, emotional intelligence plays a key role in leading us on the path to a fulfilled and happy life. This is mainly by offering us a framework through which we can apply intelligence standards to our emotional responses and lets us understand these responses to ensure that they are logically consistent with our belief systems.

With constant changes in workplaces and in the available body of research, we must understand the art of emotional intelligence so that we can work with others in an organized way and as a team, respond, effectively adapt to change and manage stress so that we can successfully achieve our business objectives. When you work on improving your emotional intelligence, you prepare yourself for personal happiness, professional success, and overall wellbeing.

Chapter 2 The Four Attributes of Emotional Intelligence

Self-Management

You may be wondering what self-management has to do with emotional intelligence. Well, one thing that is important to bear in mind is that self-management involves using what you know about your feelings so that you can manage them in such a way that they can generate positive interactions with the people around you. You want your emotions to motivate you in all situations. When you recognize that you have negative emotions you position yourself to be in control of your actions.

Think about it for a moment – if you are a manager at your workplace, do you think people would want to work with you if you don't have control over yourself and the way you react to situations? Trust me; no one wants to work – much less interact – with someone whose actions are informed by their prevailing mood. Achieving results by bullying and shouting other people is something of the past. It is something that has no place in the modern world where people are aware of their rights, and labor courts are there to ensure that workers are properly treated.

I am not saying that self-management means that you can never be angry. We all go through situations that sometimes get on our nerves and it is perfectly reasonable to be angry. However, the key to being emotionally intelligent is to make sure that you are in control of your feelings and can channel them into solving problems.

Some people have a strong tendency to exaggerate in their minds the negative aspects of any given situation. If you are one of them, you must apply the reflective cycle in such situations so that you can have a realistic view of what is happening and what you can do to yield the desired result.

127

To engage your emotional intelligence, you must use your feelings in such a way that you can make constructive decisions about your actions. When you get stressed, it is easy to lose control of your emotions. It is easy to lose the ability to act appropriately and thoughtfully. To put this into perspective, take a minute to think back to a time when you were stressed and overwhelmed. Was it easy to think clearly? Did you make rational decisions at the time?

Probably not!

When you are stressed and overwhelmed, the ability to think clearly and to accurately assess your emotions tends to be compromised. The truth is, emotions are bits and pieces of information that tell you about yourself and the people around you. However, in the face of stress and threat, they seem to take us out of our comfort zones and then we easily lose control of our abilities and ourselves.

Self-management ensures that you not only manage stress but also that you remain emotionally present in every situation so that your emotions don't override your thoughts and self-control. It allows you to make informed decisions that ensure you are on top of the situation, control impulsive emotions, actions, and manage them a healthy way. It allows you to take the initiative, commit to the things that matter most in your life, follow through on these commitments, and adapt to changing circumstances.

Three Steps of Self-Management

Step 1 Identify What You Are Feeling

When you miss a meeting, you missed a delivery date, have problems with your spouse, or long-term sentiments that something is wrong, it is important that you identify the emotions you are feeling. Is it anger, sadness, anxiety, or frustration? Whatever your starting point is, you must learn how to exercise your self-awareness before you do something about it.

Step 2 Determine the Underlying Cause

This is often a very challenging step because you need to evaluate, reflect, and honestly find out the root cause of your emotional feelings. Are you resentful of your boss because you have been told you missed the targets? Is it your spouse you suspect is having an affair and it makes you feel sad, disappointed, or frustrated? Find the root cause of your emotions.

Step 3 Act

Once you know what emotions you are feeling and where they are coming from, the next thing is for you to act. There is always something you can do to break out of the cycle of negative emotions. It can be something as simple as admitting the emotions you have are unjustified or misplaced, or that you are directing them at the wrong person.

When you recognize the truth behind your emotional feelings, you gain better control over them, so that you can manage them even when you are angry or stressed. Don't get me wrong – I am not saying that you should pretend as if these emotions are non-existent and dismiss them. No, you must accept that they are there and be willing to manage them.

When you master the art of self-management, you prepare yourself to think logically about every situation and decide on various ways you can handle them. This way you reduce the anger and fear you have and your level of emotional intelligence will rise above normal.

One thing you must bear in mind is that your team will always be looking up to you for cues on what the right behavior is and what is and what is not acceptable. If you show you cannot control your own emotions, then you are simply telling them that there is no reason to control theirs. It is this lack of self-discipline that encourages people to copy undesirable habits – what Goleman refers to as "emotional hijacking." In other words, you let your mind be taken by your primitive emotions, and once they are standing in the way you cannot make a realistic and objective assessment of the situation.

The truth is that these emotional breakdowns are building up gradually and unwillingly – and the symptoms of them are often overlooked. When you are frequently being bullied and feel unsupported, your behavior may eventually result in negative consequences. However, when you make an honest evaluation of your actions and that of the people around you, you will not only identify what the problem is, but will also find possible solutions to the problem before it gets out of hand.

In other words, the key to develop your emotional intelligence self-management is to conduct an honest evaluation of your behavior. Once you identify a negative form of behavior, you can work on removing or controlling it.

Think about it, do you often allow others' moods and attitudes to affect you? Are there times when you or any other member of your family/team has been influenced this way?

If so, then it is high time you made a conscious effort of isolating yourself so that you can be objective when evaluating a situation. Only a handful of people can have this kind of effect on you, and you must know who they are. It could be because you have a personal relationship with that person that, in a way, is deeper than a usual working relationship. It could be someone you respect, closely identify with, or admire.

The point is that you realize that they influence your emotions. Knowing that plays a significant role in minimizing the negative influence their emotions might have on you, embracing who you are so that you can learn why their moods and attitudes affect you. When you have this knowledge, you can make a conscious effort to neutralize these negative emotions.

Tips to Improve Your Self-management Skills

- Breathe
- Differentiate between emotions and reason
- Share your goals with someone important in your life – a mentor or a spouse
- Count from one to ten
- Sleep on it
- Talk to someone you trust
- Laugh it out
- Think about it
- Talk better to yourself
- Visualize it
- Get enough sleep
- Control your body language
- Workout
- Control what you can and give up control over what you can't

What did Steve Jobs do when someone in the audience attacked him publicly during the Apple Developer Conference? Well, returning to his company after a decade away, Steve Jobs was publicly attacked by someone, and do you know how he responded? He used some of the self-management tactics we have discussed here.

The first thing was that he paused for a couple of seconds before saying a word. He may or may not have counted to 10, but he paused and took a deep breath. This gave him time to compose himself, get a realistic perspective of the situation before he could say anything. He then took a sip of water and said: *"You know, you can please some of the people some of the time, but ..."*

Just doing that allowed his mind to change to a positive mindset. He then took another long pause – possibly to gather his thoughts on what to say next. You can do the same – be aware of your emotions and adequately manage your emotions. It is not about what other people say or think about you that matters; what counts is how you respond to their thoughts, actions, and words!

Self-Awareness

Emotional self-awareness is the second element of emotional intelligence. It refers to one's ability to understand your emotions and how they affect your performance. Think about what is currently going on, how do you feel about it, why are you feeling that way? How is this helping or hurting what you are trying to achieve?

Self-awareness is also about how others see you and how you can align your image of yourself with the bigger picture. It is about having a clear sense of your strengths and weaknesses, something that gives you a realistic sense of self-confidence. It is also something that gives you clarity of what your values and purpose so that you be more decisive when you set your course of action. As a leader, you can get candid and authentic, speak with conviction about your vision.

Let us consider the following example where a chief tech officer at a company unwillingly bullies other workers. The thing is that this officer is good at what he/she does, but sucks when managing others. Often would play favorites, tell people what to do, and do not seem to listen to what they have to say. Anyone he/she doesn't like is shut out. When confronted about this behavior, it comes a denial and the blaming other people or turning back on them, saying they are the problem.

What do you think about this tech officer?

Well, he/she lacks emotional self-awareness.

According to research, a boss who is arrogant, stubborn, and a bully is often considered by their subordinates as incompetent. These character traits have been shown to have a strong correlation with poor financial results, poor talent management and lack of motivation/inspiration to junior colleagues. In a work they are poor team leaders.

A study by Korn Ferry Han Group reported that among leaders with various strengths in emotional self-awareness, at least 92% have teams with high energy and performance. In other words, when you are a great leader you tend to create a positive emotional climate that stirs motivation and extra effort among employees – and this is because of a good emotional self-awareness. On the other hand, leaders with low self-awareness were reported to create at least 78% of a negative work climate.

That said, what you must bear in mind is that emotional self-awareness is not something that you can achieve at one go and be done with it. It is instead a trait that you have to keep nurturing every opportunity you get. It is an ongoing effort and a conscious choice that you make to be self-aware. The good thing is that the more you practice the more it gets ingrained in you and becomes natural. In short, being self-aware is simply regularly checking your sensory experience to allow a positive change in behavior.

The very first step to building your emotional intelligence is to raise awareness about your emotions. What you are currently feeling is often a mirror of what you experienced earlier in life. The ability to manage core emotions – such as anger, fear, joy, and sadness – all depend on the consistency and quality of your early life's emotional experiences. If your primary caretaker, as a little child, valued and understood your feelings, there is a high likelihood that your emotions are a great asset in your adult life. However, if it was the opposite, there is a chance that you will try to run away or hide from your emotions.

Take a minute to reflect on the following questions;

- Do you experience emotional feelings that flow and change from one moment to the next?
- Are your emotional feelings accompanied by strong physical sensations – such as chest pains, stomach cramps, or throat blockage?
- Do you experience individual feelings and emotions, and do they show on your facial expressions?
- Can you experience intense feelings strong enough to capture your attention and that of others?
- Do you pay close attention to your emotional feelings, and do they inform your decision-making?

If any of these experiences don't ring a bell, then the chances are that you turned off or tuned down your emotions. If you are going to build your emotional intelligence and become emotionally stable and healthy, it is important that you connect with your core feelings, embrace them, and get comfortable with them. The only way you are going to achieve this is by practicing mindfulness.

In other words, being mindful is choosing to deliberately focus your attention on the present moment without judgment. When you are mindful of what you are doing at that very moment, it helps you shift your attention and thoughts towards what you are doing at that moment so that you can appreciate the bigger picture. It can calm and focus your mind so that you are more self-aware of your surroundings.

Tips on How to Improve Your Self-awareness

Get Out of Your Comfort Zone

You might have heard the saying, "magic happens outside the comfort zone!" Well, that is also true for emotions. If you look around, you will notice that there are several instances where you run away from your emotional feelings – and you are not alone. However, one thing you must realize is that this is not a long-term plan. You must allow your feelings to surface and offer the information they carry.

Instead of trying to shove your emotions away or running from them, you must learn how to guide yourself to them and through them. You cannot ignore what you are feeling because if you do, you are not doing yourself any good because they will only disappear now and resurface sometime later.

Be aware that getting out of your comfort zone is not all that bad. If you are going to expand your frontiers you have to develop the willingness to do things that might make you uncomfortable. Trust me, with practice you will start enjoying all the fruits of your labor.

Identify Your Triggers

Think of a trigger as anything – a substance, situation, person, or condition – that makes you emotional and prompts you to act in a certain way. You may for instance have a manager that feeds on others' energy like a vampire, and that makes you angry. It could be a noisy surrounding with your colleagues gossiping and laughing loudly over the phone when you need to concentrate on some work. It could be a colleague that lacks effective communication or people management skills.

Whatever it is, most people typically respond by shutting down. If this is something that happens to you in a place where emotional outbursts are considered a taboo, be aware that keeping those emotional feelings inside for yourself will do you no good. This is because your body language will be screaming, and someone sharp enough will notice that.

When you learn to identify your triggers, you are preparing yourself for improved emotional intelligence. This is because you begin to learn how to improve your ability to control the outcome of your actions. You will learn how to calm down, take charge of your actions and keep your presence of spirit. To do that, you must identify the specific cases and begin generalizing from there. When you have a deeper understanding of what pushes your buttons, the situations become more manageable because the emotions you experience will not come as a surprise to you anymore.

It is also important that you go all the way at identifying the root cause of your triggers. In other words, you are finding out exactly why those people or situations get on your nerves. Why do you think a noisy surrounding triggers agitation or irritation? Is it because you are more skilled in reading and writing than you are in listening and talking? Or maybe the hate you have for your managers is because they remind you of a past manager who bullied you at the workplace? When you identify that your reactions are channeled to the wrong person, you might be able to get along with people better.

Don't Judge Your Feelings

Feelings are like waves of the ocean; they come and go. The truth is that they are just what they are – feelings- nothing more nothing less! Trying to label your feelings as either "good" or "bad" or as "positive" or "negative" will only cause you to lose your ability to recognize them and raise your awareness of them. It is human nature to want to judge everything that comes your way and then put them in two large boxes. The truth is that doing this will only make things counterproductive.

The thing is, everything you consider a "bad or negative" feeling will automatically be something you want to avoid at all costs. The truth is that there is some shame that comes with feeling bad or having negative feelings. On the other hand, when you have positive or good feelings, you want them to stay, and you may even see the need to reward yourself for having them. The problem is that you let them run wild, which eventually drains you of your energy.

The point is, whether the feeling is good or bad, or positive or negative, they bring certain information. Either you feel happy because you have achieved something, frustrated because the reality is different from what you expected, or sad because you lost something.

However, if you allow your emotions to come and go just as they are – without judgment – then you might just have the chance to understand what they are and what the mind is trying to tell you. In other words, your emotions will just run their course and vanish without trying to control you.

Don't Make Decisions in a Bad Mood

There are times in life when we feel as though everything else is moving in the wrong direction. Whether you call this bad luck, feeling down, or depression, the truth is that you cannot feel anything right because there is a black veil that clouds your thoughts.

The problem is that once the bad mood takes charge of your brain, it is easy to lose sight of the good things happening in our lives. You start to feel like you hate where you live, where you work, what you do, and the people around you irritate you. Even though you know deep down that what you think and feel is not true, you can't seem to get rid of these thoughts and emotions.

One thing you must keep in mind is that emotional intelligence, through self-awareness, helps us to take note of the situation and accept it as it is. And you must admit that there is little to nothing you can do to change it. The trick is to wait – with time it will just pass. In other words, try to postpone making any life-changing decisions at this point, at least until you are out of this zone!

Don't Make Decisions in a Good Mood Either

This is the other side of the balance where you don't want to make major decisions just because you are feeling good – happy, ecstatic, or excited about something. Think about it, when you are walking down the streets and meet a salesman, they try to get you excited about what they are selling to the point that you lose control of your mind. This happens in such way that when they offer you their merchandise, they get you to feel so good about having it that you end up paying more for something that is not even worth it.

Don't get me wrong – I am not saying that feeling good is a bad thing. The point is, you must careful of your good moods just as much as of your bad ones.

Get to the Birds-eye View

Have you ever heard someone tell you that you are "above things?" well, this is something applicable to emotional intelligence as well. Take a minute to imagine yourself rise above your personality so that you can watch yourself from above. Think of yourself soaring high like an eagle and then watching yourself from high up there – getting a bigger view of yourself from a viewer's eye. How many things do you think you will see and understand about yourself?

While you may not look at yourself from above, the truth is that taking on an observer's view of yourself might just be what you need to understand your behavior. It will allow you to be aware of your thoughts and emotions in every situation you go through in life. You must try to inject yourself with the trigger and reaction so that you can process the whole information and get a new perspective of things. The goal here is to constantly remind yourself of the real emotional feelings that lie under all the layers.

Revisit Your Values and Actions Accordingly

From my point of view life is pretty much dynamic. The kind of work we do every day is hard and our families are very much demanding. Even in the middle of all that, it is important that you set take time to learn something new, have fun, and be at peace. Get involved in activities that give you these things – such as playing sports with your kids, watching your favorite TV series, answering emails, and making phone calls to friends and family. All these activities are enough to fill your day. However, these things are also the reason why your focus is on the outside when you should look at what lies inside you.

One thing to keep in mind is that all these things on your to-do list can be overwhelming and draining all the energy you have left. The trick is to stop and review your values and actions.

Take time to ask yourself if your career is moving in the right direction or if your job requires you to do things you are not comfortable with, if your colleagues treat you right, whether you have enough time for the things that matter most in your life, or if your current path leads you where you would like to be in a couple of years.

All these things are not there to scare you about the present and the future, but instead to help you evaluate your values, trust, responsibilities, and determine if they are sustainable. The goal is how

DARK PSYCHOLOGY 4 IN

you wish to change the world and make it a better place for you and your family.

Check Yourself

It is important to understand that self-awareness is mostly an internal process and that there are external implications of what happens inside you. This is why you must learn to get in the habit of regularly checking yourself to make sure everything is okay.

Think about how your face looks like, if your eyes look puffy, if your makeup is right, your clothes, do they look well? Are you beginning to wrinkle? Is your working space tidy? Do you assume the right posture when working? Do you communicate with confidence? When walking, do you take long steps?

The trick is to make sure you are aware of your normal self and are alert for times when you feel stressed. Realize that everything changes, and when you are aware of the things happening in and around you, it becomes easy to identify stress factors fast enough before they can reach your conscious mind.

Fill Your Blind Spot With Feedback

You must remember the windows of knowledge – which simply refers to the intimate parts of you that no one else knows about. Each one of us has three parts. What most of us are aware of are the private and the public parts of ourselves. However, what we fail to recognize is that blind spot – the part that we do not see.

The truth is your view of yourself may not be impartial, but other people can see what you truly are. The question is, are you willing to seek help from others? You must talk to someone you trust – spouse, partner, parent, or friend – to give you feedback about yourself. Be sure to observe the rule of communication – when you ask for feedback you should listen more than you talk. You must open your heart to the truth, and instead of trying to get defensive let the people closest to you tell you truthfully their observations without trying to hold them back.

That said, one of the foundations of emotional intelligence is self-awareness. It is through self-awareness that you can learn how to spot your emotions, their root cause and your reaction to them. With time, you will learn how to control them so you can use them to serve your mind and its true purpose.

The last thing you want is to go through the motions of life without really paying attention to your emotional feelings. You don't want to completely ignore your feelings or allow them to control you and get the best of you. Realize that emotions are powerful forces that do either work miracles in your life or ruin your life completely. By mastering the art of self-awareness, you can finally take back the control of your life into your hands and steer it in the direction you want to go.

Social Awareness

One thing is to recognize and understand your emotional feelings, but quite another is to accurately pick up and understand the emotions of others and what they are going through. If you are going to improve your emotional intelligence you must be willing to hold what you like so that you can practice social awareness. You have to stop talking, running monologues in your head, anticipating another person's answers before they can even utter a word, and trying to create answers when someone is speaking.

In other words, social awareness requires that you shift your focus from yourself to look out towards others, learn about them, and appreciate them. Social awareness is all about being grounded on our ability to recognize not only others' emotions but also understand them. While we may be tempted to focus only on our emotions, that luxury is not there if you are going to work in an environment where you are not the only one that exists in it.

Realize that when you tune your emotions to other people, you allow yourself to pick up on vital signals to what is going on with them. This way you can read the room and measure your answer to be sure it is connected to the person you are directing it to.

How can you do that?

Be Sure the Lens You Are Looking Through is Clear

This simply means that you must be there and ready to give others your undivided attention. You must prepare yourself to take up the role of an observer by using your five senses and realizing that your sixth sense is your emotions.

Note that your emotions are important lenses for the brain and they are what helps you understand other people signals. Be sure you are careful enough not to over project your emotions on others. Instead, use them as spider senses to stay alert and focus on what others are going through.

Watch Their Body Language

While someone may not always find the right words to express their feelings, the truth is that body language says it all. It is constantly communicating. According to research it is not yet clear how much of the message is interpreted through body language. However, one thing you must understand is that even if there is a disparity between words and body language, you believe the latter, right?

This is why when you are evaluating a person's body language you must do a head-to-toe evaluation. Start with their eyes and let your eyes lock with theirs – are they blinking, shifting, or trying to look away? That might be indicative of deception, sadness, or depression. Look at their face, is their smile forced or authentic? What about their posture – is it upright or slumped? Are their hands fidgeting? All these cues help inform your social awareness when interacting with others.

Listen Carefully

Listening is one way of communication. There is no way someone can talk nonstop without really paying attention to what the other has to say – by listening. It is not just about words but also the tone of their voice, the speed at which these words are used, and the spacing between words.

When you are interacting with others you must learn how to make a conscious effort to stop everything you are doing to just pay attention to what they have to say, how they say, and why they are saying it in the first place. When someone is speaking to you stop answering an email, texting, or doing some other activity. Give them your undivided attention, observe, and listen so that you can accurately pick up every piece of information they are trying to deliver.

That said, social awareness goes a long way in helping us recognize and interpret non-verbal signals other people use when communicating us a message. It is these cues that help you know what other people are feeling, how their emotions are changing every moment, and what is truly important to them.

Note that mindfulness is an ally of emotional and social awareness. To build your social awareness, you must recognize the important role of mindfulness in the social process. The truth is you will not be able to pick up nonverbal cues when you are trapped inside your head, thinking about things that don't even matter. If you are going to be socially aware, then you must be present at the moment.

While you may pride yourself for your ability to multitask, the truth is that it will cause you to miss subtle emotional shifts happening in other people, which eventually gets in the way of you understanding them. The trick is to leave your thoughts aside and then focus on the interaction itself. Follow the flow of the other person's emotional response by realizing that it is a give-and-take process that calls for attention to changing emotional experiences.

By focusing on others, your self-awareness does not have to decrease. When you invest your time and efforts on others, you make it easier to gain a deeper insight into your emotional state, values, and beliefs. If you are uncomfortable hearing others express their views and opinions, you learn something important about yourself.

Relationship Management

This is about making your relationships effective, fulfilling, and fruitful. The trick to do that is by becoming aware of how effectively you can use nonverbal cues when communicating with others. The truth is it is almost impossible to avoid transmitting nonverbal messages to the people around us concerning your feelings and thoughts.

The muscles on your face – especially those around the eyes, forehead, mouth, and nose – play a significant role in conveying emotions without even using words. They also allow you to read other people's emotions. When you master how to use and interpret these signals, you can significantly improve your relationships.

The other way is by using humor and play to relieve stress. These are natural antidotes to stress, and they can lower the burden so that you can keep things in perspective. Laughter does not only relieve stress, but it also brings the nervous system into balance, calms the body, sharpens the mind, and makes you more empathetic.

Finally, you must learn to see conflicts as opportunities to get closer to others. In every human relationship conflicts and disagreements are quite inevitable. You cannot possibly have your needs, expectations, and opinions met all the time – and that is not necessarily a bad thing. The truth is, conflict is good, and resolving them healthily and constructively goes a long way in strengthening trust between people. When conflict is not perceived as threatening, it can foster creativity, freedom, and safety of relationships.

Criteria for Effective Relationship Management

Decision

You must make every decision regarding what the best course of action is in a given situation. This is something that should be informed by prior research you do to deepen your understanding of how others feel and why they feel that way.

The truth is that you will have thoughts about varied ways of interacting with others and the different reactions you are likely to get when you say or do something. There is also a chance that you will be aware of the effect this has on you and how to properly manage it.

Interaction With Others

The way you interact with others should be based by your research and you could write it down or communicate with them face to face or through group discussions.

An Outcome

You must realize that what you say or do and how you say it is informed by certain outcomes you desire to achieve. This is what makes relationship management an intentional activity.

145

Your Needs

Your desired results must be guided by the particular needs you want to meet, one at a time.

Chapter 3 Busting Myths About Emotional Intelligence

As a human being and a leader, it is kind of difficult not to see the importance of emotional intelligence. It is because of emotional intelligence that I have achieved success both in business and life in general. It is this skill that has helped me see and understand my clients' pain points, stimulate a positive working environment, and improve my relationships both at the workplace and outside.

However, despite emotional intelligence's popularity and usefulness, several myths are surrounding it. It is a real shame having them because it can be a powerful tool you can use to drive success and happiness into your life. Here are some of the misconceptions about emotional intelligence that you need to let go of so that you can make the most of it in your career and life.

Emotional Intelligence Does not Exist

There are people – including psychologists – who believe that there is no such thing as emotional intelligence. The truth is that emotional intelligence is a relatively new concept, and different people have different ways of defining what it is. One thing you must bear in mind is that testing for emotional intelligence is not a scientific thing to do.

Emotional intelligence is real, and it is something that dates back to the '30s and '40s when people were trying to express their interest in this area. Edward Thorndike came up with the term social intelligence and explained how this was an essential component in our lives and in ensuring that we succeed in what we do. Several other people contributed to emotional intelligence until Goleman took it to the next level in 1995.

Even though it took a journalist to spread the concept across to the masses, the truth is that psychologists have been trying to understand this concept for decades. While some believe that this is not something that exists, there are several other experts who strongly believe and demonstrate its existence.

It is All About Empathy

Even after decades of writing and speaking to people about the science of emotional intelligence, it is interesting that there still are people who believe in one or more of emotional intelligence myths. What is shocking is that most people think that emotional intelligence is all about empathy.

While empathy is a component of emotional intelligence, the truth is that it is only a slice of the whole ability. It is much more complicated than just being charmingly empathic. It is the capacity of one to recognize your emotional feelings and those of the people around them, how to manage these emotions, and how to effectively interact with others. It is through emotional intelligence that one learns how to strike a healthy balance between social, emotional, and intelligence competencies.

It is not About Awareness But Behavioral Change

According to researchers, raw knowledge in itself is not about a change in behavior. For instance, we all know that smoking, eating fast foods every day and lack of physical exercise are bad for our health. Even with this knowledge people still need to be motivated to change their habits so that they can make choices that support their overall wellbeing. It is about calling people into the right kind of environment for the desired result to take place.

Just because you are aware of someone else's emotional feelings does not mean that you have high emotional intelligence. It is about using this knowledge you have and the motivation to do it and the right environment that supports your actions.

If you are a manager you can use emotional intelligence to your advantage during the hiring process. While it would not hurt to screen people's levels of emotional intelligence, what is good is to train them and equip them with the right skills to improve their EQ. From now on you can build a culture and surroundings where these skills are put to use.

Emotional Intelligence is Equated with Other Personality Traits

There is no way you can equate emotional intelligence to such personality traits as optimism, calmness, kindness, motivation and happiness, among others. Even though these personality traits are very important and help one achieve success in our lives, the truth is that they have very little to do with intelligence. They have very little to do with emotions and absolutely nothing to do with actual emotional intelligence.

Unfortunately, there are trained psychologists who tend to confuse emotional intelligence with character traits. The truth is that these personality traits should be called exactly what they are instead of mixing them up in an assortment named emotional intelligence.

Emotional Intelligence Predicts Success

For decades, people have thought that those who are most successful in life are emotionally intelligent. While it is easy to see how emotional intelligence influences how a person communicates, leads and negotiates, research shows that we tend to do business with people we choose and like.

Yes, emotional intelligence plays a significant role in one's success, but it is not the only indicator/predictor. Take a look at all the top successful people across the world and rate them one by one – you will be surprised to find that most of them lack even an ounce of emotional intelligence.

What you need to understand is that people are very diverse, and there are equally diverse ways one can achieve success, become accomplished leaders, enjoy a successful professional life, and build a brilliant company. Unfortunately for some, emotional intelligence is not part of the equation. According to research published in the Journal of Applied Psychology there is no correlation between emotional intelligence and job performance.

You Either Have EI, or You Don't

Some people believe that emotional intelligence is innate. In other words they strongly think that it is something you are born with or without. The truth is that emotional intelligence is something that anyone can learn and develop.

Yes, it may not happen overnight but you can become emotionally intelligent if you continually practice self-awareness, relationship management, social awareness, and self-management. It is through these skills that you can master how to channel your emotions in the right direction and for the right reasons. The best way to start is to become mindful of your words and know your triggers. Trust me, once you step up your empathy skills, you are on your way to achieving emotional intelligence.

You Have to Give Up Emotional Intelligence to Be Mentally Tough

Over the last couple of years several people have discussed the importance of mental toughness. This is something that it is commonly directed towards people who have served in the army – specifically the Navy Seals and marines.

I have found this advice to be more useful to help yourself strengthen your focus and resilience. However, when it comes to emotional intelligence, mentally tough people tend to ignore their emotions and those of the people around them. And this is something that conflicts with the misconceptions that emotions are a sign of weakness.

If you cannot raise your awareness of your emotional feelings and those of people around you, there is absolutely no way you can say that you are emotionally intelligent. Rather than trying to be mentally tough, you must not allow other people to use your emotions against you. For instance, if you see a high-performing athlete, they might seem that they are in the "zone," but the truth is that they have no idea what is happening around them. They tend to keep a cool head just until the game is over.

Realize that mental toughness is not just about driving stricter timelines. It is about taking a pause to just listen to what lies inside you, so that you have a better understanding of yourself and those around you and where they are coming from. It is about having the discipline not to get too immersed in emotions.

There is no Dark Side to Emotional Intelligence

Whenever we talk about emotional intelligence, it is always about something positive. However, just like with any other force, there is always a light and dark side. A good example of this is leaders who drum-up fear just to satisfy their own selfish needs. In this case, it would be to keep employees in check or just have people vote for them.

When people hone their emotional skills, they increase their likelihood of manipulating others. This is mainly because when you can control your emotional feelings you tend to mask your true feelings. When you know that other people are experiencing certain emotional feelings, chances are you will pull on their heartstrings and motivate them to go against their best interests.

This does not mean that you should start being wary of emotional intelligence. If you have boosted your emotional intelligence, you will be in a better position to identify when someone else is trying to cover your eyes and cloud your judgment.

It Does not Influence Our Decisions

In reality, it is not possible to decide without have an emotional bias. The truth is that every feeling starts with an external stimulus regardless of what someone has said or what the physical events are. From that point on, the brain generates an emotional feeling that causes the body to produce responsive hormones. These hormones, in turn, enter the bloodstream to create a positive or a negative feeling.

There is no Correlation Between Emotional Intelligence and Physical Wellbeing

According to research studies, having a higher emotional intelligence is associated with improving the psychological and physical health of an individual. This is something that you and I could take for granted, right?

Having the ability to notice, understand, and fix our moods goes a long way to ensure that we make healthier decisions in life. For instance, if you are stressed you might feel the need to turn to comfort foods, cigarettes, alcohol, or something else, just to try and overcome that emotion. Unfortunately, all these things you are turning to are unhealthy vices. The worst part is that when you ignore these emotional feelings, you start experiencing symptoms such as fatigue, stomach pain, muscle tension, and other potentially life-threatening conditions like heart disease.

Chapter 4 Steps on How to Grow Emotional Intelligence

Step 1 Tapping Into Your Emotions

Note Your Emotional Reactions to Events Throughout the Day

It is easy to place your emotional feelings on your experiences throughout the day. One thing you should note is that taking the time to acknowledge how you feel about your experiences is critical to improving your emotional intelligence. Ignoring your feelings means that you are ignoring important information that has a significant impact on your mindset and how you carry yourself. You must choose to focus your attention on your emotional feelings so that you can easily connect them to your experiences.

For instance, if you are at the workplace in a meeting and suddenly a colleague interrupts you when you are still presenting your point. What emotions are you likely to experience? What if you are being praised for the good work you have done, what would you feel?

When you get into the habit of naming your emotions as they happen, you raise your awareness of the surroundings and each experience you go through along with the emotions those experiences stir up. This way, you start to gradually increase your emotional intelligence.

The trick is for you to get in the habit of tapping into your emotions throughout the day. Think about how you feel when you wake up and before you go to bed, and make it a habit.

Pay Attention to your Body

Rather than trying to ignore the physical manifestations of your emotional feelings, you must start listening to them. Realize that your mind and body are interconnected and neither can survive without the other. In other words, the body and the mind deeply influence each other.

To raise your emotional intelligence, you must learn how to read physical signals and use them to find out what emotions you are experiencing. For instance when you are stressed, you might feel like there is a knot in your stomach, a tightening on your chest, or paced breathing. When you are sad, it might feel like getting up with slow and heavy limbs. When you are happy or anxious, you might feel butterflies in your stomach or your heart racing fast.

Observe How Your Emotions and Behavior are Connected

Take a minute to reflect on the last time you felt a strong emotion; how did you react?

Often, when we feel strong emotional feelings we try to mask them so that we don't have to deal with them much less have people realize that we are going through something. Well, emotional intelligence is about tuning into your gut feeling in every situation you experience every other day, instead of choosing to react without taking the time to reflect.

Note that the deeper your understanding of what triggers your impulses, the more you increase your emotional intelligence to be in a better position to use what you know to change your future behavior.

Here are a couple of examples of behaviors and what underlies them;

- Feeling embarrassed or insecure has a likelihood of making you withdraw from others and from engaging in conversations.
- When you are angry you might realize your voice rises or angrily turns away.

- When you are overwhelmed, you might panic and lose track of what matters most in your life.

Avoid Judging Your Own Emotions

Do you know that every emotional feeling you have is valid – even if it is negative? One thing you must note is that even if your emotions are negative, judging them will only inhibit your ability to fully feel them and hence to use them positively.

Think of it this way – every emotion you are feeling carries bits and pieces of information connected to something that is happening around you. Without this information you will remain in the dark about what is the right way to react. This explains the reason our ability to feel our emotions is a form of intelligence.

Yes, this is not something you will master overnight, but with the practice of letting go of negative emotions, you can effectively connect them to what is happening around you. For instance, if you are bitterly envious, the first thing you need to ask yourself is what that emotion is telling you about the whole situation. It is also important that you fully experience every positive emotion. Try to connect your satisfaction or happiness to what is happening in your life so that you can often master how to feel them.

Notice Patterns in Your Emotional History

It is one way to learn about recognizing your feelings, but it is quite the other to connect them to your experiences. When you have a strong emotion, it is important to try and reflect the time when you last felt that way. Try to assess what happened before, during, and after the event.

This will help you see a pattern so that you can exert more control over your behavior. Take note of how you handled the situation before and what the outcome was. This way you can make a better decision this time to handle the situation differently, so that you can get the desired result. It is also important to keep a journal of emotional reactions and how you feel with each passing day so that you can determine if there is a pattern in the way you react to situations.

Practice Deciding How to Behave

One thing to keep in mind is that you cannot help the emotions you feel. However, you can choose to stay connected to everything that is happening around you. Without this set of information you are likely to be left out in the dark about how you can appropriately react. This is why having the ability to feel your emotions is a form of intelligence.

When something unpleasant happens in your life you should take a moment to feel your emotions. Allow that wave of sadness and anger wash over you. Once that wave is gone the next thing is for you to decide on what the appropriate course of action should be. Instead of repressing your feelings, you must communicate them or keep trying, instead of throwing a towel.

Don't try to escape your emotions. Yes, letting your negative feelings rise to the surface may not be the best thing to do, and you may be tempted to control them by silly drinking, burying your head in movies, or turning on habits that numb your pain. The truth is that when you do this, your EQ will start going down.

Step 2 Connecting with Other People

Be Open-minded and Agreeable

When it comes to emotional intelligence, being open and agreeable go hand in hand. When you have a narrow mind you are generally saying that you have a low EQ. However when you allow your mind to be open you not only gain understanding and reflect on what is happening internally, but it also gets easier to handle conflicts in a self-assured and calm manner. You will simply become socially aware of what others are going through, and see possibilities begin to open to you.

One of the best ways you can strengthen your EQ is to listen to debates on radio or Television. Ensure that you consider both sides of the argument and find out what subtleties require your close inspection. When someone fails to react the same way you would, don't try to be mad at them. Instead, the reasons they reacted that way and try to see things from their perspective.

Improve Your Empathy Skills

Empathy simply refers to the ability to recognize how others are feeling so that you can share emotions with them. When you are an active listener, you can pay attention to what others are saying so that you get a better sense of what they are feeling. In other words, you are using the situation to make informed choices that will help improve your relationships – and that is a sign of emotional intelligence.

If you want to grow your empathy, you must be willing to put yourself in the other person's shoes. Try to think about how you would react if you were in the same situation. When you actively imagine what it must be like to experience the same situation, you will not only identify with their hardship but will also see ways to help them through support and care.

Whenever you see someone experiencing strong emotions, the first thing you need to ask yourself is how you would react in the same situation. Being truly interested in what the other person is saying or experiencing helps a great deal in ensuring that you react more sensitively. Rather than allowing your thoughts drift from side to side, ask yourself questions and put what they are saying in summary form so that they know that you are in the conversation with them.

Read People's Body Language

You must read between lines and pick up what the other person is truly feeling by focusing on their body language and facial expressions. There are times when people say things when their body language and facial expression are saying a different thing. You must practice being observant so that you can pick up on what is less obvious – because that is where people's emotions lie.

If you are not sure that you can accurately interpret another's body language and facial expressions, try taking a quiz. When they raise their voice, it indicates that they are not only stressed but also angry about the whole situation.

See the Effect You Have on Others

When it comes to emotional intelligence, understanding other people's emotions is only half the battle. It is important that you also understand what effect you have on them. When you are around people, do you tend to make them nervous, anxious, angry, or cheerful? When you walk into a room where people are having a discussion, do they get enthusiastic and open up more, or do they retract and end the conversation?

When you put these things into perspective, you will not only identify the patterns you need to change but also see how you can appropriately change to improve the situation. If you are someone who tends to pick fights with loved ones or cause people to close up when you are around them, you should consider changing your attitude so that you can improve the emotional effect you have on others.

Start by asking your loved ones what they think about your emotionality and where you can improve, so that you become a better person. It could be your tone of voice, listening skills, or something else. Whatever it is, you can ask people you trust to help you recognize the effect you have on others and how they can help you change for the better.

Practice Being Emotionally Honest

When someone tells you that they are "fine" with a frown, it means they are not communicating honestly. The same thing happens; you are the person on the other side of a conversation. One thing you must realize is that for people to read you better you have to be able to physically open up about your emotions. When you get into an argument, tell people that you are angry, upset, or disappointed in them. When something is making you happy, share that happiness and joy with the people around you.

When you are yourself, you make it easier for other people to get to know you better. People will tend to trust you more when you show them where you are coming from. That said, one thing you must not forget is that there is a line: learn to control your emotions so that you don't hurt the people around you.

Step 3 Putting EQ to Practical Use

See Where You Have Room For Improvement

In life, being intellectually capable is very important. However, being emotionally intelligent is an essential need. When you have high emotional intelligence you are in a better position to seize job opportunities as they present themselves or lead a better relationship. The four core elements of emotional intelligence we have discussed in the previous chapter will help you figure out where you need improvement in your life. Is it self-awareness, self-management, social awareness, or relationship management? Whatever it is, you can work on improving it and boost your emotional intelligence.

Lower Your Stress Level by Raising Your EQ

When you hear someone say that they are stressed, what they are simply saying is that they are feeling overwhelmed by a wide range of emotions. Life is filled with difficult situations ranging from relationship breakups to job loss. In between these things are millions of stress triggers that have the potential of making any daily issue a challenge. If you are stressed a lot, it is hard to behave the way you want to. However, when you have a plan in place to help you relieve stress, you stand a chance of improving your emotional intelligence and all aspects surrounding it.

What triggers your stress? What can you do to help alleviate your stress? Create a list of all forms of stress relief from hanging out with friends to taking a walk to enjoy nature – anything to put it into good use. That said, if you feel that your stress levels are getting out of hand you must consider getting the help you need from a professional therapist. They can give you the tools you need to cope with stress and raise your EQ in the process.

Be More Light-hearted at Home and Work

When you have optimism it becomes easier to see the beauty in life. It becomes easy to turn your awareness into everyday objects so that you can share your emotional feelings with the people in your life. Trust me, no one wants to sit down and spend time with someone who has no optimism.

When you are optimistic, you draw people to yourself and enjoy all the possibilities these connections have to offer. On the other hand, if you are negative you will push people away instead of building your resilience. Emotionally intelligent people know how to use their humor and fun to make themselves and the people around them feel happier and safer – and they can use laughter to get through tough situations.

Chapter 5 Emotional Intelligence at School/Workplace

Each passing day, we all make emotionally charged decisions. Each time we are planning something we feel as though our plan A is better than plan B, and end up making choices based on our gut instincts or emotions. However, when we understand where these emotions are coming from in the first place, only then will we become in harmony to each other – especially when working in a team.

With the increase in globalization, emotional intelligence has found a significant place in our lives because places at school or work have become more cross-cultural and global. It is because of globalization that our interactions have become complex along with how we express these emotions.

One thing you must remember is that emotional intelligence in school or at the workplace comes down to expressing, understanding and managing good relationships and addressing problems even when you are under intense pressure from above.

Today, the conventional measure of intelligence pays attention to logic and reasoning in such areas as math and reading comprehension. The general idea that this kind of reasoning is what determines our success and productivity at the workplace is persuasive and intuitive as well. This is mainly because it measures our ability to grasp and digest facts in our surroundings.

However, the idea that there is only one form of intelligence has recently been subjected to intense scrutiny. Many psychologists now have the theory of multiple intelligences. The two major areas that are measured in tests include verbal-linguistic intelligence and logical-math intelligence. But these are only two areas out of nine different areas of intelligence with varied characteristics.

162

That said, not all these intelligences have found their way into the world of business. For instance, bodily-kinesthetic intelligence is what most dancers, athletes, and other forms of physical labor use. It is through this form of intelligence that minds have been opened to greater possibilities of thinking and achieving success.

On the other hand, the ideas about rational intelligence took root from the enlightenment that happened soon after scientific thoughts were codified for the very first time. The very early aspect used by natural philosophers was the idea of rational objectivity, which required that individuals attempt to view the world around them not as they desire it to be but as it is. While this idea may seem perfect on the surface, the problem is that it often causes people to move away from using their gut feelings and using their emotions in finding solutions to real-life problems. It is important to note that rational intelligence does not only focus on hard facts, but also logical reasoning that results from unproductive scenarios of win-lose cases.

In today's workplace, excelling means striking a balance between interpersonal and intrapersonal intelligence. The former simply refers to the ability to detect and respond to other people's emotions, moods, desires, and motivations. On the other hand, the latter simply refers to the ability to raise our awareness of self so that we are more aligned with our beliefs, values, and thought processes.

When you combine these concepts, what you get is a good overview of emotional intelligence and how it is related to business leadership. When you don't have the guiding influence of rational intelligence, emotional intelligence ends up being subjective in such a way that it is no longer useful for business goals. However, if they are properly treated, it serves as a key to drive internal collaborations and external alliances.

EI is the Key to Communication in the Workplace and School

In its most refined form, emotional intelligence offers empathy which is important to help us to fully understand others' perspective even when it contradicts our own view of things. According to research there is evidence that shows women who have high emotional intelligence tend to act in collaborative ways by embracing an inclusive leadership style, as compared to men.

It does not matter whether you are a man or a woman when you practice emotional intelligence. There are so many more benefits it has to offer at the workplace and to all stakeholders across the industry. This is by:

- Helping leaders to motivate and inspire good works among its employees by understanding other people's motivators.
- Bringing more people to the table and helping one avoid the traps of group thinking.
- Empowering leaders to not only recognize possibilities, but act on opportunities that other people may not be aware of in the first place.
- Assisting in conflict identification and resolution in such a fair and even-handed manner.
- Producing higher morale and helping other people to make the most of their professional potential.

Just like rational intelligence, emotional intelligence is something you and I can cultivate if we put an effort and take the time to study it more. The very first step to developing emotional intelligence is by strengthening your power of introspection. It is about recognizing your emotional feelings, thought processes, and biases, so that whenever you are making decisions they are not only informed but well-rounded. When you exercise emotional intelligence, you must act in confidence, rise above your fears and worries, and be able to question the status quo and avoid gut reactions.

Emotional Intelligence in Hiring Processes

Even though technical skills are things that can be imparted through training, the truth is that it is more challenging to teach emotional intelligence during the recruitment process at the workplace. While companies can integrate theories of emotional intelligence in their hiring processes and professional development in all spheres, the truth is that it is not easy to achieve that with a 100% accuracy.

For instance, when hiring entry-level employees, you may wish to test for their EQ when you have a group of candidates competing for the same new position or a promotion. Most managers, leaders, and stakeholders identified as having high emotional intelligence and high leadership potential tend to deliver better results as part of their development process.

Even though most roles at the workplace could benefit from emotional intelligence, the truth is that not all roles require highly developed emotional intelligence. The higher one climbs in the career ladder, the more valuable emotional intelligence becomes.

This explains why professionals such as the Human Resource or Public Relations departments benefit a lot from emotional intelligence because they are mostly involved in the hiring process. This is mainly because their emotional development plays a significant role in helping companies maximize their contributions and optimize their investments for future growth and development.

Emotional Intelligence in the Globalized Economy

Just as the global economy has developed into a system of partnerships, negotiations and communications, emotional intelligence plays a bigger role in the public sphere. This is why emotional intelligence is strongly correlated to such traits as self-control, perseverance, and increased performance and productivity, even under pressure. It is what offers leaders with the emotional strength to adjust and adapt to change, deal with setbacks, and achieve goals no matter their skills.

It does not matter how the economy changes. What matters most is that conventional intelligence will always be the center of success in the global economy. That said, bear in mind that even the most technical of all roles requires one to greatly expand networks with diversified stakeholder portfolios, taking up roles in complex atmospheres and investing both emotional and mental capital to handle the most unexpected of situations. Both rational and emotional intelligence are here to stay, and it takes brilliant leaders, managers, and students to exhibit both.

Chapter 6 Emotional Intelligence and Health

Physical Health

According to research, there is evidence that shows emotional intelligence has a significant and direct impact on our physical health. Instead of using a traditional aspect of emotional intelligence, you better use a trait meta-mood scale (TMMS) that directly relates to the core aspect of EQ;

Attention

This refers to the ability to take note and focus our attention on our feelings.

Clarity

This simply refers to the ability to clearly understand the nature of your moods.

Repair

This refers to your ability to maintain a positive mood, repair negative emotions were necessary to achieve your goals.

When you look at things from this perspective, what you will note is that emotional intelligence can affect physical health. For instance you have the power of attention, clarity, and repair. There is a high likelihood that the following scenario holds to you.

First, you could begin to feel easily irritable and cannot seem to put your mind on one thing. After a couple of considerations you realize that you didn't have your breakfast because you woke up late and had to prepare the kids for school and get ready for work. You realize that all you have had are two cups of coffee since you woke up. What you are essentially feeling is hunger pangs. You decide to take a break to go into the breakroom to fix yourself a healthy snack because you can't hold till lunch, which is still two hours away.

In the above rudimentary example, the truth is that you paid attention to your mood, identified the reason that underlies it, and exerted your effort into repairing the negative emotions you are feeling before they get out of hand – by coming up with a solution that will address your needs and contribute to your desired outcome.

What do you notice about this example? Well, the truth is that emotional intelligence positively affects one's health.

Several research studies that have been conducted relate the elements of emotional stress and the behavioral response of cardiac, hormonal and enzymatic activity. Some research participants are writing about their traumatic emotional events – including recall and evaluation. During these sessions, their blood pressure was measured.

Without offering an exhaustive account of the research studies, the results showed that people who accurately perceive their emotional feelings could cope with stressful situations. They also demonstrated the ability to overcome hesitancy by seeking medical help, accepting changes in their bodies, and proactively seeking a resolution to achieve better health.

This is something that can be done with such habits as an improved diet, overcoming alcohol addiction and a regular workout regimen. All these behavioral patterns are associated with strong emotional intelligence, increased level of dynamism, acceptance of personal reality, and responsibility for your own well-being.

In other words, self-awareness, motivation, and self-management increase your likelihood of enjoying a positive health regardless of how and when they manifest in your life.

Mental Health

According to research, mental health conditions are linked to lower levels of emotional intelligence. For instance, someone with borderline personality disorder (BPD) has shown greater sensitivity to expressing emotional feelings. What is interesting is that people with BPD often struggle to label their emotions and what they truly mean. The downside to this is that they cannot seem to control their emotions.

Someone with depression has been shown to have a lower EQ score. These kinds of people tend to show less sensitivity to changing emotional contexts, hence causing them to get stuck in negativity.

Social anxiety, on the other hand, has also been linked to a low EQ. Such a person tends to fear what others will think or say about them. They have a high likelihood of perceiving neutral expressions like hostility, which causes them to misinterpret social signals.

The other thing that is important to note is that substance abuse contributes to serious deficits in aspects related to emotional intelligence. Unlike the conditions we have already mentioned, drug abuse contributes to impaired emotional perception and regulation.

What is even interesting is that research studies have shown that there is a link between low emotional intelligence and self-destructive habits. In other words, some people use self-harm as a way of regulate their emotions. By improving your emotional intelligence, you significantly impact your mental health, so that people can have reduced tendencies for aggression and quickly recover from trauma.

This explains the reason why mental health awareness is on the rise and risks reaching proportions that will stretch services. While there have been more studies on mental health, the truth is that no one should doubt the fact that we need more information in this area.

Mental health is a condition that can strike anyone at any age, gender, profession, or culture. There are several reasons mental health issues occur, and yet there is no single case that can be considered the same as the other.

That is why we propose emotional intelligence in support strategies that help people recover from mental health issues. Don't get me wrong; I am not saying that you should replace therapy and medical attention with emotional intelligence. However, people with mental issues at the lower end of the spectrum could greatly benefit from EI.

Through self-awareness, you can identify your strengths and weaknesses and leverage them to your advantage. When you know your weak areas, you can better position yourself to improve your mental balance. Remember that self-awareness is a central component of emotional intelligence and has been tested in a wide range of fields. When someone has mental health problems, increasing their awareness of their emotions allows them to recognize their issues before they can get out of hand – prevention is better than cure!

That is why self-awareness is integral to our mental balance. For instance, if you are aware of your emotions and actions and can recognize that there are certain areas where you need help to controlling your emotions, you can learn how to effectively manage them. This is because your awareness will focus on your emotional feelings and the strategies you can use to manage them. Instead of taking on more tasks than you can handle, you take on projects you can complete, lower stress levels, and achieve mental balance. Doing this will not only help you get better but will also improve your self-confidence, create positivity, enhance your mindset, facilitate balance and happiness in your life.

There are so many ways you can improve your mental state and boost your emotional intelligence. One of them is through the practice of mindfulness. Mindfulness plays a significant role in helping people deal with their current situations. For instance, when you pause to just take in a deep breath, you not only allow your mind to shift to the present moment, but also allow your mind and body to regain balance and more control.

The other way you can achieve mental balance is through meditation. While not everyone will feel comfortable with meditation, the truth is that it is very effective. You do not have to be religious to practice meditation. When you meditate you give focus and scope to your mind. It needs to deal with emotional imbalance. One thing with mental health is that it is associated with a lack of energy and motivation. However, when you meditate and allow your mind to feed on positive self-talk and affirmations, you not only release all negativity but also allow the mind to see possibilities where the balance was lacking.

Yes, someone with mental health issues might not feel positively changing their thought process. However, small changes here and there go a long way in bringing positivity into your life. Instead of thinking that you cannot do something, you can simply turn that into something positive like *"I've got what it takes to do this."*

The other trick is to use music, something that has been shown to boost emotional intelligence. It does not only improve one's mood and emotions but also encourages one to use a reflective process, which offers you the opportunity to evaluate yourself, your emotions, thoughts, and progress.

For you to grow you must learn to motivate yourself to meet both your intrinsic and extrinsic needs – which can be physical, mental, nutritional, physiological or a combination of all. The best way to use motivation is to effectively direct it through the use of process goals. Within the facet of mental health, one of the key drivers is the use of motivation to create energy. According to research, when you have not motivation you risk having one aspect of mental health. Adopt

171

motivation strategies – such as positive self-talk and goal setting – to reverse this trend.

Finally, how many friends do you have? Are these quality friendships? Well, it is one thing to have many friends but it is quite another to have friends who look out for you and who help you become each day a better person. This is what quality friendship is all about, and is the kind of support needed by mental health cases. To improve your emotional intelligence you must look for opportunities to meet new people and build new relationships. While this is something that can be challenging for people with mental health issues, the truth is that positioning yourself within the right time and space makes it possible, when your purpose of building new friendships and growing the existing ones allows you to open up and achieve consistency of trust.

Chapter 7 Emotional Intelligence and Relationships

The secret to a lasting relationship is emotional intelligence. This is mainly because emotional intelligence makes people extremely aware of changes happening around them –small or big. When you build your emotional intelligence you simply boost your sensitivity that we all are seeking in our partners. Through active awareness and empathy you will gain the ability to sense when there is a slight change in the dynamics of your romance so that you can act accordingly.

Realize that you have the potential to attain the kind of love you have always dreamed of. A relationship where you enjoy deep intimacy, real commitment, mutual kindness, and soulful caring. This is simply because of empathy – out innate ability to share our emotional experiences with others.

However, for anyone to reach this height of intimacy and romance, you need all the skills of high emotional intelligence – sharp emotional awareness, acceptance, a vigilant active social awareness. Your emotional awareness will help you avoid making mistakes by getting lustful or intoxicated in love. Acceptance, on the other hand, goes a long way in helping us experience emotions that have the potential of harming us if left unattended. Finally, active vigilance is what helps us to evaluate our relationship so that we know what is working and what is not.

So, how we can then build emotionally intelligent romantic relationships?

One thing you must realize is that you don't have to choose the wrong lovers and end up in a failed marriage. You don't have to sit back and watch romance seep into your long-term relationship. Look inside your relationship and determine whether there are conflicting needs and wants that might come between you and your partner. The truth is, you deserve a loving and healthy relationship filled with romance.

173

The last thing you want is to resign yourself to boredom or fighting in your love life.

The truth is that you have the potential to attain the kind of love you have always wanted. This does not mean that your emotional intelligence should be at a peak before you can find love. Research shows that falling in love helps most people stay motivated to educate their hearts. This explains why most deeply passionate lovers are in their eighties because they find out that a high emotional intelligence in both partners adds up to romance that never stops growing, does not lose its spark, and always seeks to strengthen them – both individually and collectively.

Here's how you can boost the EQ in your relationship;

Actively Seek Change in Your Relationship

Look around you. Everyone you know are in relationships, but none of them likes change. People fear change because they think that it will destroy their romance and attraction to each other. However, the opposite is true. Change helps you realize everything you have been missing.

One thing to keep in mind is that change does not necessarily have to mean worse. Research shows that things often come out better than ever on the other side of change. Think of your romantic relationship as an organism, that by nature, must change. It is through change that a relationship gets to grow. Your ability to embrace change plays a significant role in helping you gain courage and a sense of optimism.

Take a minute to think about your relationship – what is it that your partner needs most from you? Is it something new? Do you need time to reassess things together? Are there external influences in your life that are demanding some change in the roles in your relationship? Do you consider yourself happier than you used to be?

Without emotional intelligence these questions are very challenging and scary to answer, and that is the reason why several lovers ignore the signals of change until it is out of control.

Look at Challenges as Opportunities Instead of Problems

Did you know that courage and optimism are what help people view dilemmas as challenging opportunities rather than problems?

Take a minute to think about how creative you and your partner can be. This is the point where you don't need to blame each other for emotions. In other words, you are not controlled by negative emotional influences. You are simply alert enough not to repeat the mistakes you have made in the past.

With high emotional intelligence you are free from resignations and routine, so that you start looking at problems as opportunities for growth. You are not afraid when the problem comes up because you know that you can simply come down and do some brainstorming to solve the problems. You view differences as opportunities to come together and get closer, so that you can both come out on the other side of victory stronger, together and individually.

Respect All the Feelings You Have for Each Other

The truth is that none of us is delighted by the discoveries we make about our partners. However, one thing you must realize is that when it comes to emotions, you must accept them all. Falling in love with someone does not mean that you will never be angry, disappointed, jealous, or hurt.

The truth is that it is up to you how you respond to these emotions. What matters the most is that you feel them. Several relationships have been ruined by blame, and millions of couples have dismissed their need for deep intimacy because of shame. The truth is that these

175

things are cruel reminders of fear, anxiety, and anger. If you have done what it takes to build your emotional intelligence, you will choose to experience the emotions together so that you can get on with your lives together.

Keep Laughter in Your Love Life

Several couples intellectualize their emotions without even realizing it. If you are one of them, you need to realize that acceptance is what you need, and a large part of that comes with lots of laughter. To be accepted in your relationship, you must learn to laugh with each other.

If you cannot laugh together, chances are you will not be able to stand each other's unique flaws and inevitable stumbling blocks any more than you can tolerate your own. You will not have the ability to accept surprises no matter how pleasant they might be. However, when you work on growing your emotional intelligence you will not only ensure that you constantly improve your relationship but also ensure that you never get trapped by expectations of perfection.

Pay Attention to How You Feel When Your Spouse or Partner Is not Around

Fortunately there are several ways you can use to monitor precisely how your relationship is going. These are the three-gauge means of measuring your well-being when trying to figure out how the rest of your life is supposed to be.

The first thing is to ask yourself whether you feel restless or irritable? Do you find yourself dragging through the day after a night of marital bliss? Do you find yourself resenting family and friends even though you are both spending time alone together?

One thing you must realize is that love never feeds on tunnel vision. Realize that no matter how you coo like a dove with your partner if you lack energy, clarity of mind, and benevolence at all times. Yes, you may enjoy all the sex you have together, but if you lack energy the morning or day after, then something is wrong.

So, how can you then know that the other person is "the one?"

Well, the truth is that when you are first falling in love, you must know that the person you are about to settle down with is "the one." The last thing you want is to make a mistake, get in the wrong marriage and end up in a lifeless union. Here are some of the tips that will help you know;

Listen to Your Body And Not Your Mind

Unfortunately, most people choose their mate for reasons that have nothing to do with what they feel and instead have to do with what they think. What is more, we tend to drive our relationships based on how things should be or have been.

This is where you go wrong!

The truth is that you don't lose at love because you allowed your emotions to run away from you, but because you let your mind run away from you.

You may think that you are in love for so many reasons – such as infatuation, lust, status, security, or social acceptance. You think that you have found true love because your current partner meets your expectations and some image you have created in your head of your dream partner. What you must realize is that unless you know how you feel, your choice is only destined to be wrong!

177

Whenever you imagine your dream partner, the best thing is to transport that form of mental debate to justify your choice so that you can check it with your body. Take in a deep breath, allow your mind and body to relax, and focus by getting out of your head and into your body. What does your gut feeling tell you? is there a persistent feeling that keeps growing inside, saying that something is wrong? If so, then chances are that your choice is wrong!

The truth is, if you allow your mental image versus physical sensation to lead you, you will never know what you *truly* want.

Notice the Messages From Your Whole Body

When you are in a new relationship it can be difficult to get clear signals from the rest of your body because they are likely drowned out by all the sexual desires running around. This explains why you need to pay attention to other important and more subtle feelings – migraines, lack of energy, muscle tension, and stomach pains. These feelings could simply mean that your desires are not really what you need.

However, if you find yourself glowing of love, have liveliness, and a spark of energy, this could be the real deal. If it is only lust or infatuation, chances are that you will feel it in other parts of your life and relationships.

Take a moment to ask yourself the following high emotional intelligence questions;

- Does this relationship energize me and my whole life? Has my work life improved? Am I taking better care of myself?
- Are my head and focus straighter? Am I creative and more responsible?
- Do my "in love feelings" go beyond positive feelings of caring about the other person in the relationship? Am I more

DARK PSYCHOLOGY 4 IN

generous, more giving and empathic towards the people around me than I was before?

The truth is, if the responses you get from your body are not exactly what you wanted to hear, it is time to push beyond your fears of loss so that you can look at things from a bigger picture perspective. Finding out at this point that you have not found your true love will spare you of all the heartache, pain, and a pile of negative emotional memories you risk experiencing down the line. Consider this a legacy that can keep you from making the same mistake again and ending up in sour love in the future.

Take a Chance on Reaching Out

When you are in a new relationship, there is always that feeling to be on your guard. We tend to automatically put up barriers and walls when it comes to knowing each other deeply. When you leave yourself open and vulnerable at this point in the relationship, you tend to feel scared, when in the real sense you are trying to find out if the love you feel for the other person is real.

You must become the first person to reach out. This is something that will reveal an intimate secret, demonstrate affection, laugh at yourself when everything seems scary. Think of it – do the other person's reactions fill you with vitality and warmth? If they do chances are that you have found a kindred soul. If not, you have found someone with low emotional intelligence and it is time for you to decide how you wish to respond.

What You Need to Feel Loved vs. What You Want

If you are going to find someone you truly love, then you must know the difference between what you would like, from what you cannot live without. These are some of the exercises that will help you get it right;

Start by selecting at least five features or traits in the other partner you feel are most important to you. Order these character traits in descending order. Some of them may be neatness, adventurous, humor, emotionally, open, considerate, smart, affectionate, monetarily successful, well respected, famous, charismatic, spiritual, empowering, nurturing, and conversational, among others.

As you consider each trait, ask yourself if they make you energetic, calm, and emotionally stir you. Find out if these traits make you feel pleasant, unpleasant, or indifferent.

Realize that a desire will be fleeting and superficial, while something you consider a need will automatically register on a deeper level of feelings.

Repeat this exercise over and over again so that you gain a deeper insight into the differences between what you need in love, and what you want. Ask yourself if the other person in the relationship thinks that you are in love to meet these needs.

How to Respond to a Low EQ Partner

One thing you must realize is that we don't all grow our emotional muscles at the same rate. If you have a high emotional intelligence compared to your lover, the most important thing is to learn how to respond to them.

What words do you want your partner to hear? You must take the time to reconsider what words to use. If you are not sure about what exactly you need and the reasons you need this, there is a high likelihood that your message will be mixed up.

You must choose a time when you and your partner are not in a hurry to take a walk together, go on a date, or brunch. While at it, ensure that you are intimately into the conversation so that at the end of it, you both can remember the discussion. During the day send your partner "I feel" text messages concerning your needs. This will help your partner see what is wrong with them for a chance to improve. For instance, you can text them, "I feel like making love every day, but I don't like the smell of garlic and onions. Would you be willing to brush your teeth before we go to bed?"

There is a high likelihood that partners will respond defensively. If they do, you must repeat their concerns back to them. Repeat the message and pay attention to what they have to say about it. If possible, keep repeating it over and over again until you are satisfied that they heard what you communicated to them.

Chapter 8 The Interaction Between EQ and Social Intelligence

It is important to note that social intelligence is about developing experience with people and learning from our failures and successes in our surroundings. In most cases social intelligence is what people commonly refer to as tact, street smartness, or common sense.

What you will note about people with high emotional intelligence is that they carry on conversations with different kinds of people and can verbally communicate with the right words – hence referred to as social expressiveness.

Additionally, such people are adept at learning how to conduct a wide range of social roles and responsibilities. They are well versed on the informal rules of the game, are excellent listeners, and can thoroughly analyze what makes tick the people around them. They know this by focusing their attention on what others have to say and their behaviors.

They not only know various ways of conducting a wide range of social roles but also can put their skills into practice so that they are at ease with a wide range of personalities. In other words, they are careful what impression of themselves they create in other people. This is something that not everyone can do because it needs a delicate balance between controlling and managing your self-image before others and ensuring that you are reasonably authentic in letting others see your true self.

That said, one thing you must bear in mind is that social intelligence is more about the future. It came about just so that people could strive to survive and figure out the best way to get along with others, get out of situations, and earn a favorable outcome. It does not matter whether you have paper qualifications in social intelligence. What matters the most is that if you don't know how to apply it in life, you might end up straining or ruining your relationships and lose opportunities.

Yes, there are times when you want to give people feedback so bluntly, but editing your words to convey the message constructively goes a long way in ensuring that you don't end up putting your foot in your mouth. Unlike social intelligence, emotional intelligence is more about the present, hence its close relationship to emotions and feelings. When you read someone's facial expressions, you can easily tell whether they are happy or not. You can tell whether they are nervous, shy, or angry about the situation at hand.

But, what are some of the social competencies of emotional intelligence?

Read on!

Social Competencies of EQ

Empathy

When we want someone to see things from another's perspective, the first thing we tell them is *"put yourself in their shoes."* Well, that is what empathy is all about. It is the ability to communicate and lead by understanding another person's views, thoughts, and feelings.

When we improve our empathy, the truth is that we become better versions of ourselves. We strengthen our relationships and make them more meaningful. We strive for success in the workplace. We realize it improved health and overall quality of life.

If you look at the top performers in your company, what you will notice is that 90% of them have high emotional intelligence. This is because the more people understand their thoughts, emotions, and feelings, the better they get at understanding someone else's thoughts, emotions, and feelings. When we become better at listening to others, we become better human beings.

But what happens when you lack empathy?

Well, according to research studies, scientists have linked a lack of empathy to a wide range of societal vices – such as theft, murder, and drug dealing among others. Think about the prisoners, are they empathic people? Most likely not. Most of these people lack empathy and didn't care to think about what their victims might have been feeling. If they had empathy, there is a high chance that would have prevented them from committing acts that put them in prison in the first place.

One thing you must note is that empathy is the ability to trust other people. The truth is that when your friends feel that you care, you earn their trust. If they trust you, that simply means that they will be willing to take risks with you and become more open with you. The reason why your friends communicate with openness with you is that they have built their trust in you.

In other words, as trust continues to grow, it promotes the sharing of information, thoughts, and feelings. It is this form of sharing that expands the foundation upon which you and the others relate with each other. Think about it for a moment, when your friends talk about their interests and ideas, what do you do while you listen to them?

Simple – you stop what you are doing to give them your undivided attention. With empathy you can raise your awareness of other people's feelings during the conversation. When someone asks you for help, it is important that you understand what they are not saying in their words but are saying with their body language.

You must bear in mind that a significant portion of communication is often related in non-verbal signals. The truth is that we may not even realize it, but when we communicate with our facial expressions, noise, gestures, among others, empathy allows us to understand what these non-verbal cues mean. When you master what non-verbal cues mean, you become better at understanding how the other person truly feels.

A solid foundation in emotional intelligence begins with a show of empathy!

You can grow your empathy with practice and the use of the right process. It is possible to take empathy to the next level, something that, in turn, boosts our overall emotional intelligence. When you have the right tools, the process of learning about empathy does not necessarily have to be costly or complicated.

Types of Empathy

There are three types of empathy;

Cognitive Empathy

This simply refers to the kind of empathy that helps us know what the other person is feeling and what they might be thinking. It is often referred to as "perspective-taking." This type of empathy is connected to the intellect, thought, and understanding. It goes a long way in helping people negotiate, stay motivated, and understand a wide range of perspectives.

The only pitfall to this is not putting yourself in another person's shoes to feel what they are feeling.

One thing you must bear in mind is that cognitive empathy is all about thought as much as it is about emotions. The truth is that understanding sadness is not the same as feeling sadness.

If you came home upset about losing your job, your partner would respond in this manner. It is the same way a doctor looks at their patients to try and understand their illness. They don't dive into the patient's emotions. In other words, cognitive empathy is about responding to problems with brainpower.

This can be a great asset in situations where you are required to get into the other person's head so that you can interact with their circumstances with tact and understanding. Think of cognitive empathy as mixing apples and oranges. This implies that for you to truly understand what another person is feeling, you have to feel them in some way.

Emotional Empathy

This simply refers to the ability to feel physically along with another person as though your emotions are contagious. It is concerned with mirroring neurons in the brain, physical sensations, and feelings. It plays a significant role in helping people close their interpersonal relationships and careers.

The pitfalls to this are the fact that emotional empathy can be overwhelming and even inappropriate in some circumstances.

It helps to think of emotional empathy as sound because it involves directly feeling the other person's emotions. Have you heard of the term empath? Well, this means a person with the ability to fully take on the emotional and mental state of another person. Unfortunately, this form of response can seem disconnected from the brain and thinking. However, emotional empathy is deeply rooted in the human mirror neurons.

Each one of us has neurons that fire in certain ways whenever we see someone acting in animal-like behavior. It makes you relate to their actions both in the brain and body. This is exactly what emotional empathy does – feel someone else's experiences in reaction to certain situations.

Think about your loved one for a second – they come to you in tears. What do you feel? Well, the truth is that you will tend to feel a pull on your heartstrings. When you connect with someone in this way, you strengthen your intimacy and promote a strong bond between the two of you.

Just like cognitive empathy, emotional empathy has its flip-side, and this happens when you cannot manage your distressing emotions. This often leads to emotional burnout. In other words, when you feel too much of what another person is experiencing, you risk making even very small interactions overwhelming.

Compassionate Empathy

This is the kind of empathy in which you not only understand another person's predicament but also feel with them. You are spontaneously touched to help. It is concerned with actions, emotions, and intellect. This plays a significant role in helping you become fully considerate of the other person.

The downside to this kind of empathy is that we are always striving to have it, but we cannot fully have it. In most instances, compassion is necessary. It may be fitting for monetary negotiations, political convincing, among others. It is the first response we give our loved ones, and it strikes a powerful balance between the two parties involved.

It is important to note that the heart and thoughts are not opposing each other. The truth is that they are intricately connected. It is through compassionate empathy that we honor the natural connection we have with others. When your child comes to you in tears, you are driven to understand why they are crying and want to comfort them by sharing in their emotional experiences and helping them heal. It is a lot to handle.

There are times when we feel going one way or the other with more feelings, thoughts, fixation, and continual changes. The thing about compassionate empathy is that it is about taking the middle ground and then using our emotional intelligence to properly respond to the situation. It is about thinking what the other person might want – to be held, to act to help them fix their situation or just give them a listening ear. You do this without necessarily feeling overwhelmed by sadness or the need to fix things.

In other words, compassion gives us that mindful touch to handle even the toughest of situations.

However, one thing you must remember is that empathy is a teeter-totter. In other words, if you go too far into another person's psyche, do you risk losing yours? If you dive too deep in their world, are you risking missing out an integral part of the human experience? If you feel too much, is it inappropriate? If you feel too little, does it hurt?

You must understand that not all situations are the same, just like not all the types of empathy are the same.

Take a minute to think about a real-life example in your own life where each type of empathy is applicable. I believe that you must have found compassionate empathy at some point in your life. Realize that any type of empathy takes practice to gain emotional fitness – just like any other balancing act. Finding a sweet spot where you can empathize effectively is worth the work.

Do it today!

How to Improve Empathy for a Successful Life

- Be quiet inside and out
- Watch as well as listen
- Ask yourself what you are feeling
- Test your instincts
- Challenge yourself
- Get feedback
- Explore the heart and not just your head
- Walk-in other people's shoes and examine your biases
- Cultivate your sense of curiosity

Social Skills

This is a broad term that refers to the skills we need to handle and influence other people's emotions in an effective manner – in the context of emotional intelligence. While this may sound like manipulation, the truth is that this is as simple as understanding that giving others your smile makes them smile too. Because of your smile, you can make someone feel much better and positive than they were before.

Think of social skills as the last piece of the emotional intelligence puzzle. Once you can understand and manage yourself, only then will you be able to understand other people's emotions and feelings, and influence them.

Some of the most important social skills include;

Communication Skills

This is a vital piece of emotional intelligence. You must pay attention to what others have to say and also convey your thoughts and feelings to them in an effective manner.

You may be wondering what makes a good communicator. Well, if you can listen well to people around you, understand what they said, and seek open and full information sharing, then you are a good communicator. If you are prepared to hear others' problems and not just ready to only hear good news, then you are a good communicator.

Good communication means dealing with tough situations, setting them straight, and not allowing annoying problems. You must ensure that you register and act in emotional signals in communicating so that the message is right.

Leadership Skills

This may sound strange, but one thing you must note is that leadership skills are all part of social skills. Emotional intelligence is a huge part of leadership and not vice versa. What you must note is that leadership skills and emotional intelligence are inextricably linked to each other. As we have mentioned earlier, only people who are tuned into their emotions and that of the people around them have the hope of influence.

One of the key aspects of good leadership is influence, and having the ability to bring others along with you. You may refer to this as charisma, but the truth is that leadership is much deeper than that. In short, it is good emotional intelligence.

To be a good leader you must have the ability to articulate a vision and motivate others with it. It does not matter if you are formal or informal; the trick is to ensure that you offer leadership, support, and guide the performance of the people you work with, hold each person accountable, and lead by example.

Persuasion Skills

Persuasion simply refers to the art of motivating people, winning their hearts to your ideas, and leading them on your proposed course of action. If you look around at people you know are persuasive, you will realize that they not only have to influence but also have the ability to read others' emotions in a given circumstance and fine-tune their words so that they appeal to the people around them.

Conflict-management Skills

We all know that conflicts can arise at any given time. They seem to appear out of thin air. However, the art of resolving conflicts as soon as they arise is crucial both at home and in the workplace. It all begins by raising our awareness to the importance of diplomacy and tact, and how these can be used to address difficulties in various situations.

Being a good conflict manager means that you have to be willing to bring disagreements out in the open when resolving them. You must ensure that you use information sharing as a way to encourage debates and open discussions, minimize hidden currents, help each party recognize other's feelings and logical position so that you can obtain a win-win solution.

Chapter 9 Understanding Emotional Drain and Dealing With Them

Life is not easy, we all know that. There are so many ups and downs, mountains and valleys, highs and lows, and you never really know what to expect. There are times when life is even a little tough for us to handle anything at all. It does not matter what the reason might be, but the truth is that it finds a way of kicking us when we are down.

One thing we fail to realize is that when we suffer we get emotionally and mentally drained. The thing is that the effects of these shows in ways we can see. Our energy gets sapped to the point that we feel physically exhausted, and what we can do at that point is to break down. You must know when life is too much so that you can position yourself to better control and manage your emotions. Here are some of the signs to look out for:

Hopelessness

This is a sign that you are emotionally drained. When you have pushed, fought, and clawed through the storms, all your energy gets sapped, and you begin to ask yourself why you are even bothering when things don't seem to get better. This is the point of hopelessness and is very dangerous. When you get to this point, you risk making your pain and suffering permanent because you have accepted that this is your way of life. If you are at this point, it is high time you seek help.

Crying Often

For most people, crying is something they left behind during their teen years. As we grow older we get to manage and control our emotions better and we only cry when something big happens in our lives. However, some have been pushed to the limits and crying has quickly become their way of life – a sad movie makes them cry, someone wrongs them and they cry, or an old friend seeks forgiveness from them and they cry.

When you are crying easily like this, it shows you are emotionally exhausted. In other words, even the smallest emotional push brings you into tears.

Insomnia

Are you experiencing trouble getting sleep? This might have something to do with your emotions. When you are emotionally drained you risk suffering from insomnia. You may think that just because you are stressed you will fall asleep easily. However, insomnia occurs often because you are spending most of the time in deep thought, fighting with the demons in your head and have trouble getting a good night's sleep.

Lack of Motivation

When you are emotionally drained you don't seem to care about striving for anything. You no longer have goals that wake you up in the morning. You are just going through the waves of life, and you let it take you in whatever direction it likes. You find yourself neglecting your work, health, hygiene, and family.

Detachment

If you have been punched hard by life, it is easy to detach yourself from the rest of the people around you. You have allowed the pain to become part of your life so that you have become numb to it because you have gone through way too much that the reality no longer exists for you.

You must find out what is making you emotionally drained. Is it your partner, family, friends, work, boss? How do you do when someone is sucking your energy reserved dry?

- You think about them all the time
- You are physically exhausted
- You find happiness when they leave
- They don't lift you up
- Once you have been together you feel the need for some downtime
- They demand too much of you
- When they talk they leave you feeling more frustrated than you were before
- You can't seem to say what you mean when you are around them

Things You Can Do if You Are Experiencing Emotional Exhaustion

Exercise

Whenever you are exhausted, exercise is usually the last thing you can think of – after all working out is a form of physical stress. However, research shows that when we exercise we relieve mental stress. It will not only help your mental balance, but it will also bring changes to your body, heart, spirit, and metabolism. It offers stimulation and a calming effect against depression and stress.

Research has shown that working out can reduce the levels of body stress hormones – like cortisol and adrenaline, and it promotes the release of feel-good hormones called endorphins – natural painkillers and mood elevators – which tightens the muscle.

Breathing Exercises

Breathing has been shown to help relieve stress and increase relaxation. When someone is panting fast and has a form of erratic breathing, this is an indicator that they are under duress. However, when you take in slow and deep breaths, it has a calming effect. You must learn how to control your breathing to mimic relaxation.

The best way to breathe is to do it slowly and deeply while focusing your attention on the movement of your diaphragm – up and down. Then hold your breath for at least seconds before you exhale thinking about relaxation for another five seconds. Repeat this process for about 15-20 times while ensuring that you do it slowly and deeply.

Meditation

This is a practice that has been shown to help relieve stress and calm the mind. This is by lowering both the heart rate and the blood pressure – physiological signs of stress.

The first thing is for you to choose a place and time when there are no distractions. Then get comfortable by finding the right posture that will promote relaxation. Allow your mind to get into a passive mental state. You must allow your mind to go blank so that thoughts and worries don't get in the way of your relaxation. Watch your thoughts come and go without necessarily passing any judgment.

The trick is to focus your attention on a mental device. You can use simple words of affirmation or mantra so that you repeat them over and over. Alternatively, you can choose to focus your attention on a fixed object within your space. The goal is to ensure that you block out any form of distraction as much as you can. Once you have mastered this, you can dedicate at least 20-30 minutes to meditation every day.

Journaling

If you thought this was just for professional writers, you better think again. If you ask anyone who has been journaling, they will tell you how much it benefits their mental health by releasing emotional drains.

This is mainly because journaling allows you to write down all your deepest thoughts, emotions, and fears, which is a great way of understanding, managing, and letting go emotional drains. Research shows that journaling plays a significant role in lowering anxiety, boosting better sleep patterns, improving memory, minimizing depression, and making someone kinder.

One Last Word

Indeed, emotional intelligence is one of the most important things one must have in life to ensure success in every situation.

One thing that is important to bear in mind is that emotional intelligence is not a trend! It is here to stay. According to reports and statistics compiled by major companies across the world, it is evident that people with emotional intelligence undoubtedly affect their bottom line. For instance, if an employee has a high level of emotional intelligence, they will not only be productive and generate revenue for the company, but will also achieve their personal and career goals.

You probably know other people who have mastered the art of managing their emotions. Instead of getting angry when provoked by a stressful situation, they choose to look at the problem from a different perspective to calmly find a solution. These people are excellent decision-makers and have mastered the art of listening to their gut feeling. Irrespective of their strengths, they have the willingness to look at themselves with an honest eye. They take criticism positively and use it to improve their performance.

Well, I am here to tell you that you can be just like these people. As you begin to accept emotional intelligence into every area of your life, you will begin to see an improvement in your technical abilities, interrelationships, and overall success. It is through emotional intelligence that you can fuel your performance. It impacts your confidence, optimism, self-control, empathy, and social skills, so that you can understand and manage your emotions and accelerate success in every area of your life.

It does not matter what your profession is, whether you work for a small or large organization, whether you are senior or junior in your company. What matters is that realizing how effective you are at controlling your emotional energies is the beginning of a successful adventure. Yes, emotional intelligence may not be something taught and tested in our educational curriculum, but the truth is that it is really important.

Take a look at your life –chances are that you will notice how hectic and busy your lifestyle is. It is this kind of life that makes it easy for you to lose touch with yourself and your emotional feelings. You must try to reconnect with your feelings by setting a timer for various points throughout the day. As soon as the timer goes off, you stop what you are doing, stand on your two feet, and take in a deep breath. Then bring your thoughts to what you are feeling in that moment, where the emotions are coming from, and where you feel the sensation in your body and what it feels like. Realize that the more you practice this, the more you make it your second nature.

The key to emotional intelligence is to celebrate and reflect on all the positives in your life. No one has a perfect life – we all go through ups and downs. It does not matter whether you have more positives or negatives in your life—the trick to celebrate every win – whether small or big. When you embrace the positives in your life, you allow yourself to develop more resilience and increase your chances of enjoying fulfilling relationships so that you can successfully move past adversity.

No matter what life throws your way, you must not forget to take time to just breathe. Taking time to take deep breaths will not only help you master how to manage your emotions but also help you avoid outbursts. Just walk out the door and wash your face with cold water, take a walk, or just take in fresh air – anything to calm your nerves. This goes a long way in helping you get a hold of what is happening so that you can effectively respond to the situation.

That said, emotional intelligence is a lifetime process! It is not something you develop overnight. The truth is that to grow your emotional intelligence; you have to train your mind to accept continual improvements along the way – so that you can be better with each passing day.

So, what are you still waiting for?

Start working on improving your emotional intelligence and watch how your life changes for the better.

Best of Luck!

© **Written by:** JOSEPH GRIFFITH

Introduction

Living with pain and being in emotional distress is never easy, especially when you are suffering from anxiety and depression, which in general makes your pain even more intense and even more so overwhelming. What CBT, Cognitive behavioral therapy, teaches us is that our thoughts are connected to our emotions and our behavior, that way presenting the solution for resolving mental problems such as depressive disorders and different types of anxiety disorders. DBT, Dialectical cognitive therapy, is based on CBT and studies how depression and anxiety can be successfully treated by applying two opposite actions: acceptance and change. By merging studies behind DBT and CBT, we have created a guide that should help you learn more about depression and anxiety, while also being introduced to helpful techniques, skills and practices that are based on CBT and DBT, created to treat anxiety and depression in an efficient and effective way. By starting with the Dialectical and Cognitive behavioral therapy guide we have created, you will be able to identify your symptoms and get a better insight into what your mental state is depriving you of, while also gaining direct access to helpful strategies and skills that should help you solve your problems and ease your emotional pain and anxiety and/or depression symptoms and causes. This guide contains a compilation of handy and simple, yet effective and efficient practices, that were created as a result of decades of researching and studying CBT, and consequently DBT that was created based on CBT to specifically treat patients with tendencies towards harmful and destructive behavior. Regardless of how hopeless you may feel, beaten up by depression and anxiety, there is a solution and a way out waiting for you on the following pages. Learn more about your condition, CBT, DBT, techniques and skills that should help you heal and successfully treat your mental condition while embracing a more positive way of life.

Chapter 1:

Introduction to CBT and Dialectical Behavioral Therapy

Our emotions are not separate from our thoughts, and although logic is often viewed as pure opposite to emotion, cognitive behavioral therapy, known as CBT, proves otherwise with the help of decades of extensive and intensive research. Although cognitive behavioral therapy revolves around treating various mental conditions through the power of talk therapy, psychotherapies weren't always focused on defining patients' emotions, especially not in relation to patients' thoughts.

Cognitive behavioral therapy is defined as a form of talk therapy where patients are taught how to reflect on their thoughts in order to calm emotional confusion. This emotional turmoil is in many cases the main trigger of negative mental states, commonly depression and anxiety. Cognitive behavioral therapy is used on patients who are suffering from autism, posttraumatic stress disorders (PTSD), bipolar disorder, fear and phobias, anxiety and panic attacks, stress, various forms of addiction, and even procrastination, lack of social skills and difficulties with communication.

CBT was first used, although not under today's known term – Cognitive Behavioral Therapy – by Aaron Beck. Aaron Beck was a psychotherapist who managed to note that many of his patients who were suffering from different mental illnesses, had something in common regardless of how different their mental conditions and their characters were altogether. Beck noted that this thing they all had in common was a concept they all held onto – producing negative thoughts.

These negative thoughts reflected negative impressions Beck's patients had on external factors, their environment and surroundings. What is interesting in this case, is the fact that patients were able to develop negative thoughts on any kind of situation they alone found disturbing although that situation by itself could be positive. Beck noticed that his patients were heavily affected by their own negative perceptions, trusting their impression as they would trust their own logic.

Beck called these negative thoughts "automatic thoughts", and started studying how thoughts are related to our emotions. Beck can be called the father of Cognitive Behavioral Therapy as CBT received its first form thanks to him. However, many psychotherapists who decided to continue Beck's work managed to provide decades worth studies and research that brought a final conclusion on how our emotions coexisted in relation with our thoughts. What CBT proves is that we can create negative emotions by creating negative thoughts, and these negative thoughts are usually created due to negative perception of reality that is in many cases actually positive.

Thanks to the overall effectiveness and efficiency of Cognitive behavioral therapy, CBT is used alone as the main form of talk therapy, as well as in combination with different therapy types, in order to treat various mental conditions. Some of the most common mental conditions that every third person has are depression and anxiety. What CBT studies managed to prove after decades of extensive research and testing, is that depression and anxiety can be developed by having negative emotions as triggers, otherwise known as "automatic thoughts" as defined by Aaron Beck. Soon enough, thanks to many years of research and applied techniques under Cognitive behavioral therapy, CBT has become one of the most popularly used talk therapies, as CBT techniques revolve around identifying triggers of negative emotions that cause mental conditions such as trauma, phobia, depression and anxiety, while CBT is designed to treat more severe mental conditions such as PTSD and bipolar disorder, as mentioned before.

CBT therapy usually revolves around talking in an attempt to first identify the core of the problem a patient is suffering from. The patient also needs to be taught to be in control of their own emotions and emotional responses by remodeling the way they think and perceive. What CBT studies managed to determine is the fact that negative thoughts trigger negative emotions, where negative emotions create negative behavior patterns. That means that CBT not only reflects on thoughts and emotions, but also on the final product facilitated by negative emotions and thoughts – negative behavior patterns. Negative behavior patterns are then defined as mental conditions, forming certain patterns that appear difficult to be broken, as patient is not aware of the trigger causing negative behavior. As CBT proves, negative thoughts otherwise known as automatic thoughts, are the main trigger of negative emotions that affect behavior of patients in a negative way. The solution is found in CBT as talk therapist explore the way patients are perceiving their surroundings and environment. During therapy, CBT therapist show patients that by changing the way they think and perceive things around them, they are also changing the way they behave, gradually reducing their initial problems.

While other forms of therapies may require months and even years in order to come to a solution of problems, cognitive behavior therapy may only take several weeks until patient is able to feel a difference in behavior and emotional responses. That is how CBT became one of the most popular and most effective forms of psychotherapy. CBT revolves around showing the patient that their emotions and the way they behave can truly come to a positive change if only they change the way they perceive experiences and situations. A part of the therapy requires patient to accept how they feel before they are able to determine why they feel the way they do. The next step would be implementing healthier habits, such as changing negativity to positivity, until a final result is provided in the form of a resolution and a successfully treated mental illness. Depending on the severity of patient's condition and the type of mental illness, some CBT therapies may last longer than other forms of talk therapies. However, depression and anxiety are usually successfully treated within only several weeks. In order for a CBT therapy to be as successful as possible, patients and therapists must work closely and with honesty, while the patient must put up with their problems with motivation, devotion and effort. While talk therapies usually take place once or twice a week during the treatment, patients are also given "homework" to be completed at home. Homework in CBT represents various tasks and challenges the patient should go through to successfully solve their mental health problem. Although therapist's help is of essential importance for patients, a lot of work is done through "homework" and psychology-based techniques the patient is getting as a part of the CBT therapy. There are more than several CBT techniques as well as several types of Cognitive behavioral therapy, one of which is especially useful in treating depression and anxiety – dialectical behavioral therapy or DBT.

To understand how DBT works, one must learn how Cognitive behavioral therapy works, as DBT is based on CBT as an extension created for forming a type of therapy that is most effective in treating problems related to harmful and toxic behavior, and unstable emotional state. Depression and anxiety are described, although different in core, as mental conditions determined by harmful behavior and unstable emotional patterns, which is why these conditions are usually efficiently treated with DBT.

While CBT focuses on studying how emotions are related to thoughts and behavior, finding solutions in this unbreakable relationship between our logic and emotion, DBT emphasizes the importance of emotions and social aspects. Furthermore, CBT and DBT are frequently combined in order to provide an efficient treatment for patients, especially those struggling with self-harm and negative thoughts against themselves. DBT has a goal of teaching patients how to best accept who they are and learn how to make the best out of what they have in themselves. Still DBT is much similar to CBT, as it also has a goal of teaching patients how to change negative behavior which is not part of who they are, all in order to have a quality and happy life. Both therapies are based on providing viable solutions to accept yourself and make a change that will allow you to live a happy life, and

DARK PSYCHOLOGY 4 IN

more importantly, both types of therapy teach you how to cope with how you feel.

Before we get to how psychology-based techniques help you treat your depression and anxiety in accordance with teachings of CBT and DBT, we are going to define CBT and DBT and the way these therapies work on patients with different mental disorders.

Chapter 2:

Defining Cognitive Behavioral Therapy: How CBT Works on Depression and Anxiety?

Cognitive behavioral therapy works on efficiently moving the core triggers causing various mental conditions, which includes, but are not limited to, depression and anxiety. Cognitive behavioral therapy uses connection between emotion, thought and behavior, to address the issue noted in a patient, towards ultimately solving the negative mental state that is causing the patient to be unable to lead a healthy and happy life. Although Cognitive behavioral therapy is used for treating severe mental disorders such as posttraumatic stress disorder, bipolar disorder, and various types of personality disorders, it is equally efficient in treating less severe mental conditions like depression and anxiety.

Depression and anxiety are some of the most common negative mental conditions in the modern world, and are usually developed due to repeated negative experiences, constant emotional disorders or inability to cope with the way you feel. CBT is working on finding specific triggers causing these mental disorders to appear and stay with patients, along the way offering viable and non-intrusive solutions for resolution of depression and anxiety. CBT offers various techniques within talk therapy that would help patients cope with depression and anxiety by recognizing negative patterns in present thoughts and emotions, and displayed behavior patterns. CBT techniques help patients learn how to recognize negative thoughts and cut them to the core so that emotional triggers can be removed and isolated before being completely mitigated. By helping patients solve their negative thoughts by recognizing negativity defined as automatic thoughts, CBT therapy is then looking into teaching patients how to change their behavior by adopting a more positively-oriented perception of experiences. Furthermore, CBT is relying on the fact that our thoughts alone can trigger negative emotions when challenged by a situation or experience we perceive as negative. When patients can distance themselves from those negative perceptions they are able to realize that the very negativity causing the problem is not in the problem itself but in their thoughts – that means that the way they think is dictating the way they feel. Consequently, negative emotions will trigger negative behavior, feeding their anxiety and/depression and creating a perpetual problem that may lead to self-destructive behavior. When self-destructive behavior appears, the problem multiplies as patients are no longer in control of emotions, adopting a mental state where emotions appear as unstable and less likely controlled. In cases when self-harm and self-destruction pose as a part of the problem, DBT comes in as one of the most effective and efficient ways of dealing with depression and anxiety.

Over the decades of studying, research and randomized controlled trials, a great number of scientists and psychotherapists specialized in CBT techniques, determined that CBT talk therapies have the same effects on depression and anxiety as medications used specifically for treating these mental disorders. Unfortunately, most psychiatrists will decide to treat patients suffering from depression and/or anxiety with less specific therapies in oppose to CBT, as well as choosing medication treatments. The main problem with medication, however, is that depression medicine will not remove the core problem – it will only make it silent and in order as long as you are taking your medication. On the other hand, CBT is working on removing the core problem and changing behavior through talk therapies and a variety of tasks and practices posing as effective techniques for treating depression and anxiety. Moreover, in case of major depressive disorder, CBT can be combined with medical treatment to provide better results – still working on removing the main triggers of negative mental state with a little help from depression medicine.

How Cognitive Behavioral Therapy Works on Treating Depression and Anxiety?

Cognitive behavioral therapy can find a solution for mental disorders such as depression and anxiety, as CBT focuses on distorted cognition of self. What does that mean?

Distorted cognition is a state of perception where you are unable to perceive yourself, your emotions, experiences and other people for what they represent in reality. Your mind may be playing tricks due to the fact that you feel vulnerable. CBT focuses on discovering your vulnerability in order to find the main trigger of negative emotions, while negative emotions are triggered by negative thoughts. What if there is no true reason to feel the way you feel, behave the way you do, or think in a negative way? What if your mind remembered a single bad experience, triggering negative emotions whenever you are reminded of it? Not to be mistaken, CBT is not focused on helping you forget the "bad stuff" – it's quite the opposite – CBT is due to help you realize what is actually the problem while helping you change.

Depression can be defined as a result of distorted cognition where a patient is no longer able to perceive any or barely any experience as positive, always managing to overshadow positive with negative thinking. When talking about distorted cognition of yourself, we also need to emphasize that mental disorders may be caused by a combination of negative perceptions regarding experiences, situations, surroundings, others, and your own self. There are numerous factors that may call for a CBT intervention, where CBT techniques can effectively deal with any of these factors, ultimately leading to a successful end of therapy.

Perhaps the best way to describe what CBT is looking to solve through talk therapies and specific techniques and practices is to use a real-life case as an example. Let's say that you have had several bad experiences in the past that made you feel apathetic, demotivated, stubbornly sad, and ultimately depressive. Later on, you have had a particularly bad week that somehow managed to pull out all the negative things that happened in your past, so you can feel like you are slipping away to depression, even slowly feeling comfortable in your gradually developed state of depression. While depressed out of several reasons – you might have lost someone you love, did not complete an important goal or you are having troubles connecting with people – you will reflect your past negative experiences on all future and present opportunities to feel better about yourself. Before you know you stop to appreciate your own life, which is only a step closer towards becoming self-destructive and start thinking about self-harm. In this case CBT takes the patient to a talk therapy where the affected person is helped on their way towards realizing what went wrong. i.e. what led to severe/mild/major depressive disorder.

One of the most important techniques in this stage of CBT therapy (the very beginning) is to rationalize the way you feel – in a way your perception will be gradually changed to help you adopt more constructive patterns in your life – patterns that will help you get rid of depression.

With rationalizing, there comes acceptance of your own fears and triggers that are causing you to feel depressed. CBT is thus focused on helping you recognize negative patterns of thoughts and behavior so you can learn how to control negativity and implement positivity.

After patients are able to rationalize negative thoughts and behavior, the next step is implementing techniques that are due to help patients adopt more constructive behavior by starting to change their mindset from negative to positive. Anxiety treatments are much similar, although patients suffering from anxiety are battling with different emotions than patients suffering from depression. Let's say that a patient has social anxiety, described as inability to communicate and connect with other people. The reason for that sort of inability lies in the fact that the patient believes that he/she has nothing to offer to their potential connections, considering themselves boring, uninteresting or dull, and are convinced that anyone and everyone can see their flaws. The fact is that the flaws the patient is referring to are not an actual and realistic image of patient's characteristics, while you may also notice that this social anxiety is created in their mind and encouraged by negative, automatic thoughts. In both cases we have presented, the patient with depression and the patient with anxiety, both consider to be worthless and do not have respect for their own personal value – moreover, they don't perceive themselves as valuable human beings at all, also failing to realize that all negativity they are experiencing is actually coming from within distorted self-perception.

CBT is then implementing behavioral component in form of (behavioral) activation (BA), which means that patients are getting help through several steps that are usually implemented in talk therapies and workout techniques created for work at home.

Patients who are treated for anxiety or depression with CBT techniques will be encouraged to:

- Increase experiences and behavior that feel rewarding and that can make them feel like they are achieving something and actually making progress in general
- Decrease toxic behavior patterns that support depression or anxiety – main triggers must be defined and identified so that the patient would be able to renounce destructive behavior that is keeping the symptoms of mental illness up to date
- Patients will most certainly experience setbacks in the form of inability to engage in new constructive and positive behavior and experiences in the beginning of CBT treatment – patients need to be encouraged to overcome these barriers in order to engage in constructive behavior

One of the main issues for patients suffering from depression and anxiety is their inability to find pleasure even in things that were once considered pleasurable. This type of negative behavior will only strengthen the feeling of despair that goes hand in hand with depression, anxiety and other mental problems. Inability to feel pleasure might be related to social factors, as well as by physical changes, changes in surroundings, emotional disbalance, anxious outbursts, unrealistic fears and expectations, and frequent depressive episodes. Patients suffering from depressive disorders and anxiety are more likely to choose social and physical intervention. This is why CBT dictates techniques that represent creative solutions for creating more positive opportunities for constructive behavior and rewarding experiences.

The main goal is to help patients realize how mood and overall emotions are affecting other aspects of their personal life as well as life of people around them.

Mood is related to actions, physical reactions, emotions, behavior, events, thoughts and communication with other people. By exploring these aspects, therapist is able to create valuable practices with CBT techniques that should help the patient recover by adopting more constructive behavior. The connection between these aspects is mutual, which means that it goes in two directions. For instance, feeling down and sad may affect the patient to retreat physically and socially, cutting communication with others. In case this negative behavior is extended, patients are more likely to lose all social connections, which will result in feeling down and sad again. Mood affects patients decisions, and the result of their decisions affects the mood. Over time, this cycle may appear as a vicious circle, which in a way it is.

What is important in this case for the patient to note is that each of these reactions and actions can be changed for better. Equally essential is to educate the patient on the matter of relationship between emotion, behavior and thoughts, so that the patient could get a sense of control. Once the patient is able to break the pattern of connection between thoughts, behavior and feelings, and the ability to control emotions and change behavior by changing automatic thoughts to a positive mindset, a great part of the work towards full recovery is done. During treatments, which will be presented in the form of techniques and practices further in the book, the patient will be taught how to relax, learn self-appreciation and self-respect, as well as learning new skills and behaviors by being exposed to various scenarios.

You should note that no specific technique is related to Cognitive behavioral therapy as there are many different strategies implemented and backed by CBT for treating anxiety disorders and depression. Further in the book, you will be able to get involved with some of the most effective treatments facilitated by CBT research and studies as a well-established way of treating severe and moderate mental disorders.

Chapter 3:

Defining Dialectical Behavioral Therapy: How DBT Works?

As previously mentioned in the book, DBT, or Dialectical behavioral therapy, is actually based on CBT, Cognitive behavioral therapy. While CBT values cognition of emotional responses and thoughts, DBT is focusing on facing two opposites – acceptance and change, to help patients live a healthy and happy life. As you are progressing with the book you will be able to read more about differences between the two types of therapy which are narrowly related and are more similar than it might appear at first.

For now, we will discuss the definition of DBT, while taking advantage of how DBT works in treating mental disorders such as depression and anxiety.

DBT was first developed based on cognitive behavioral therapy with the goal of treating Borderline Personality Disorder (BPD). However over time of practicing this type of therapy it was determined that DBT can effectively treat mental disorders such as depression and anxiety. While CBT therapy teaches patients to relate their emotions to thoughts and behavior, DBT focuses on teaching patients different techniques and new skills that would later help them overcome difficulties that come with depression and anxiety. Whenever a patient is faced with anxiety episodes or is experiencing depressive mood swings and unstable emotions, the patient can turn to these skills and techniques to battle negative emotions. Depression comes with many different symptoms, each related to negative emotions and behaviors, while DBT has proven to effectively work on treating some of these symptoms.

DBT has proven by far to be effective in helping patients with the following symptoms of depression:

- Physical pain such as chronic pain, headaches and other physical issues that cannot be treated with traditional solutions – depression comes with intensive negative emotions that may cause malnutrition and lack of appetite, increased necessity for food, persistent headache, aching muscles, lack of sleep, etc.
- Suicidal thoughts and thoughts of self-harm and death – patients suffering from depression place little value on their own life which may result in suicide attempt. DBT is working on removing factors that represent the cause behind suicidal thoughts to prevent self-harm
- Lack of motivation and lack of interest for things the patient once viewed as pleasurable – patients often lose the ability to enjoy and find pleasure in things and activities that were once considered pleasurable
- Difficulties with focusing, remembering and memorizing, as well as thinking – patients feel unable to think on their own, usually relying on automatic thoughts as their reality of perception, while frequent or constant negative feelings are causing loss of focus
- Frequent and constant irritation with minor nuisances - patients may feel irritated even to experiences and situations that are not otherwise considered irritating
- Frequent and constant sadness – the patient is usually caught up with perpetual feeling of sadness, feeling down even when something pleasant happens

Based on CBT, psychologist Marsha Linehan developed dialectical behavioral therapy. DBT was formed as a type of treatment by Linehan to treat women who displayed suicidal behavior. The main idea behind the treatment is to face two opposites considering that these opposites are not that different in the first place. DBT is set to learn patients suffering from depression and anxiety how to evaluate themselves and learn to accept who they are and how they feel, while changing negative behaviors to positive behavior patterns. The idea is to help people suffering from these types of disorders to live a happy life, day-to-day, revoking what they've been taught every time a depressive or anxiety episode emerges. Skills that are to be learned through DBT for successful anxiety and depression treatments are defined as:

- Skills that should enable patients to deal with intense emotions
- Skills to help patients solve internal conflicts by learning to trust their own emotions and thoughts
- Skills to help patients regulate emotional distress and battle toxic emotions
- Learning how to regain focus even in most stressful situations – practicing mindfulness is one of the top techniques for achieving focus
- Skills that should help the patient put up with emotional pain and negative emotions

Based on the group of skills a patient is set to learn through DBT techniques, treatment can be divided into four different stages of skill development. All stages are worked on simultaneously.

- Tolerance to emotional distress – patients will learn how to handle intense emotions
- Mindfulness – patients will learn how to focus on the moment and current experiences, being fully aware of what they are feeling, thinking and how they are behaving
- Interpersonal skills – patients will learn how to solve internal conflicts, as well as how to build and develop relationships with other people in their life
- Regulating emotions – patients will learn how to effectively and efficiently change the way they feel whenever a negative emotion strikes

All stages of DBT skill learning are applied in treatments for patients with anxiety, as well as to patients with depression and are considered to be fully effective in treating this type of disorders. Next we will present the main differences between cognitive and dialectical

215

behavioral therapy, so you would be able to get ahold of types of treatments and techniques you will use for treating depression and anxiety

Chapter 4:

Difference Between Cognitive Behavioral Therapy and Dialectical Behavioral Therapy

DBT is based on cognitive behavioral therapy and as such, dialectical behavioral therapy has much in common with CBT. However, regardless of the mentioned similarities and connection between two types of therapy, CBT and DBT practice different approaches on the same set of problems, i.e. in treating mental disorders, in this case depression and anxiety.

For starters, cognitive behavioral therapy focuses on teaching patients how their emotions are related to their thoughts and behavior, i.e. if you are having negative thoughts on experiences and situations around you, you will start to feel negative emotions over time, and these negative emotions will also affect your behavior. This relationship is complementary and may even change the course – for instance, you feel bad and because of your feelings you are expressing negative behavior such as social isolation. Since you are alone and isolated negative thoughts appear, creating a vicious circle when emotions may affect thoughts and behavior, thoughts may affect emotions and behavior, and behavior may affect thoughts and emotions. CBT teaches patients to change their thoughts and perception in order to change the way they feel and behave, starting from the idea that patient's perception is distorted.

On the other hand, DBT focuses on acceptance and change through four stages of developmental skills that we have already listed in the previous chapter. Both types of therapy involve talking as an important part of the treatment, while both CBT and DBT place a special emphasis on learning skills that are due to help patients change negative behavior to be able to live a quality and happy life. DBT focuses on emotional and social aspects rather than exploring the way behavior is related to thoughts and emotions. However, DBT

217

practices teaching mindfulness, which in a way involves cognition as well, which is no wonder since DBT is based on CBT. DBT was first used for treating patients who are expressing toxic behavior and have suicidal thoughts, as well as inclination towards self-harm. DBT thus teaches people how to regulate their emotions in order to be able to cope with mental disorders such as depression and anxiety.

The main difference between DBT and CBT is perhaps the way these therapies are observing validation of problems and relationships that patients have with others. CBT teaches patients how to change perception from negative to positive in order to adopt new skills that will create a healthier perception of experiences and situations, that way treating mental disorders. DBT, on the other hand, teaches patients how to accept themselves for who they are and how they feel while learning new skills that should help them become efficient in dealing with negative emotions they are experiencing due to their mental condition and the way they feel about themselves, others, and their surroundings. DBT also places a great value on relationships you have with other people, emphasizing the importance of developing and nurturing meaningful relationships with them. Although the approach that both types of therapy have is different, both CBT and DBT are proven to efficiently solve mental disorders such as depressive disorders and anxiety.

Before we present you to useful techniques facilitated by CBT and DBT treatment plans, we will introduce you to the way anxiety and depression are formed and developed. In order to battle your problems, you need to know your "enemy."

Chapter 5:

Depression and Anxiety: How Everything Starts

To be able to effectively battle your issues with anxiety and/or depression, you first need to understand how anxiety and depression develop, which is why we have dedicated an entire chapter to the topic on how these mental disorders are formed and how everything starts. After you have gone through the history of these two common mental disorders, you will also be able to understand how CBT and DBT techniques may help you overcome issues you are experiencing with depressive disorder and anxiety.

How is Anxiety Developed?

Regardless of how different we are we all have fears. Some of us are afraid of dark (no shame in it!), some people are afraid of more abstract things like changing and trying out new things, some people are afraid of public speaking – whichever the fear and whatever the reason, the bottom line is that feeling fear is normal. Fear is actually a natural response our mind has in order to help us survive, which means that being afraid may make you cautious of some things that may pose as a threat to your well-being. If you see a man in a hood stalking from an alley in the middle of the night, you are more likely to feel fear, which is a good thing since you are being alarmed by your mind that something is wrong, which further causes a response set to protect you from harm. However, feeling anxious and having an anxiety disorder will prevent you from truly living and enjoying life.

We now know how fear is formed and why, but how is anxiety formed and developed and why some fears transform into anxiety disorder?

Anxiety is a serious problem especially when allowed to develop freely, which usually occurs when a person affected by this disorder feeds their fears and doubts. Anxiety may cause physical weakness, heart palpitations, tremors, difficulties with breathing, nausea and even seizures in more progressive cases of anxiety disorder. But how is anxiety developed?

219

It takes years for anxiety to fully develop, while in this process each negative experience builds one upon another until the feeling of anxiety becomes completely debilitating for the person suffering from this disorder. Even though it may sound simple, anxiety is formed by a combination of different factors, where take part past and present experiences, traumas, personality and hormones created by your brain. Scientists also believe that anxiety, as well as many different mental disorders may run in the family, so genetics is one of the recurring factors as well. Beyond genetics, a person may develop anxiety disorder when frequently or periodically faced to stressful situations that cause a natural defensive response in our brain, known as "flight or fight". Our body is a complex mechanism, designed to protect us and keep us going. One of these complex mechanisms is the "flight or fight" mode which is triggered whenever a stressful or dangerous situation appears. Some of the most common triggers of anxiety disorders are extremely stressful situations such as being in a toxic relationship, working on a job position that you do not enjoy and find stressful, continuous stress, feeding your personal fears as well as inability to recognize situations and experiences as non-harmful. Anxiety is usually developed in early adulthood and childhood, which means that the way you are raised may also create anxiety disorder, as well as traumatic experiences you have gone through later in your life. Abuse and neglect are some of the most common factors for developing anxiety in early childhood, while finances and unhappy love life are said to be the most common stress-inducing factors that feed anxiety and help its further development. The bottom line is that many different factors may cause anxiety to develop over time, but regardless of the reason, the most important fact to note is that anxiety IS treatable with CBT and DBT techniques, proven to be some of the most effective treatments in anxiety disorder.

Another important thing to note is that every person is faced with everyday anxieties as we all have worries and fears, but in case the feeling of anxiety is prolonged to the point where fearing and worrying becomes a normal part of your life, you need to seek help and solve your mental condition to be able to live a happy life.

Symptoms of Anxiety: How is Anxiety Displayed?

People suffering from anxiety disorder will experience different symptoms caused by excess worrying and fearing, which may further lead to developing heart problems, seizures, difficulties with breathing, as well as insomnia.

The following are the common symptoms by which anxiety is usually diagnosed:

- Excess worrying – you are worrying too much about everything and anything, to extent where you are unable to focus on present problems and commitments, as your mind is set on a specific issue that is causing you to feel anxious.

- Suicidal thoughts and thoughts of self-harm – the feeling of self-harm and suicidal thoughts usually arrive once anxiety disorders have long progressed into a severe disorder – in case you are having thoughts of self-harm, you need to react and seek for help. DBT therapy is especially effective in treating harmful behavior.

- Frequent tension, pressures and feeling nervous – feeling a strong combination of tension, pressure and stress may be another symptom that anxiety disorder exists. Constant feeling of tension and pressure, and the feeling that something is expected from you or that something is lurking to hurt you or make you feel miserable is a common sign of anxiety.

- Sense of danger and panic – patients with anxiety disorder will experience the feeling of constant to frequent sense of danger, doom or panic, having the feeling like something bad is going to happen any time.

- Increased heart rate, heart palpitations – one of the ways your body is reacting to anxiety as your brain is in constant distress.

- Trembling and sweating.

- Physical weakness, nausea, feeling tired – the constant worrying and fearing is taking a toll on your body, creating a stressful environment that causes you to feel physically ill, which may further lead to seizures.

- Issues with appetite and gastrointestinal health – constant worry may affect your body in a way to convince it that you are really in distress. As your body believes you are in danger due to frequent fearing and displaying of anxious behavior, you may start losing your appetite – this condition may further create gastrointestinal problems.

- Problems with focusing – as you are constantly obsessed about issues that make you anxious, you may be experiencing difficulties with focusing on your job and other important day-to-day activities.

- Insomnia and difficulties with sleeping – due to constant and continuous worrying and fearing, you might have troubles sleeping as you could get rid of anxious thoughts and problems that you feel you need to solve but don't know how. Over time you may develop insomnia.

- Inability to control worry – you would like to quit worrying, but you cannot control the extent of the worry you are experiencing.

- Avoiding anxiety triggers – as you are battling with coping with your anxiety, you have probably noticed that you are avoiding scenarios and situations that can trigger your anxiety.

Even thinking about situations that make you feel uncomfortable are making a debilitating effect on you, alongside making you more anxious and worrisome.

Types of Anxiety Disorders

There are more than several types of anxiety, while some people may suffer from more than a single type of anxiety disorder, making their mental state even more complex. Whichever the type of anxiety disorder you are suffering from, DBT and CBT techniques and skills can help you treat your mental condition.

Types of anxiety disorders are the following:

- *Generalized Anxiety Disorder*

Generalized anxiety disorder is usually combined with other types of anxiety disorders and involves worrying about everything and anything, which includes trivial activities and ordinary experiences and events. A person with a generalized anxiety disorder will worry at all times and whenever something happens or is about to happen, regardless of how trivial a certain situation is.

- *Social Anxiety*

People with social anxiety disorder tend to avoid social gatherings, considering the experience to be embarrassing and believing that everyone is judging them and can see the worst of them. People with social anxiety are highly self-conscious, but their perception is distorted in a way that doesn't allow them to see through anxiety and into reality. People suffering from this type of anxiety disorder are more likely to develop depression alongside suffering from anxiety, due to social isolation.

- *Phobia*

Having specific phobias related to certain unexplainable, but strong fears, is also a type of anxiety disorder. Patients with phobia will avoid specific triggers at all costs in order to prevent phobias from triggering into anxiety seizures or panic attacks.

- *Substance Anxiety*

Anxiety often develops due to substance abuse. Symptoms of substance-induced anxiety are displayed in strong panic attacks that appear as a result from drug abuse, medicine overdose or withdrawal from highly addictive drugs. Such anxiety disorder is more likely to be urgently treated with medication. CBT techniques can be effectively used for treating drug addiction as well.

- *Selective Mutism*

This type of anxiety disorder usually appears and develops in early childhood. A child suffering from selective mutism will have difficulties speaking in certain situations, which includes communicating with others rather than family members, speaking in public, speaking in school. The child will have no problems with communicating with family members and people the child is close to, however, this condition may stand in a way of a normal social life, school success and later on in adulthood may prevent the patient from having a job and functioning well as an adult.

- *Panic Disorder*

Panic disorder involves episodes of intensive feelings of fear and anxiety where the patient feels like something is awfully wrong although nothing too intensive happened in reality. During panic attacks the patient will display difficulties with breathing, staying short of breath, while experiencing heart palpitations, chest pain and constant fear that seems to never end. When a panic episode is over, the patient will try to avoid situations in which panic attacks happened, also fearing about the next panic attack, which only creates more triggers for panic disorder and anxiety involved.

- *Medical Condition-induced Anxiety*

Anxiety can also be caused by a physical condition, in which case this state is usually treated with medications in combination with talk therapy if necessary, alongside prescribing suitable medical therapy.

- *Separation Anxiety*

This type of anxiety disorder usually appears in childhood and continues displaying symptoms of trauma in the later years of the patient's life. Separation anxiety is developed in childhood when a child is separated from parents, a parent, or a person that carries a parental role in child's life.

- *Agoraphobia*

Agoraphobia is a type of anxiety disorder that involves avoiding places, usually wide-open places that feel threatening and unsafe, which can trigger panic attacks. Persons suffering from agoraphobia tend to avoid different places that might make them feel trapped, threatened or humiliated.

DBT skill training can successfully treat most anxiety disorders, as well as depression. Before we get to useful techniques on how to treat anxiety and deal with it, we will also find out how depression is developed.

How is Depression Developed?

A great number of factors are noted by psychologists and doctors in connection to developing depression. While there are numerous different factors that can affect a person towards developing depressive disorders, one thing is certain and is common to all cases of depression – just like it is the case with anxiety, depression develops over a longer period of time and is actually a result of more than several negative experiences and factors that are defined as triggers.

In some cases depression is diagnosed as a result of chemical imbalance. However, development of depressive disorder is far more complicated and complex. Life events may trigger depression and feed already present risk factors, while a single event may cause depression to appear in case a patient already has symptoms of impending depression. In most cases, a series of negative experiences and traumas need to take place over a longer period of time in order to get depression as a result. Frequent exposure to stress and stressful situations, as well as events like losing your job or experiences such as being in a toxic relationship, may all affect the patient in a way to develop depressive disorders. Stress is most certainly one of the main triggers of depression, and while all people in the world are going to stressful situations, not all develop depression as a result, which means that risk factors need to be already present in order to cause symptoms of depressive disorder. Often, patients are suffering from chemical imbalance, specifically related to the part of the brain designed to regulate mood. Another risk factor and a probable cause of depression in combination with chemical imbalance and external factor is genetics. There are certain groups of genes that prove that depression can be inherited through DNA in case there is a history of mental illness running in the family.

Besides from changes in the brain and the way your brain is releasing essential chemicals in combination with other risk factors such as genetics and stressful life events and experiences, depression is more likely to develop due to certain personal features that a person might have. Personality also plays a major role in development of depressive disorder, so in case you have low self-esteem, tend to worry a lot about everything and anything, and if you are inclined towards criticizing yourself and developing negative case scenarios in your mind, you are more likely to become depressed and develop depressive disorder.

Abuse of drugs and alcohol may also lead to a state of depression, as well as serious medical conditions that are physically exhausting. Whatever the case and whichever combination of risk factors leads to depression, it is important to remember that depression is not just "sadness" or "feeling blue" – depressive disorders represent serious mental condition and should be treated accordingly. CBT and DBT are proven to have successfully treated numerous cases of depressive disorders over the course of several decades. Most commonly, in order for depression to develop to the extent where the patient needs to seek medical attention, more than several traumas, losses and negative experiences need to "pile-up" so that depressive disorder would be triggered. Depression can be recognized by various defined symptoms that indicate that a person is suffering from depressive disorder.

Symptoms of Depression: How is Depression Displayed?

In order to confirm that you are suffering from depression, there are more than several symptoms and warning signs that indicate that you should start treating your condition before it progresses to more serious mental illnesses. In case you have carefully read the previous section where we have listed anxiety symptoms, you will notice that people who are suffering from anxiety are also displaying symptoms that indicate the presence and devastating effects of depression as well.

The following are the most common depression symptoms:

- Easily irritated and frustrated most of the time – people who are suffering from depressive disorders are more likely to get easily irritated, where irritation may be triggered by most trivial experiences and by on the first look harmless situations. Frustration is frequently, if not constantly, present.
- Lack of confidence and self-esteem – depressed people are having issues establishing confidence and lack self-esteem, which is why it is easy for them to blame themselves for anything and everything, which only leads to further developing depressive disorders.
- Feeling guilty – the presence of guilt on patients who are suffering from depression is almost inevitable. Patients with diagnosed depression will feel guilt even for things and case scenarios that don't directly involve them as decision-makers or active participants. The guilt may enhance if the person notices that their depression is hurting and affecting others.

- The feeling of being overwhelmed – negative emotions are not easy to bear, especially when combined with negative experiences and traumas, so patients with depression will feel overwhelmed with emotions they are experiencing, unable or almost unable to cope with their emotions.
- Lack of motivation – patients with depression lack motivation even for completing important tasks and developing professionally and personally. Lack of motivation can be displayed even in most trivial actions, such as for example getting out of bed in the morning.
- Social isolation and lack of social interaction – depressed people will avoid social contact, feeling uneasy and exposed on social gatherings, followed with lack of communication and social isolation. Lack of social interaction might result in losing friends, which eventually only strengthens depressive disorders.
- Lack of focus and concentration – depression comes with lack of focus, which means that people who are suffering from depression might have a hard time completing tasks and focusing on important day-to-day activities. The mind is so obsessed with negative thoughts and overwhelming feelings, which is how patients with depression are having a hard time focusing.
- Inability to enjoy – inability to find pleasure in things that were once considered pleasurable is one of the most common signs that a person is suffering from depression. Even when something nice happens, a depressed person won't be able to truly enjoy, which is usually followed by being misunderstood by people around them – people can mistake this sign of depression with a personal choice, making the situation more difficult for the patient
- Withdrawal from those who care – inability to enjoy pleasurable things and lack of social interaction may further lead to withdrawal from family members. Once the family becomes interested in what is going on with you, you may

decide to retreat and avoid those who care, believing that you are getting in the way of their own happiness. Depression may also make you feel like you are worthless and hurting others by the way you feel and perceive.

- Substance abuse – just as substance abuse may lead to depression development, depressive people may turn to substance abuse, i.e. alcohol and drug abuse in order to be able to feel something positive, which only leads to more severe problems, alongside developing addiction.
- Total unhappiness – you feel unhappy, sad, moody and discontent almost all the time. Sadness and unhappiness have become your center emotion.
- Inability to make plans and decisions – patients suffering from depression will have a hard time making plans since seeing a future worth living is slowly becoming a problem. The lack of self-esteem and indecisiveness is additionally getting in the way of normal and happy living.
- Feeling tired and fatigue – depression also has physical symptoms, one of which is feeling fatigued and tired. The constant sadness and lack of motivation in combination with other symptoms is slowly starting to reflect on the way you are functioning physically. You may feel ill for days at times, while fatigue and the feeling of being tired may persist in the long run.
- Problems with sleeping – obsessive thoughts of self-resent in combination with emotional and physical pain may impose difficulties with sleeping. Your sleeping patterns are changing as you are having issues with both, falling asleep and getting up once you manage to get some sleep. Insomnia may also develop over time.
- Loss of appetite and problems with gastrointestinal health – loss of appetite and nervous gut may be another one of symptoms that people with depression are experiencing. The lack of will to live is affecting appetite and food consumption,

which may lead to more medical problems in case depression is not treated.

- Weight loss/gain - extreme weight loss or weight gain is another one of side effects at people who are suffering from depressive disorders. While some people may feel lack of appetite, others will try to fill emotional void by finding comfort in food.

Types of Depressive Disorders

There are more than several types of depressive disorders, displaying differences in behavior, emotions, signs and symptoms, while all of these conditions are categorized as depression and can be treated successfully with CBT and DBT techniques. The following are types of depressive disorders:

- *Situational Depression*

Situational depression is otherwise known as adjustive disorder, or reactive depression, and it represents one of the most common types of depressive disorder. Situational depression usually appears when a traumatic experience occurs or when a person is exposed to a highly stressful situation, such as loss of loved ones, divorce, losing a job, medical illness and other serious and significant, yet stressful changes in life. Situational depression has the same symptoms as major depression while the difference lies in the fact that situational depression is a short-term condition. However, situational depression can reappear in numerous future scenarios although it lasts for a short period of time, especially when compared to major depression.

- *Manic Depression*

You might know manic depression under its second name, bipolar disorder. Manic depression or bipolar disorder, involves major and unpredictable mood swings which may take the person suffering from this condition from suicidal thoughts and inclination at one moment, to total happiness and joy. Depending on the severity of manic depression, patients may have major mood swings as often as weekly to as rarely as once or twice a year. Manic disorders can be related to mood swings triggered by certain situations, as well as to chemical imbalance.

- *Atypical Depression*

Atypical depression is in many ways similar to situational and major depression; however, it doesn't involve endless sadness in combination with negative emotions. Atypical depression is displayed through symptoms such as oversleeping, overeating, increased physical and emotional sensitivity, irritability, lack of tolerance for rejection, and having troubles in having normal relationships. What is interesting about atypical depression is the fact that patients who are suffering from this depressive disorder can recover from depressive state in case something positive happens to them.

- *Major Depression*

Major depression, otherwise known as clinical depression, is perhaps the most complex form of depressive disorder due to the fact that this mental state takes months and years to develop, while persistently torturing the patient with perpetual sadness and total lack of motivation for external stimuli. Patients suffering from major depression will have all previously listed symptoms, or at least five symptoms for more than two weeks in order to confirm diagnosis as clinical depression. Main signs of major depression are lack of interest in things that were once found pleasurable, as well as constant feeling of sadness.

- *Psychotic Depression*

Some people who are suffering from depressive disorders may be experiencing psychotic episodes, which usually happen after suffering for years from untreated depressive disorders. Psychotic episodes may include delusive behavior and disorganized thoughts, while the patient will also deal with false convictions and beliefs. Hallucinations during psychotic episodes are also a common symptom that a person is suffering from psychotic depression as a result of severe depressive episodes.

- *Seasonal Affective Disorder*

Seasonal depression or Seasonal Affective Disorder is another type of depressive disorder that involves feeling depressive triggered by the change of seasons. Seasonal changes may affect some people to feel depressed, followed by symptoms such as heaviness in limbs, fatigue and feeling tired, having problems in relationships with other people, and craving for food more than usual. The symptoms of seasonal depression are more likely to appear with the beginning of fall and end with the end of winter. However, some people may experience negative changes with the beginning of spring and summer.

- *Persistent Depressive Disorder (Dysthymia)*

People who are suffering from dysthymia often appear to others as if they are moody, pessimistic or not enough motivated. However, people who are suffering from this type of depressive disorder are actually battling a serious mental condition. Dysthymia is actually a long-term type of depression that lasts for years, while symptoms may disappear for some time. Even though symptoms may not be displayed for weeks or months, dysthymia persists and always returns as a chronic mental illness. Dysthymia is thus making patient's everyday life more difficult whenever the symptoms appear.

- *Postpartum Depression*

Postpartum depression is also known as "baby blues" and appears on women who had just given birth. It is a perfectly normal thing to be stressed about becoming a parent, while hormones may play a major role in allowing the feelings of anxiety, fatigue and sadness. However, in case the symptoms persist for more than several weeks, the patient is more likely to be diagnosed with a case of postpartum depression, and should be treated accordingly as a serious mental problem.

- *Premenstrual Dysphoric Disorder*

PDD or Premenstrual Dysphoric Disorder, is a type of depressive behavior that appears as a result of hormonal disbalance. PDD is a mood disorder and it may appear at some women periodically during the premenstrual phase. Symptoms include anxiety, depressive mood, mood swings, irritability and sadness. Many girls and women are having a hard time coping with premenstrual hormones. However, not all display symptoms typical for PDD. In case this behavior is repeated over the years ahead of every menstruation, the person experiencing these issues is more likely to be diagnosed with PDD.

- *Disruptive Mood Dysregulation Disorder*

DMDD, or Disruptive Mood Dysregulation Disorder usually appears at young children who are reacting with moods and emotions that are not appropriate for their age. Children suffering from DMDD will have frequent emotional outbursts of rage that are less likely to be contained even when the external irritation is not categorized as particularly negative for the child. The patient will feel irritated during, after and before these episodes of emotional outbursts.

Now that we have gone through all forms of anxiety and depressive disorders, we are certain that you could find your own symptoms somewhere among the list of depressive disorders and types of anxiety. As we are starting with useful techniques that are set to improve your health and help you deal with your emotional turmoil, don't be afraid – the journey of healing and treating mental illness starts by identifying triggers and symptoms of your mental condition. Starting with the next chapter, you will be able to access simple but effective CBT and DBT techniques for depression, followed by more useful lessons that will help you treat your anxiety with success.

Chapter 6:

DBT Techniques for Treating Depression and Anxiety

CBT and DBT are proven to gently work to remove factors that create the environment for the development of depressive disorders, treating depression with well-rehearsed techniques and lessons that are formed based on extensive research on CBT, which took decades to reach the current level of effectiveness. With DBT techniques as additional aid on your road towards healing, you are getting closer to solving your mental state and living a happy and normal life. We will start with useful techniques on how to treat depression and anxiety with DBT, by following the four stages of skill learning: practicing mindfulness, distress tolerance, interpersonal effectiveness and emotion regulation.

Practicing Mindfulness with DBT

Practicing mindfulness is equally efficient in treating both depression and anxiety as a part of DBT treatment that is proven to be effective in treating these types of disorders. By implementing practices and techniques that are due to teach patients the art of mindfulness, patients should be able to live in the present moment without judging themselves, and having the ability to focus on the moment they are experiencing in a given moment. What is important for you to remember is that you also need to let go of judging other people, as well as forget about judging your own judgments. To be able to perceive reality as it is, you need to let go of negative presumptions and judgments and focus on how beautiful you are just the way you are. Perhaps the most painful feeling of all when it comes to absence of mindfulness is thinking that you should be someone else, while believing that you are the worst version of yourself. There is no better or worse version of oneself in DBT – you are who you are and DBT practices are set to help you understand and accept yourself, while implementing healthier practices into your everyday life. Remember that DBT combines two opposites during treatment, which are accepting and changing. You need to accept yourself as a beautiful and valuable person, but you also need to be aware of the fact that you will only be able to grow if you decide to go for options that are better for your own mental health, i.e. you need to accept change as well as accepting yourself.

Mindfulness Practice #1: Observation

The first practice that will take you closer to mindfulness is learning how to observe, before you can learn how to describe and participate, which are all part of DBT skills to achieve mindfulness. In the beginning you may find it difficult to focus on what you feel instead of focusing on what you think or believe, but the trick in observing, as one of the key skills you need to learn to achieve mindfulness, is to learn how to focus on what you feel, see, taste, touch and experience through your senses. Our brain has a tendency to label things and explain and define what is happening, so we could grasp internal and external experiences. That is why it may be hard for many people to live in the moment and just feel – try focusing on what you feel in this moment. What can you sense with your touch, with your eyes, with your ears and through your emotions without trying to define what you are experiencing? How do you feel when you try to relax and just live the moment? You should feel relieved and enter a state of mind where you are acting only as an observer of what is going on around you. In case you are finding it difficult to focus on how you feel without pressing labels upon sensations you are picking up, try visiting a place that makes you feel comfortable and pleasant in your own skin. Is there are a park or a garden you specifically enjoy, or you used to enjoy before you started battling your anxiety or depression? Revisit that place and try observing it with a different perception – observe everything around you, touch a flower, smell it, see what is going on around you without trying to judge your environment or define what is going on – just try and live in the moment as if you are experiencing everything for the first time without any previous knowledge on the world around you.

What you need to learn from this DBT skill practice is to allow things to happen without feeling the need to change it, or make it go away by pushing these experiences away. The main idea behind learning the skill of observance as practiced through DBT treatment is to learn to allow things to happen without labeling or judging experiences that seem to be taking over. Another important thing that you need to understand as you are learning the skill of observance is that observing must represent experience, rather than intellectual understanding – you need to learn to observe and live through experiences without the need to explain everything that is going on. Your experiences need to be pure, judgment-free and without needing to label every experience you have and everything you feel. Understanding the skill of observance alone is also not enough in order to learn the skill – you need to experience observance. You may learn to do so by getting involved with some simple exercises:

- *Breathing*

Try focusing on your breathing. Breathing is one of the most essential practices to relax and also to practice mindfulness. Being mindful means that you are perfectly aware of everything that is going on around you, but without the pressure of defining your experiences as good or bad. Make sure that you are in a position you consider to be the most suitable and comfortable – lie down, sit down, it doesn't matter as long as you feel comfortable. Try focusing only on the way you are breathing without thinking on anything else – just breathe and try to relax as you are inhaling and exhaling. Observe your belly rising and deflating as it is filling in and then out. Similar to meditation you are focusing only on the way you are breathing, without giving much thought to how you breathe. You can use this practice on a daily basis as an introduction skill for learning how to be mindful based on DBT.

- *Listening*

To achieve mindfulness as the first stage of DBT skill training that should help you get rid of your anxiety and/or depression, you need to start training your senses as an important part of your experiences. Try turning your mind off for anything else rather than just listening. Try listening to the sounds around you, try to pick up everything you hear but without trying to make comments, label the sounds you hear or define what you hear. There are no pleasant or unpleasant sounds at this moment – you are just listening and experiencing sounds that you are able to pick up in your surroundings. In the beginning, it may be a bit difficult not to think about what you are hearing, but as you are trying to relax, you should be able to pick up sensations and experience sounds without adding labels to what you hear. If you are trying not to think of the sounds you hear or make comments, try using the breathing exercise before you get involved in exercising listening to the sounds around you. That way, you may relax and let go of any judgments and the need to label and define everything you are experiencing.

-   *Seeing Without Labels and Judgment*

When talking about observing and perceiving without labeling and defining everything around you, we include another handy and effective practice that should help you observe without getting involved in labeling and judging. Try taking a walk to the park and sit on a bench. In this practice, as you are comfortably seated on a bench in a park, you will try to observe only the things that are in front of you, which means that you will observe passengers and everything else happening in front of you, but without looking around or observing stimuli that are not in front of your eyes. Make sure to only see things in front of you without putting labels on what you see. Try not to judge things passing by, and try not to guess what they are about, who they are and where they are going. What may be a handy push into succeeding in this practice is to pose as an observer and not a participant of what you are experiencing. By experiencing these skills, you will be able to understand mindfulness better than trying to intellectually understand the concept of mindfulness, as this state of mind is strictly related to experiencing and not to understanding.

The Goal of Learning DBT Observance Skill:

The goal of practicing observance is to help you live the moment without getting back to past experiences, which also includes unpleasant memories, overthinking, past traumatic experiences and even grudges you are holding against yourself and others. Mindfulness means teaching yourself to take the best of the present moment and enjoy the NOW, as you would enjoy a present given from a loved one. You also need to distance yourself from your personal anticipations of the future – you must learn to live in the present in order to achieve the state of mindfulness and learn how to cope with all the problems you are going through due to your condition. Once you learn how to live the moment, you will be able to take each moment of your life gradually, without considering past influences and future anticipations – you will learn how to become aware, more secure and focused on what you are experiencing in the moment.

Mindfulness Practice #2: Describe

After learning how to observe without triggering the need to define, judge and label, you will be able to extend your mindfulness skills by adding up the skill to describe, which acts as an extension to the previous skill – Observance. You previously practiced how to distance yourself from recognizing experiences and just focusing on what you are able to sense in the moment. With the next skill – Describe – you will learn how to describe your experiences. However, you will be challenged to learn how to describe your experiences using only pure facts that describe what you feel through your senses, without involving your personal impressions, assumptions and interpretations. This skill might be a bit trickier to learn as we all tend to define things around us through our subjective perception, which is basically the thing this practice is asking you to avoid.

As you are practicing mindfulness through the second skill, Describe, you will be describing your observance through pure facts. You will have to describe thoughts, emotions and sensations as they are: thoughts, emotions and sensations, without adding your opinion, labels, judgment, assumptions and concepts. This practice is set to teach you how to describe your thoughts, emotions and sensations in a factual way, without attaching a biased interpretation of reality. If you for instance are thinking that you are not loved or that you are not worthy of love, that is your thought and not a fact. If you tend to jump to conclusions without first considering the facts, which is making you sensitive to outside stimuli, this skill should help you base your thoughts on facts and not on personal fears and doubts, which should eventually help you avoid scenarios where you are making yourself feel bad by inducing false presumptions and twisted perceptions on how you are perceived by yourself and others.

Let's take an example to show you how you can practice the skill to describe what you observe, using pure facts instead of your own assumptions and judgments. For instance you have met your boyfriend and the two of you are having lunch. You notice that your boyfriend is looking around, appearing more distant than usual. You begin to doubt yourself, convincing yourself that you are the reason for the behavior you are observing. You conclude that he is bored by your presence, that he would be better off without you and that he might wish he were somewhere else. Your thoughts are becoming chaotic and you start to doubt the honesty and stability of your relationship. "Why is he looking around? Is he bored my me? Am I boring? Did I do something wrong? I must have made a mistake to make him act the way he does. He probably doesn't even want to be here; he probably doesn't even want to be with me. Why is he with me? Does he really love me?"

In case you noticed in our example, the girl in our case scenario (can also be a young man and his girlfriend) presented as a potential case scenario, started to describe what she observed in her boyfriend's behavior, immediately concluding and labeling his behavior based on personal fears and doubts – that is not a way to describe what you see and notice by observing. The right way to observe the situation would be: "My boyfriend is looking around – and that is all there is." If there were facts that would show you that something is wrong between you and your boyfriend, proving to you that something is really wrong, then the internal negative conversation you would be having with yourself could be justified, but in this case, what you observed was only a boyfriend looking around – that's a fact. We used this example to show you that describing your sensations during observance should be only based on facts, i.e. information on external stimuli that you can confirm with certainty as facts.

To get back to the example, the correct way of reacting in that sort of scenario is to ask your boyfriend about what you have noticed. You may refer to the situation by asking him: "Is everything all right? I noticed that you are looking around, did something happen?"

He will provide you with an answer for sure, then you can get involved in concluding based on the answer you get – his answer will thus represent a fact that you can work with to describe your experience. Perhaps he is just nervous because something happened at work, but you shouldn't run to conclusions on any potential case scenario until you have viable facts to work with.

Whenever you catch yourself jumping to conclusions based on what you are observing or thinking about in a given moment, stop yourself and go through the facts related to that case – you may only use facts to describe experiences, regardless of whether these experiences are related to your thoughts, emotions or sensations. The way you are experiencing things around you is based on your own perceptions, and by basing this perception on facts, you are actually able to see reality as it is, freeing yourself from fears and doubts.

The Goal of Learning DBT Describe Skills:

This practice has a goal to teach you how to become able to base your conclusions on facts instead of jumping to conclusions based on a clouded judgment, personal fears and doubts, as well as based on bias assumptions. You only need to use facts for creating your opinion on external experiences you are able to pick up – otherwise, you would be creating a different reality for yourself, weaved by negative assumptions and your own negative opinions you have about yourself. One of the main reasons behind holding grudges against yourself and attaching negative labels to your own character is the fact that you are basing your opinion on your doubts and fears and not on real facts, which is why the describe skill is very important.

Mindfulness Practice #3: Participate

Starting from teaching you how to observe and how to describe events and experiences you are able to observe, we have arrived to the point of mindfulness practices where you will need to learn yet another essential skill – Participate. Participating represents just what you expect it does – the exact opposite of observing. Gradually progressing towards achieving the state of mindfulness through learning how to distance yourself from jumping to conclusions and living in the past and through future anticipations, the next thing is learning how to get involved, i.e. to participate. Let's define the term of participating from a closer stance – participating means that you are set to join different forms of activities without taking your self-consciousness, fear and doubts with you. Participating means that you are actively involved in your experiences, representing a participant, i.e. a person of action. If this doesn't sound like you at all, that only means that you did not take time to leave your self-consciousness behind, and that you are still struggling with your fears. If this is the case, we suggest you get back to previous practices of mindfulness before continuing with practicing participation.

In case you are observing the way in which children are participating in different activities, you will notice that most children are able to participate in activities such as playing with others without giving much thought about what others think about their participation. Children will not include inhibition in their decision to participate, which is the exact mindset you should learn to adapt over time as you are practicing mindfulness. Let's say that you are invited to a party. You know that people you don't know will also attend that party, and in most cases, you would decide to skip and stay home and do something that is more inclined to your comfort zone. Before you decide to skip that party, ask yourself Why? Why did you decide to skip the party? Do you believe that people will judge you, observe you and analyze you? Do you think that you are not interesting enough or don't have anything to talk about? None of these reasons represent facts – these are only your false beliefs and assumptions, and if we have learned anything in the previous skill training, you should describe sensations, thoughts and emotions only by using facts. So, the bottom line is that there is no valid reason for you not to go to that party and participate with others by opening yourself to a new experience that you can learn from. Another example where we can make a valid point on what participation means in general and for your mental health is dancing. Yes, dancing. Dancing to the rhythm of music without paying attention to other people around you and without thinking about what other people think of your dancing moves is the perfect example of practicing mindfulness through participation. By dancing surrounded with other people, you are participating while with leaving your assumptions, judgments and inhibitions behind, you are participating through mindfulness. With participation, you are actually practicing all three essential skills that define mindfulness: observance, defining and participating.

Remember, instead of thinking through your activities, you should fully experience them by not thinking about the way or the reason you are participating. You may practice participation through mindfulness through daily mundane activities, such as cleaning, doing dishes, dusting, or spending some time in the bus, car or metro on your way to work. Driving to work doesn't need to be a negative experience where you start reflecting on everything you believe is wrong about you – you may become an active participant and create a positive experience that is also good for your health. Let's say that you need to take a bus on your way to work, or anywhere you need to go by bus. Normally you might feel uncomfortable, thinking that people are looking at you and judging you as they are observing, you may believe that they know who you are and that they can see the lack of worth you are able to see in yourself. Note that these are not facts and if you are still struggling to separate facts from false perception, wrong assumptions and self-judgment, you should definitely dedicate more time to the previous skill training – Describing.

Instead of thinking what other passengers on the bus think of you, focus on sensations around you and participate by observing your surroundings. Take a look through the window and see your home city passing by you as you are riding a bus. You do not need to make any plans or think about the past – just enjoy the ride and embrace the moment you are experiencing.

To be able to truly participate in different activities without thinking through every action you take and every experience you find, you need to understand that your self-consciousness is getting in the way of truly living through your experiences. Self-criticism is another factor getting in the way of participating freely and without judging yourself. It is very important to remember that you need to rely on facts, that way preventing yourself to get involved with self-criticism – if there's no evidence on what you think, feel and sense, then it is about your perception of reality, and you should always try and trust facts – not biased opinion and assumptions. In case you are prone to addictions, such as drugs or alcohol, don't mistake participation for addiction you might be sharing with other people. You may feel like you are living in the moment when consuming alcohol or drugs, but once again, that would be wrong assumption.

The Goal of Learning DBT Participation Skill:

Remember that example we used about dancing and living in the moment by participating without self-consciousness or self-criticism? It is important to understand that in this case it doesn't matter how good or bad you are at dancing – you could be a treat to watch while dancing, or not, but what counts is not how good you are at dancing as long as you can get a quality experience out of your participation. The goal of learning DBT participation skill is to achieve mindfulness, while you should learn how to start enjoying every moment you get.

243

By participating, you are actually diminishing the feeling of being alone and alienated, which usually poses as a major problem for people who are suffering from anxiety and/or depression.

Mindfulness Practice #4: Letting Go of Judgments

As learned through the skill of describing sensations, thoughts and feelings by only using facts, letting go of judgment is based on a similar philosophy which dictates that you should never think of any experience as right and wrong, or good and bad. If you try to describe your experiences as good or bad, wrong or right, you are not using facts to describe what is going on – you are using your personal perception of experiences around you, which is the exact opposite of mindful describing, which means that you are actually judging (others, yourself and experiences you are going through). We tend to mix up facts with our own convictions and judgments, often allowing our personal judgment to overshadow reality and truth. Judgments don't have to have a negative connotation, as there are also positive judgments, and in this case, DBT suggests to let go of any type of judgment, positive as well as negative. At first, it may appear as if we want to get rid of negative judgments, there are no valid reasons not to get into creating positive judgments. However, it must be taken into account that positive judgments often turn to negative, so this could backfire and you will end up disappointed. Let's say that you love and cherish someone so much that you could say that he/she is the most wonderful person in the entire world – this is a positive judgment. Thinking that someone is the best, or the most wonderful person in the world is not the same as appreciating and loving someone, so by creating this positive judgment, you are actually leaving room for this assumption to become a negative judgment. Let's say that "the most wonderful person in the world" happens to disappoint you, which eventually inevitably happens in any type of relationship as conflicts are a perfectly normal thing – the positive judgment you have made about that person can then turn into a negative judgment due to the disappointment and false expectations you have previously created. You need to try to describe thoughts, emotions, experiences and sensations without judging and by using facts as the only viable proof of reality of things. Instead of characterizing something as good or bad, right or wrong, you should try answering the following: who, what, when, where, how, why. Even WHY can be a bit overwhelming and should be perhaps avoided. When describing many WHYs usually we do not come with a solid and direct answer, i.e. "Why would someone do something like that?" – people sometimes do unexplainable things without knowing why themselves. That is why you might want to avoid asking WHY when something happens.

Mindfulness Practice #5: Letting Go of Negative Thoughts

DBT is based on CBT, so it is no wonder that DBT suggests letting go of negative thoughts. Even though DBT is about accepting yourself and changing at the same time, practicing the opposites this way, DBT still supports the cognitive part of CBT, which is the way we think and perceive experiences. However, while CBT considers that you should change the way you think to fit a more positive behavioral image, DBT states that you shouldn't indulge in thinking that you should be better than you already are, considering that thinking how you should be different and better in any way also represents negative thoughts. This negative statement is making you feel bad and it is also worsening your condition along the way, which is why you should avoid thinking that you should be someone else – you should accept yourself as you are through CBT and DBT practices and decide to change some aspects of your perception in order to live a happy life: no judgment, no negativity – observe, describe, participate, live in the moment.

Practicing Distress Tolerance with DBT

After going through the first stage of DBT practice, i.e. mindfulness, you are set to practice skills that should help you develop distress tolerance. As someone who is suffering from anxiety and/or depression, you are sensitive to external stimuli that may affect you in a way that you feel like you are threatened and in distress. Everyone in the world is going through some kind of emotional distress – the loss of loved ones, break up, losing a job, moving, and many different external factors may make a person feel emotional pain while experiencing distress. People who are suffering from anxiety and depression tend to feel distress in a more intensive way, which makes them unable to focus on other things rather than experiencing emotional pain. This emotional distress may take the best of anyone and everyone, which is how it is very important to learn Distress Tolerance, and the way this skill may help you treat anxiety and depression alongside the skill of mindfulness. When it comes to being in emotional distress, people who suffer from depression and anxiety are more prone to suicidal thoughts and self-harmful behavior, while commonly being toxic for their own selves. Emotional distress appears as barely bearable to patients who are diagnosed with anxiety or depression, and it is that pain that can push a person to the limit and inject suicidal thoughts in the patient's mind. By learning how to cope with distress through distress tolerance, suicidal thoughts alongside self-harmful behavior should be diminished, while successfully treated.

Distress tolerance techniques can be divided in three different types of skills, which includes: crisis survival techniques, sensory body awareness, and reality acceptance. Since DBT is based on acceptance and change, distress tolerance skills are also revolving around these opposites as well as practicing mindfulness.

Crisis Survival Skills

Crisis survival skills are designed in accordance with DBT treatment with the goal of providing solutions for surviving emotional crisis. Patients who are suffering from anxiety and depression can use these survival techniques in cases where it is almost impossible to get over intense emotional or physical pain, but it can be also used in various situations that can be categorized as the time of crisis.

In case you wish to act upon your emotions even though it is obvious that emotional response would only make things worse, you can use crisis survival skills. Crisis survival skills can as well be used in situations that can be described as emotionally overwhelming, where the patient is usually not able to cope with intense emotional experiences. In case when you feel like you are able to settle down a certain situation that can't be resolved immediately, crisis survival techniques may also come as handy.

Although it may be tempting to use crisis survival skills in your everyday life, and even for the most trivial case scenarios, these techniques should be used only in times of crisis as the name suggests. You will use these skills to pull yourself out of unpleasant situations that can be described as emergency. During the time of emergency, you are usually not able to see through the moment of crisis, which is making it difficult for you to find a solution that would help you resolve a critical situation.

Crisis Survival Practice #1: Stop Skill

Stop skill is one of the simplest and perhaps most effective practices of crisis survival strategy and can be used when you are preparing to act upon your emotions even though it is obvious that you will make things worse by doing so.

Sometimes it is the best to just stop where you are, take a step back and distance yourself from the moment of crisis in order to be able to make an action once your mind is clear and your logic is ready to step in. When facing the moment of crisis, you should first alert yourself to STOP and take a moment to try and make a safe distance between yourself and the challenge you are facing. Let's say that you are about to enter a conflict with a friend – your friend managed to make you furious, sad and disturbed at the same time, and as you are facing a hurricane of emotions, you just want to react in accordance with how you feel. You don't have enough facts in line that would prove that your friend indeed deserves that sort of emotional reaction, which means that the best solution would be to stop and take a step back before you make things works and act in accordance with false assumptions and judgment.

Each letter of the word STOP, represents a letter of action and a step towards mastering the stop skill.

S – stop and consider why you shouldn't take action even though you wish to show how you feel about the negative situation you are facing. You should be in control of how you feel, while controlling the way you are showing your emotions. Just stop and remain still for a few moments until you can process the entire situation in a more logical way.

T – take a step back. You need to distance yourself from the situation that is making you feel emotionally overwhelmed. By taking a short break, you are preventing yourself from acting based on your emotional distress. Acting on your impulses could only make things worse, which is why you should take a deep breath and move onto the next step of the stop skill.

O – observe. This is where your practice of mindfulness will come more than handy, as observe is one of the key skills that should be mastered towards achieving mindfulness. As you remember, observing includes analyzing the situation by picking up external and internal sensations without labeling and with no judgment allowed. After you stop for a moment and take a step back, you should use objective analyzing while observing the situation you are in. While observing the situation of crisis, you should take a note of what is going on around you, as well as how you feel about what is happening right now.

P – practice mindfulness. After you have observed the situation and collected all facts on how you feel and what other people who are involved in this situation are saying, and how they are acting, you can proceed with practicing mindfulness in a way that will allow you to apply what you have learned with mindfulness techniques. Consider what is your goal in this situation, how you can make things better, and which action you should not take to prevent things from getting worse.

Crisis Survival Practice #2: Listing Pros and Cons

Everyone has a weak point: yours might be a form of addictive behavior, negative behavioral patterns that are getting in the way of a quality everyday life, harmful behavior, or perhaps you are having difficulties with motivation to complete tasks that need to be done. Whenever you are faced with some of these situations, you can make a list of pros and cons, which represents a form of crisis survival practice. Whenever you are facing a moment of crisis, you may write down a list of all things against you are struggling with, so you can get a clear overview of the situation and create room to make a decision you would act on. Whenever you are having doubts about how you should act and react, you can use pros and cons lists you create to get back on the right path, which will help you build an appropriate action and reaction to the situation you are struggling with.

Crisis Survival Practice #3: Short-term Distraction – ACCEPTS

Sometimes you may be overwhelmed with emotions to the extent where you are no longer able to make decisions that would work in favor of resolving the problem you have, but will only make things worse. When you feel that you cannot create a response that would make a negative situation better, you can turn to creating a short-term distraction that will set your mind to a different thread of thoughts, that way preventing you to act based on an impulse. You should note that your short-term distraction should not turn into a long-term way of avoiding problems, as problems you tend to avoid and ignore usually find a way back to you. There are several techniques that you can use as a crisis survival practice for creating short-term distractions – an easy way to remember these strategies is to list them by an acronym ACCEPTS. Each letter in the acronym stands for one crisis survival technique.

A – activities. You can use different types of activities to put your mind at ease and step away from an overwhelming situation, so you can get back to it once you are ready to face your problem. This solution should only work as a short-term relief. You can exercise, go for a walk, read a book, paint, get involved with gardening, take a ride on a bike.

C – contribution. By contributing to someone else's happiness – of course, not at the cost of your own – you may find a short-term distraction from overwhelming situations and experiences. Help a friend, make a donation, gather some things you don't need and give them to someone who needs them, or simply be there for someone.

C – comparison. Comparing your own situation to other people's misfortunes and past times you went through, and that were much harder than the situation you are currently in, may help you feel better about where you currently are. Surely there are many people in the world who are suffering from more severe problems when compared to the situation you are experiencing.

E – emotions. Don't try to get away from emotions and make yourself numb. Allow yourself to experience a wide range of different emotions by listening to emotional music, watching a drama, watching a horror movie or reading an emotional book. Emotions triggered by emotional books, music and movies may briefly distract you from the emotional turmoil you may be going through.

P – push away. You need to resist the temptation of progressively thinking about the problems you are going through. Push away all negative thoughts that are making you feel bad and at least for a while decide to think about something more positive. By pushing away negative emotions you may replenish your emotions and your mind, until you are ready to deal with your crisis situation.

T – thinking. Whatever you do during the moment of crisis, refuse to think about the problems you are having a hard time currently dealing with. Try finding something that has the ability to make you switch your thoughts from your problem to something that will help you as a distraction. You can solve a crossword, read a book that will make you think about something else or try to solve some puzzles.

S – senses. Make your senses busy with an overwhelmingly pleasant activity such as taking a shower, making a bubble bath, or dancing to loud music. Make sure to take care of your crisis problem after you have rested your mind with distractions.

Crisis Survival Practice #4: Improving the Moment

Another one of useful crisis survival practices is improving your present moment. This skill should make you improve the overall state of emotional distress and as such is a rather useful DBT technique. You may use your imagination to create scenarios where you are safe and settled in your favorite place. You are protected in this place and nothing can touch you or affect you in a negative way. Praying for peace is yet another handy practice that can help you improve the moment – try praying calmly, opening yourself to whatever you believe in. Pray for calmness, peace and serenity until you feel that you are indeed becoming more settled and calm even though you are going through emotional distress.

Try improving the moment despite the negativity the moment may bring, by trying to find a positive thing in distress you are going through. Focus on the good side of a bad situation you have found yourself in, and try to understand that you can still learn something positive out of a negative experience. A brief vacation may also provide you with a break you need – take at least one day off so you can enjoy resting in bed, watching TV or reading a book, preparing your favorite meal or watching your favorite series.

Sensory Body Awareness

Sensory body awareness skills present another way of fighting distress and you may use it alongside crisis survival skills. In case you have carefully read the part of the book where symptoms of anxiety and depression are listed, you have surely noted that depression and anxiety can affect you physically as well as emotionally. Suffering from anxiety or depression you can surely feel tired even when you have not been physically active to the extent that activity can cause exhaustion.

You may also feel muscle pain, have difficult time with frequent headaches, nausea and other forms of physical pain and distress, which is a common side-effect of anxiety and depression. Our body is constantly communicating with our brain, which is how you can feel your muscles stretching or your limbs moving, while also being aware of body movement. Most of the time we are not even aware of how our body is connected to our brain, but by practicing sensory body awareness we can become more connected to the reality of things, making it easier to accept different experiences.

Sensory Body Awareness Practice #1: Rethinking and Paired Relaxation

Paired relaxation is a fairly simple skill that can be practiced every day as a part of sensory body awareness skills. Paired relaxation has a goal of helping you relax through becoming more aware of your body, muscles and breathing. You can perform simple breathing exercises similar to the ones proposed in mindfulness practice, by finding a quiet place where you can relax and choose a position that feels most comfortable to you. Breathe in and breathe out. As you are breathing, feel your belly filling up and out while you are holding your hands on your belly. Stretch your arms and feel your muscles stretching as you are exhaling and inhaling. Move your shoulders and your fingers, become aware of every move you make, and continue to breathe in and out. Once you feel that you are fully aware of your body and that your body is relaxed, you may start including positive affirmations that should help you to rethink the current situation that is making you feel stressed, more depressed, more anxious, or emotionally challenged. Try switching negative thinking patterns with more positive affirmations. As you are breathing in and out you can also pep-talk yourself, using this practice to get you through difficult times when it feels to you like there is no easy way out. You can use encouraging thoughts such as: "I can do it." and "I am stronger than this." Create your own affirmations and repeat it as mantra while you are practicing paired relaxation.

Sensory Body Awareness Practice #2: Willing Hands and Smiling

We use our hands as well as our face through facial expressions in order to communicate with others aside from talking. Hands and face are thus important tools for communication with ourselves as well as these body parts can pose as perfect tools for inviting serenity and peace into your body and mind, which is especially helpful in stressful situations. You can practice this skill on a daily basis. Willing hands are created by opening your palms facing upwards. You need to relax first, also loosening and relaxing your shoulder before you open your palms upwards. In case you are seated when practicing willing hands, you can place your hands in your lap and open your palms with your shoulder relaxed. If you are standing, place your arms beside your body and open your palms by slightly raising your arms up as you are opening your palms upwards. As you are creating willing hands, start working on relaxing your face. Start from your forehead and head area around your eyes Make sure that you are not frowning and that you are relaxed. Start thinking about every part of your face, gradually relaxing bit by bit until you can feel that your entire face is relaxed, from your forehead to your chin. Now, as you are holding your palms open and your entire body and face is relaxed, make a half-smile. As you are smiling, try to adopt the feeling of peace that the smile describes. Everything will be just fine! You can repeat this practice whenever you feel upset and need to make peace with yourself.

Reality Acceptance

Reality acceptance is another technique under distress tolerance skills, and it represent a handy way of helping patients suffering from anxiety and depression to accept pain as a natural part of life. We all suffer and we are all faced to painful experiences and events during our lifetime. We can choose to grieve and gradually get over painful experiences, while remembering our past sufferings. Some people, however, rather choose to push the pain away by not solving painful experiences. By pushing the pain away and trying to get away from grief and painful situations, you are allowing pain to turn into suffering, where it might turn into long-term distress. Emotional distress will thus get in the way of a happy life you can have by accepting pain as a natural part of everyone's life. There are some simple and effective acceptance skills that you can practice in order to learn how to accept pain and grief.

Reality Acceptance Practice #1: Mind and Perception

When we are in pain, there are basically only two paths we can take. One path will take you to suffering and pain and the other one takes you to acceptance. Choosing the path of suffering means that you are holding grudge against past experiences and situations and against yourself, as you are holding onto the feeling of anger and bitterness. In case you are thinking in a way "Why is this happening to me? What did I do wrong for this to be happening now?" means that you are not accepting the reality as it is. You need to note that sometimes bad things just happen and there doesn't have to be any good reason for that. By accepting that fact and accepting reality as it is while trying not to hold onto anger and remorse, you are choosing the path of acceptance so you can easily move on and accept that bad things are a part of life as well as good things. Be prepared to accept the bad and welcome the good into your life. Accepting does not mean that you are actionless in your pain and that you shouldn't do anything to improve your life. It just means that you are refusing to allow the pain to turn into long-term suffering.

Reality Acceptance Practice #2: Be Willing

In order to accept and face reality, one must develop the skill of willingness. You need to wish to feel better and you need to actually want to accept reality. Willingness means that you are ready to change your ways towards more positive behaviors so that you would be able to free yourself from suffering. Practicing willingness might not be the easiest practice in reality acceptance as it requires only your will and a dose of convincing yourself that you are able and willing to work on feeling better and accepting reality as it is.

Reality Acceptance Practice #3: Radical Acceptance

We sometimes tend to battle reality and get involved in fights against what is real, that presents itself as just different experiences in our life. These experiences are often negative, so sometimes we tend to react in a harmful and impulsive way, as we are having a hard time to accept that some things are not going that way we imagined or in our favor. Radical acceptance represents the end of fighting back, and signifies the state of accepting reality as it is without responding impulsively. To be able to completely accept reality we need to understand our past and present and consider how our past experiences and present decisions may affect our future. Even if your past experiences are making you feel uneasy or uncomfortable you need to understand the facts related to your past and present in order to accept reality and embrace radical acceptance. A change is made when you are able to see reality as it is even when you do not feel comfortable about it, while you are also aware that the reality you are able to see is not acceptable as positive. Only then you can make a change. You cannot change what already happened, but you can surely make your present more positive with the looks of a bright future if you are ready to make a change starting with yourself and accepting that there are no Whys in life. Life just happens, and you need to participate.

Practicing Interpersonal Effectiveness

Emotional distress and pain that goes hand in hand with anxiety and depression can be overwhelming for you, as well as for people around you, while it is commonly the case that your emotional distress is preventing you from having healthy relationships with other people. Practicing interpersonal effectiveness is due to teach you how to decide what you want and need and how to get it, as well as working on improving your interpersonal skills, social skills and your relationships with others. Having functional and healthy relationships with other people is extremely important for your health, which is why interpersonal effectiveness skills are very important. Here are several practices for developing interpersonal skills that can help you improve your life and your health.

Interpersonal Effectiveness Practice #1: Empathy Through Thought

Your emotional distress can keep you busy with your own feelings and emotions that can sometimes be so intense and overwhelming that you may be having a hard time understanding how other people feel. You may be blind to other people's emotions as your own emotions are hard to bear, which is how your relationships with others may be jeopardized. Try placing yourself in other people's shoes when working on a relationship with someone. Empathy through thought can help you relate to other people by relating to their emotional state. This can be very handy for resolving conflict with other people as you can take a moment and consider how they see the situation you are in together. If you are angry the other person may also be angry as well. You know the reason behind your anger, but does the other person has the same reason to be angry with you? How does it feel to be the other person and why did the conflict happen in the first place?

In order for a relationship to work you must understand each other, regardless of the type of relationship we are talking about, and understanding is best achieved through empathy. Try to fix issues between you and other people by understanding where their own emotions come from. As you are resolving the conflict, try noticing what the other person wants to see in the end: whether he/she wishes for the conflict to be solved or they want to increase the overall tension created by the conflict. In case you notice that the other person is trying to be kind and solve the conflict with honesty and readiness to work on your relationship, you should respond in the same manner if you care for the other person. Practice understanding others through empathy even when there is no conflict in the middle so you could become better in solving these types of conflicts.

Interpersonal Effectiveness Practice #2: Conflict and Self-respect

When we are in conflict with someone we care about, we sometimes tend to set our self-respect aside in order to solve the conflict and save our relationship with that person. While forgiveness and acceptance show readiness to work on a relationship and preserve it along the way, this case must go both ways. You cannot step over your own values and truth in order to preserve your relationships with others. You should also never apologize in case you have done nothing wrong, while making sure that you are fully aware of the facts that describe the reality of your conflict with that person. When solving your conflicts with others, you need to remain true to yourself but you also need to be fair to the other person. Being fair in conflict resolutions means that you will not use judgments and express dramatic, i.e. unfair behavior. Always stick to the facts and try to solve conflicts while preserving self-respect. You might have a difficult time finding your own self-respect when you are beaten up by anxiety and depression, but by practicing mindfulness and other DBT techniques for treating your mental condition you will gradually get to the point where you can use facts instead of judgments, that way seeing yourself as a person who indeed deserves self-respect and respect from others.

Interpersonal Effectiveness Practice #3: Give, Receive and Communicate

Having a healthy and functional relationships with your family, friends, and your boyfriend, husband, wife or girlfriend, may sometimes look like something difficult and almost barely achievable goal. However, when you care for someone you will try to give your best to improve and maintain your relationship. Note that the other person you are sharing a relationship with should want the same thing and be ready to act upon that wish. It is very important to give in a relationship but also to be able to receive as well as you are ready to give. Although you may already be a giver with readiness to always be there for someone you care for, you might not think that you deserve the same from the other person, which is how you may be pushing away all the love installed for you as a reciprocal result of your own giving. Communication is also important, which means that you need to practice listening, observance and presence, as well as practice telling how you feel, what you want and what you need. Don't be afraid to tell what you want and how you feel, while you should also be ready to hear the same from the other person.

Always try to use a gentle approach when talking to the other person you are sharing a relationship with – be interested in how they feel and how their day went, get involved in listening, but also provide your own response. Relationships need to work both ways in order to function. Practice being present and involved by communicating with your partner, friends and family. As you are there for them, expect the same from them. Perhaps the most important thing about practicing communication, giving and receiving in relationships, is to be present and there for others even when it feels like you cannot handle your own emotions. Be ready to share your "bad" times as well as "good" times.

Practicing Emotion Regulation

It may seem that controlling your emotions is the most difficult thing you have ever been challenged to do, as your first and initial emotional reactions to negative emotions and experiences you are perceiving as negative can be more than overwhelming. Emotion regulation thus represents a part of DBT treatment for anxiety and depression that should help you learn how to control, overcome and regulate impulsive and overwhelming emotional responses. The goal of emotion regulation practices and skills is to teach you how to deal with your emotions before they turn into distress, which could make it even more difficult for you to control your emotional reactions. Emotion regulation practice should teach you how to control and regulate your own emotions, reduce sensitivity and vulnerability to external stimuli, learn how to prevent yourself from acting impulsively, as well as how to solve your problems in ways that are helpful and not based on judgments and emotional distress.

Emotion Regulation Practice #1: Describe and Label Your Emotions

Describing through labeling and judging is against the practice of mindfulness as a part of DBT treatment for anxiety and depression. However, labeling and describing your emotions can help you get a better understanding of how you feel and what your emotions represent. To be able to regulate your emotions you first need to identify them. That way you will be able to understand why you feel the way you do, providing you with a chance to control your emotions in a way that allows you to solve any negative feelings you might be experiencing. You first need to learn how to differentiate primary and initial emotions from secondary ones. Primary emotions are initial emotions that appear as normal reactions to experiences and external stimuli. Primary emotions are anger for example when you get into a conflict with someone, or grief and sadness in case a loved one dies. Secondary emotions appear as results to primary emotions and can be developed from primary emotions through thinking patterns. By describing and labeling your emotions, you are able to identify how you feel and why you feel the way you do, which gives you with the opportunity to make peace with how you feel, by explaining your emotions. You may use descriptive adjectives to define your emotions which will give you enough time to avoid acting impulsively and allow you to consider your options as you are choosing an appropriate emotional reaction. By describing pain, for example, and identifying the source of your pain, you will be able to find the right solution, without allowing the pain to turn into perpetual sadness and emotional distress.

Emotion Regulation Practice #2: Letting Go of Negative Emotions

We tend to ask "Why?", "Why is this happening to me?" when we are faced to pain and emotional distress. These questions are often keeping us tied to pain and negative emotions that are getting in the way of a healthy and happy life. You may catch yourself obsessed about the pain you are feeling to the extent where you feel like you are not able to bear the way you feel any longer. Obsessing about pain and negative emotions can consequently lead to destructive and harmful behavior, which can further make your mental condition become worse. This case scenario takes us back to the need to accept, as although it may sound contradictory, accept that we feel pain and distress is a normal thing, it can help you get over negative emotions. Instead of obsessing about the way you feel or trying to get away from your emotions you may try observing your emotion from an objective point of view. Identify your emotion, describe it and explain it. Make sure to acknowledge the fact that the emotion you have truly exists, but try and imagine that you are only an observer of that emotion, standing and observing from a safe distance. Try imagining that you are drifting across the ocean. The weather is perfect and you can feel the waves carrying you back and forth. The ocean actually represents your emotions. If you accept the waves you will float and be carried across the ocean. However, if you start struggling and swimming against the waves, you will sink and drown. That means that if you accept the pain you are more likely to deal with it and understand it before you decide to act. In case you try to fight the pain by force, you will remain overwhelmed and get stuck with pain, obsessed with negative emotions.

Emotion Regulation Practice #3: Creating an Opposite Action

Every action has an equal or opposite reaction – a rule of physics that can as well be applied to emotion regulation. Every emotion likewise has an equal reaction that appears as a result from experiencing emotions. For example, if you are angry with someone, you are most likely to start an argument. If you are sad you are most likely to start crying and retreat to solitude, and so forth. The bottom line is that every emotion has a reaction, and sometimes these reactions are not healthy for us. By creating an opposite action as an emotion regulation practice, you are actually learning how to stop intense and overwhelming emotions from progressing towards toxic behavior and impulsive emotional reactions. Just as emotions can prompt certain behavior, certain behaviors can prompt specific emotions. So, instead of starting a fight when you are angry with someone, try talking calmly towards to solving your issue. Take a moment, take a deep breath and create an opposite action. Practice emotion regulation by creating opposite reactions to prevent impulsive reactions.

Emotion Regulation Practice #4: Filter Positivity

Sometimes we tend to filter negative things, emotions and events to the extent where it might appear that there are no positive things in our life. Just as you have the ability to filter negativity and focus on negative things in your life, you can also filter positivity and focus on positive aspects and events in your life. In case you catch yourself thinking too much about all the negative things happening in your life, you may try to switch your focus by looking for positive things around you. You can start with small positive actions, such as watching a good movie or eating your favorite meal without rushing through it. Try to pick at least one positive activity every day, while thinking about positive things you already have in your life. Whenever you feel that your attention is drifting towards negative experiences and emotions, try thinking about positive things you have and feel grateful for everything that is positive in your life.

Chapter 7:

CBT Techniques for Treating Depression and Anxiety

Cognitive behavioral therapy resulted from decades of studies and research that were first used treating patients with different traumas. Today, therapies and treatments such as DBT are based on Cognitive behavioral therapy, while CBT is used for treating different mental disorders, which also includes treating depressive disorders and anxiety disorders. Although DBT is more specifically designed to treat patients who have been diagnosed with depression and/or anxiety, there are more than several CBT techniques and skills that could help you on your way to recovery.

CBT Practice #1: Keeping a Journal

Cognitive behavioral therapy is treating mental illness by applying the rule that says that our thoughts and the way we think and perceive reality are narrowly linked to our emotions and behavior. Based on this statement, changing one of these aspects should cause a chain reaction in which other aspects would also change as a consequence. In order to be able to change our behavior to a more positively oriented, and to learn how to regulate our mood, emotions and emotional responses, we first need to learn how to identify and track our behavioral, thought and emotional patterns. One of the best ways of doing so is to start keeping a journal. Your journal should contain your emotions, as well as the cause of them, the emotional response that you used as well as hold information on how well you believe you have handled intense and overwhelming emotional situations. By keeping a journal of your emotions and other related information that can describe your behavioral, thought and emotional patterns, you are actually learning how to identify your patterns in order to be able to change them to a more positive behavior.

CBT Practice #2: Identify Distorted Cognition

CBT proves that a great part of emotional turmoil, stress and distress, which builds up to create anxiety and depression, are related to negative thinking in relation to emotions and behavior that consequently become negative as well. Given the fact that negative thoughts represent false perception, i.e. distorted cognition, it is very important to be able to identify distortions in thoughts and perception. CBT explains distortion in perception through automatic thoughts, i.e. negative thoughts that appear due to a false perceiving of reality. By managing to identify automatic thoughts and separate them from reality, you should be able to stop automatic thoughts and switch them to more positive thoughts, which should result in development of positive and constructive behavior and positive emotions. Considering that automatic thoughts are able to trigger negative emotions and harmful behavior, by identifying automatic thoughts you are gaining control over how you feel and how you react to your emotions and external stimuli. Whenever you catch yourself in a thread of negative thoughts, try to identify the reason why you are thinking in the way you do. In case you are setting your mind to negative thoughts, you need to determine facts from self-induced and automatic negativity.

CBT Practice #3: Changing Cognitive Patterns

After you are able to trace and identify distortions in your own cognition, you can start determining the initial cause of these distortions. Every false cognition has its own roots, which means that you must have adopted your false convictions in some point of your life, probably as a cause of past trauma or negative experiences. To avoid evoking emotions tied to trauma and negative experiences we tend to suppress them in hope the feeling of fear and anxiety would go away. The fact is that the more you try to suppress negative emotions, the more likely is that those emotions are going to backfire. What you want to change in order to change negative behavioral patterns, are your false beliefs that appear as a product of distorted cognition.

These false beliefs might prevent you from developing individually, romantically, professionally, emotionally, and even intellectually. Let's say that you think that you are not good enough and that you are somehow not worthy. Are there facts to prove that you are right? We are guessing NO. You only believe that you are not good enough, which is a false belief that you have adopted. Ask yourself why do you think like that about yourself? When did you first develop that opinion? By exploring past experiences you can determine the source of your cognitive patterns, making it easier for you to change negative behavior to more constructive behavioral patterns.

CBT Practice #4: Expose Yourself

In order to test how likely you are to refrain from responding negatively to external stimuli you find stressful, exhausting, overwhelming or emotionally intense, you need to expose yourself to factors you consider to be your triggers. The key is to start with less intensive emotional experiences where you will do your best in trying to divert your thoughts to a more positive mindset, as learned in the techniques of DBT mindfulness. Try observing the situation and describing it with facts before participating. By taking a moment to consider your actions and describe the situation you are in, in a realistic way, you are more likely to refrain from having a negative reaction to your triggers. Don't run away from discomfort – try to face it so you can overcome it. Use facts to describe experiences, thoughts, and sensations, so you would be able to come up with a solution.

CBT Practice #5: Imagine Worst-Case Scenarios

In most cases thinking through worst-case scenarios is rather harmful for your emotional state as you may get upset solely by imagining the worst thing that can happen. Having your nightmares playing in your head, over and over, in periods when you are obsessing with your fears may only feed your anxiety and doubts. However, when it comes to practicing exposure, you will be required to imagine the worst thing that can happen and that is related to your biggest fears. By playing out that scenario in your head, you can predict the worst scenario of your worst fears. This practice is due to show you that there are no such things as non-manageable problem as every problem comes with a solution, we just need to find it. By exposing yourself to uncomfortable scenarios not only that you will be able to realize that everything is manageable regardless of the result, but you will also try to develop immunity to your worst fears.

CBT Practice #6: Progressive Relaxation

Whenever you feel overwhelmed you tend to react in accordance with your emotions, which means that you may rarely take time to consider your emotional reactions. This can further involve intense emotional reactions that may only make things worse for your situation. Progressive relaxation is an excellent and a simple way of calming yourself down and calming your nerves whenever you feel exhausted. You just need to take a moment before you take a deep breath. Inhale and exhale and try imagining your muscles relaxing, one by one, bit by bit, starting from your forehead and the tip of your head and going down to your toes. As you are breathing in and out, try to address every body part in your head, relaxing each part of your body. Feeling the connection between your body and mind through the ability to relax each muscle on demand, will surely help you calm down. When your body feels calm and relaxed, it is easier for your mind to follow.

CBT Practice #7: Analyze Your Behavior

CBT treatment includes changing your behavior as well as changing the way you perceive and think (cognition). Behavior is a product of numerous factors which includes thoughts, external stimuli such as past experiences, the way you were brought up, your emotional state, as well as your character. In this practice you will write down all behaviors that you believe are negative and are not appropriate, and which you would like to change for better. Besides, the list of negative behaviors you are ready to change, you will write down all factors you believe represent triggers for negative, harmful and destructive behavior. The third sheet should contain consequences that appeared as a result from practicing negative behavior. By listing unwanted behavior, factors, and consequences, you can get a better overview of your behavior patterns, thus being better prepared for changing your behavior to more positive patterns.

CBT Practice #8: Considering Future Outcomes

Sometimes our thoughts and emotions can be so overwhelming that it becomes hard to handle the level of distress we are experiencing. When facing such case scenario, we tend to create drama by seeing negative situations as catastrophes, which can cause a sense of doom. In this case it may appear as if there is no way out. When this happens you can prevent yourself from getting into the feeling of doom by trying to place yourself in the future where your present problem does not exist anymore. Imagine yourself a month from the present. How did you manage to solve the problem? Imagine all potential results of your situation, and try to imagine how your decisions affect your future. Considering the fact that you are not the only person in the world who is going through a certain situation may also be helpful in overcoming the moment of crisis. By imagining the future you will also realize that your problem is not there to stay and that it cannot last forever. Make sure to imagine all positive experiences you have gone through, making a list of all things that are worth living and keep trying, whenever you are faced to a situation that appears to be unbearable to manage.

CBT Practice #9: Productive vs Unproductive Worry

People tend to worry about many different things at the same time as there is always a problem waiting to be resolved – that is just the way it is in life. Worrying almost feels like a part of the solution as it can appear as if you are preparing to solve your problem by spending some time worrying about solving it. Sometimes worrying about something can actually help you find a solution to your problem, as you can focus on your problem as you are considering your options and potential results. However, in many cases, worrying only contributes to feeling anxious about situations that can surely be solved if you take a break and consider solving your problem with a cool head. That is how we can conclude that worrying can be productive and unproductive. By determining whether your worry is productive or unproductive, you are more likely to solve your problem that it would be possible if you were to start to be obsessed about it. There are several ways to tell when worrying is everything but productive. Usually, if you find yourself worrying for longer than 10 minutes, your worry is less likely to turn into a viable plan that can pose as a solution to your problem. By trying to limit your worry, you will also limit the level of stress you are exposed to, due to your problem. Worrying too much and obsessing over problems can contribute to strengthening your anxiety which is the opposite of what CBT and DBT prescribe to patients who have been diagnosed with anxiety and depression. In case you know that some things are beyond your control and you are still worrying, then your worry is not productive and you should stop yourself as soon as you realize that your worry is futile as it cannot result in a plan or a solution to solve your problem. You can only solve problems that are in your control and by realizing that some things go beyond our control will help you stop worrying about everything. Even productive worry should be reduced to minimum and approved, as long as you are sure, that it can take you to a solution you can use.

CBT Practice #10: Thoughts As Guesses

You are probably able to catch yourself doubting more than once a day, and these doubts are usually related to distorted perceptions of your own self. You can get easily discouraged, you tend to retreat on the first sign of discomfort, you are likely to withdraw from others and seek for shelter in solitude, while that same loneliness will only make you feel more alienated from the rest of the world. Those who are suffering from depression and anxiety often find themselves struggling with seeing anything that's "good", usually emphasizing all the negative things, some of which do not even exist as facts. Thoughts that start with negative attitude will only make you additionally overwhelmed, encouraging your mental illness and discouraging your willingness to get better. As you are working on treating your anxiety and depression, it would be helpful to start observing your thoughts as guesses. As long as you cannot find the facts that would support what you think, you may consider your thoughts to be nothing more than guesses. So, when you say that you are not good enough, or that you will never be able to do this or that, if you don't have a proof that these statements are facts, you need to treat your thoughts as guesses. You will also be able to note that these guesses are coming from the negative perception that appears due to distorted cognition. By questioning factuality of your thoughts, you are actually allowing yourself to draw conclusions that could prove your initial thoughts as false beliefs and not facts.

CBT Practice #11: Activity Scheduling

People who are suffering from anxiety and depression will often have a lack of motivation for doing things they would normally be interested in, if the situation was different regarding their mental condition. Patients who suffer from anxiety will even have a hard time participating in activities they once considered as pleasurable and pleasant, which is how DBT created a way to motivate patient to participate in various activities. This is achieved with a skill called activity scheduling. Activity scheduling involves creating a list of activities that should be done periodically and usually at specific times, so that the patient would be able to create a healthy routine that will surely replace unhealthy behavior patterns. Scheduled activities should be pleasurable and rewarding to increase the level of motivation.

CBT Practice #12: Problem Solving

People diagnosed with anxiety and depression may also have a difficult time with solving problems, as they are more likely to be obsessed about problems and focus on worrying on demand rather than approaching the problem with a cool head and trying to find a viable solution. That is why DBT recognized that teaching patients to solve problems is more than necessary and helpful when it comes to treating anxiety and depressive disorders. Problem-solving starts with recognizing and identifying the problem. Sometimes we cannot be sure what is exactly our problem, although we are aware that something is wrong, which is why analyzing the problem in its core is how problem-solving begins. Once you are able to identify your problem you will be able to work on finding a solution. Next, you need to approach the problem in a relaxed state as overwhelming emotions can prevent you from finding solutions to your problem. Once you are able to relax you will become more focused to find a solution than to worry about solving the problem. Keeping your head cool in stressful situations is anything but easy. However, once you are able to relax you will note that your problem might have more than a single solution which might encourage you to approach it without feeling stressed. The last part of problem-solving is taking action. As someone who is just learning how to effectively solve problems, you should plan only what you are certain you can achieve. By gradually taking smaller actions, you are more likely to solve your problem without feeling overwhelmed.

CBT Practice #13: Calm Your Body to Calm Your Mind

Breathing is very important as a form of relaxation technique, while practicing your breathing technique can also help you relax and regain your ground in intense and overwhelming situations where it may seem as you are unable to handle the level of distress you are experiencing. By calming your body you can actually calm your mind, just as emotional distress may reflect on your body and create physical symptoms of anxiety and depression. Physical symptoms such as nausea, dizziness, headache, heavy limbs, shortness of breath and heart palpitations can be reduced and calmed with an appropriate breathing technique. Whenever you feel like you need to relax as your body and mind are not able to handle the level of stress you are experiencing, you can turn to breathing. Inhale and exhale by using your nose for inhaling and your mouth for exhaling. Breathe calmly and take your breaths with ease as you are feeling your muscles relaxing in the rhythm of your breathing. You will be able to feel the burden of distress slowly leaving your body. You can use a simple breathing technique as used in previous skills and practices, whenever you feel overwhelmed.

CBT Practice #14: Practicing Fairness

Anxiety and depression go hand in hand with distorted perception, which is how it may appear to you as if you always have a point and that you are always right. While you might be obsessed with the fact that life is not fair, having a hard time to accept the fact that bad things happen just as good things do, you can forget how to act fair in your relationship with others. Instead of presuming that you are right which is often the case due to distorted perception, you should rely on facts as the main tools for achieving fairness. Whenever you are faced with a similar challenge, ask yourself why do you think you are right, also listing facts that can indicate that the other person is right. By placing yourself in different shoes, it may become easier to see beyond convictions that you are right, and even though you feel that you are right, you need to use facts to confirm your assumption, that way practicing fairness. Practicing fairness should help you solve conflicts in a thought-through and calm way without acting upon intense and overwhelming emotions. Additionally, this skill should help you develop healthy relationships with others as you will be able to understand a different point of view that is not affected by distorted cognition. Remember to always rely on facts when in doubt.

CBT Practice #15: Responsibility Assignment

Whenever something bad happens that affects us in a negative way, we feel like assigning the blame to someone or something, often missing the point that sometimes things just happens and that there is no need for finger-pointing and assigning responsibility. It is easier for us to assign responsibility to a third party for something that happened to us, as it may be easier to find the source of the problem by creating one instead – by placing a blame on something or someone without checking the facts that would support that blame, we are actually trying to make a safe distance from the negative situation and deny our own responsibility. According to CBT, you are the only responsible person for the way you feel and act while others have nothing to do with how you decide to act and react. Instead of placing the blame on others and assigning responsibility to others for the way you feel or behave, you should reflect on your own responsibility for actions you take and emotions you are experiencing. Only then will you be able to solve your issues – by taking matters into your own hands.

CBT Practice #16: Emotion Doesn't Equal Truth

Feelings can be so overwhelming that it can appear to us that whatever we feel and experience through our emotions is actually true. This is a perfectly normal case as we are all humans after all, and humans are rather emotional animals. The mere power of emotion can be easily noted in the fact that emotional distress may lead to general dysfunction and physical pain, making us feel debilitated and unable to live a normal and happy life. Most of false beliefs are born precisely from the feeling that our emotions represent truth – emotions are so overwhelming and present that we start to believe that the extent of our emotional experience can be factual – it isn't. Our emotions are only forging our perception so we believe that what we feel must be a general truth. It may be difficult to look beyond the way you feel – for example, if you feel like you are boring and uninteresting, you will start to believe that these are truly your characteristics because "Why would I feel this way if it wasn't true?" That is how you must always try with reasoning your emotions, while you will do so by only using firm facts. So, if you start believing that you are boring and uninteresting, try finding the facts that would support your theory/conviction. In case you are not able to prove your opinion with facts, you are dealing with emotional distortion and not the truth.

CBT Practice #17: Gradual Concluding

People with anxiety and depression tend to jump to conclusions without revising facts that would support their conclusions, which is how you may have difficulties understanding others and having others understand you. Instead of jumping to conclusions based on something, you notice and that is out of the usual trajectory – i.e. your friend is usually talkative and he is quiet today; why is that so? Is it about you? Are you the reason behind the silence? – you may start making conclusions that are perfectly detached from reality simply based on minor changes in patterns that you have managed to notice. Before you start arriving to wrong conclusions based on the lack of facts and your own emotions, you should first step down and think through the situation. Instead of concluding that you have done something wrong to make your friend quiet today, you can ask him if everything is right. Once you get an answer you will surely notice if your friend has provided you with an honest answer, also realizing that you have done nothing wrong as your initial conclusion suggested. Make sure to take time when making conclusions instead of making fast assumptions that are based solely on your fears and doubts. You will not be able to see things clearly until you include facts in your reasoning.

CBT Practice #18: Communicate

Communicating when suffering from depression and anxiety can be as overwhelming as symptoms that follow these mental conditions, which is why people who are diagnosed with depression and anxiety often have difficulties communicating with others and maintaining healthy relationships. Being overwhelmed with a wide range of intense emotions may also get in the way of understanding others, which consequently leads to alienation and isolation from others. As isolation may only make your emotional state even worse, it is important for you to learn how to communicate with others in a constructive way that should work both for you and others. One of the main things to note is that you should never jump to conclusions if you do not have facts to support your assumptions. Allow others to express themselves without having you impose your own conclusions on them. Likewise you should not refrain from expressing yourself as any relationship needs to go two ways. Another important thing to note is that you are NOT too difficult to handle. Due to your condition you are often faced to a distorted belief that you are not worthy of attention as well as that there is no one in the world who can handle yourself, while you may also feel like you are barely handling yourself. Make sure to be open about what you want and what you need, but also be prepared to listen to other party's needs and wishes. Make sure to cherish connections that are valuable to you - stop convincing yourself that you are too difficult to bear and address negative thoughts as assumptions and guesses that appear as a side-effect of having low self-appreciation, which can be easily overcome by relying on facts.

Conclusion

You have arrived at the end of your journey towards treating your anxiety and depression. However, the work you are left with is not over with the conclusion of this book. Successfully treating anxiety and depression is extensive and intensive and should be practiced on a daily basis with the help of DBT and CBT techniques, strategies and skills. The fact that you are more informed about Dialectical and Cognitive behavioral therapy, as well as more aware of the causes and symptoms of your mental condition, may only take you closer to a resolution of your issues.

Always return to CBT and DBT techniques and practices when you feel the need to, and when you need something to rely on in your battle against anxiety and depression. Remember that getting to the point where you can say that you feel better may take some time, while willingness, dedication and determination to get better are the key essentials of the road towards healing. You can combine CBT and DBT techniques we have provided in the guide to change your weakness to strength and strengthen the faith you have in yourself. Perhaps you could not realize how strong you are, or that you have faith in yourself at all, but the mere fact that you have arrived to the end of our guide on CBT and DBT techniques for treating anxiety and depression, speaks in favor of your strength and faith.

Note that you are a beautiful person despite difficulties you might be facing, and with a little push from this guide, you will remember that as a fact.

© **Written by:** JOSEPH GRIFFITH

How to Deal with Difficult People

Smart Tips on How to Handle the People Problem and Get the Best Out of Your life

Katerina Griffith

Book Description

Have you ever encountered someone who is frustrating to the point you feel like pulling your hair? Has someone ever driven you so crazy that you feel like screaming out loud?

Look around you – there are people in your life that are difficult to work or deal with.

You are not alone!

One thing that I have found over the years is a fair share of difficult people – friends, family, and coworkers alike. These are people who don't bother to turn in their work within the agreed timelines, who hold on tightly to their views without caring about anyone else at all. People who do not want to collaborate with others in a team. Those who push back on work they are supposed to do in the first place – so much more!

Here, we will discuss;

- How to identify a difficult person: The big five
- Types of difficult people
- Common traits of difficult people
- Why you must deal with a difficult person
   o At the workplace
   o At home
- Identifying the issue
- Three lenses to look at the world
- How to manage your reactions
- Leveraging self-control
- Steps on how to deal with a difficult person
- What do you do when all this does not work?
- Expert techniques to handle difficult people
- Actionable tips and tricks

So, what are you still waiting for? It is time to handle those difficult people in your life gracefully, and survive the drama they attract.

Read on and find out more!

Introduction

Are there difficult people in your life? I guess that's why you are here. If you have not encountered difficult people before, then it is high time you start preparing for when that happens – because it will!

The thing with difficult people is that they often defy logic. Unfortunately, some of them are happily unaware of the kind of damage their attitude has on the people around them. Others are aware of the negative impact their actions cause but yet choose to derive their satisfaction from stirring up chaos and pushing people's buttons hard to know how far they can go. Whichever the case, their actions create unnecessary complexity, stress, and strife.

I run a business where we have over 200 employees. As we collaborate on various projects from time to time, there are instances where we find problems to reach a unanimous agreement on something because each member of the team is strongly opinioned. When I just started the company I used to get bothered and so worked up in such situations. Each time I would think, "Why are these people so difficult to deal with? What an irresponsible group...I don't even want to work with them anymore; I will fire them all!"

After some time, I realized that difficult people are everywhere. Even at home, I was dealing with a difficult teenage daughter who thought that she knew everything, and nothing you told her made any sense at all! The truth is, no matter where you are at or where you go, you will never be able to hide from such people. While it might be possible to avoid the first 1 or 2 of them, what about the 3rd, 5th, ...n^{th} ones out there that you have not met yet? Avoiding these people is not a permanent solution unless you are willing to quit your job or move away from your home and never have anyone around you.

I don't know about you – but I think that this is not possible! Instead of running each time and trying to find solace where you will never find it, why not learn some incredible skills that will help you survive difficult people with so much ease and grace?

According to research, it is evident that difficult people can cause stress to those around them. What is even more disturbing is that fear has been shown to have a lasting negative impact on the human brain. When you are exposed to stress even just for a few days, the effectiveness of the neurons in your hippocampus – the part of the brain that is responsible for memory and reason – becomes compromised. If the stress goes on for several months then the neurons are likely to get damaged. In other words, anxiety is one of the formidable threats to achieving success. If it gets out of control, then the chances are that your performance is affected.

The good news is that some of the common causes of stress are very easy to identify. For instance, if your company is working towards getting a grant for you to work on, chances are you will feel stressed and learn how to manage it. However, when the source of stress is unexpected, then chances are that it will take you by surprise, and this is what causes the most harm.

According to research from the Department of Clinical and Biological Psychology, Friedrich Schiller University, an exposure to a stimulus that causes a negative emotion is the same as when one is exposed to difficult people. The two experiences cause one's brain to have a massive response to stress. In other words, when one is negative and very lazy, that alone is put the mind in a state of anxiety.

It is important to note that your ability to manage your emotional feelings and stay calm, even when you are under so much pressure has a direct association with your performance. According to findings by Talent Smart, over 90% of top performers in any organization are skilled at managing their emotions during stress periods. What is interesting is that the reason why they have control over these stressful situations is that they have learned how to neutralize difficult people.

While there are several strategies I have learned over the years from some of the top performers – who are my role models – on how to effectively deal with difficult people, I choose to share them here with you. If you are going to effectively deal with difficult people, then you need an all-encompassing approach to things you can eradicate. What you need to understand from now on is that you are in control of how you respond to different situations more than you can imagine. Take charge today with the following strategies, and your life and experiences with people will never be the same again!

Keep reading!

Chapter 1
How to identify a difficult person: The big five

It is important to note that difficult people come in all forms and sizes. There is a wide range of ways in which difficulty can manifest itself. This can be somebody spreading false rumors, seeing negativity in everything, lack of cooperation, and those who don't see value in others' contributions and views, among others. The thing with difficult people is that they look for opportunities to make trouble. They tend to use passive resistance to bring down your efforts to move ahead.

Note that, at the end of the day, the definition of 'difficult' is something rather peculiar to every individual. In other words, what you consider challenging to you may not be the same thing to someone else. You must therefore take into account your personality, triggers, and preferences, so that you are better prepared to take note of situations and people that get on your nerves.

Emotional Stability

This is also referred to as neuroticism. You may be wondering what this is. Well, neuroticism is one of the factors that go a long way in determining one's level of emotional stability. How do you react or respond to a stimulus? If your score is high, then this indicates that you are no stranger to such emotional feelings as anger, anxiety, and depression. There is a high chance that you experience these emotions on an ongoing basis. In other words, if you score highly on neuroticism, this indicates that you are emotionally reactive as opposed to those who score lower.

The thing with emotional stability is that it indicates how prone you are to intense stimuli. However, what is important to note is that these emotional outbursts often tend to erode one's ability to think logically, make complex decisions, and cope with stress effectively. A high level of neuroticism manifests with a high level of negativity – which exacerbates the slightest setback resulting in one having a bad mood.

On the other hand, a low neuroticism level is indicative that you are emotionally stable. You are less prone to emotional outbursts and are calm. However, what you need to note is that having a lower level of neuroticism does not mean things will always be favorable on your part. Extroversion has a direct correlation with positivity. If you are going to deal with difficult people, then you have to learn how to break free from emotional setbacks.

Extraversion

The chances are that you are already aware of introvert-extrovert binary, right? What part of the scale do you fall in? Well, one thing you need to note is that extraversion is a factor that determines how you interact with the world around you.

If you rank highly on the extraversion scale, you are an extravert. The good thing with this trait is that you tend to possess a can-do it spirit. These are the kind of people who are always beaming with so much energy. They do well in social gatherings and when having physical experiences with the outside world.

On the other hand, there are the introverts. These are the ones that rank low on the extraversion scale. An introvert is someone that is more laid back with a very minimal need for social interactions. While they are not so positive minded as the extraverts, the truth is that they are not always depressed or shy. However, you must note the fact that they find physical and social stimulations somewhat overwhelming. This explains the reason why prefer solitude – to process their emotions – but also a little bit of social intimacy.

Openness

282

Each one of us has a certain level of transparency. It is our level of openness to experience that goes a long way in determining how one embraces new ideas and experiences. When one is open to experience, they are said to be artistically curious, intellectual, and with a very strong sense of beauty. The good thing with openness is that people with this trait excel in creative roles often seen in people in the upper echelons of designs and academia. However, these kinds of people tend to stay away from tasks that require compliance with a set of guidelines, rules, and regulations.

Well, this is not to say that there are closed-minded people. The truth is that those who do not rank high on an openness to experience tests are often called "closed." These are the people who often have very few common interests with others. This explains why they tend to oppose ambiguity and subtlety – mostly strongly in conversations – and do not respond well to change.

While people who are "closed" don't often light the world with innovations, the truth is that they have superior roles and performances in such areas as police work and sales, among others – where protocols, rules, guidelines, and regulations are what take precedence over all else.

Agreeableness

This is a measure of one's willingness and ability to engage with others in social events. While people tend to think that this trait is a universally beneficial feature from the outset, this is not always the case. Several people believe that agreeableness is something positive, but the truth is that just like all other traits, it also has its downsides. For instance, agreeable people are often afflicted with indecisiveness – especially when they are trying to complete high-stress or complex tasks.

The good thing with people with this trait is that they understand the importance of getting along with others. They hold a high consideration for others' emotions and goals – even higher than their interests. They are very friendly, relentless, helpful, and optimistic. To the onlookers, they are trustworthy and honest.

On the other end of the spectrum lie the disagreeable people - known to elevate their interests above anything else in this life. The thing with them is that they do not concern themselves with the wellbeing of those around them. Instead, they choose to pay attention to advancing their agendas and goals. Disagreeable people are very unfriendly, uncooperative, and do not give a rat's ass about anyone else. Such people are often found in science, business, military, among other professions.

Conscientiousness

This is a trait that measures the extent to which we can control our emotions. The truth is our conscientiousness determines the scope of our success, possible experiences, and the best way to attain them.

According to research there is evidence that shows that highly conscientious people often have better control over their emotions. Even though such people tend to come off as dull and rigid, the truth is that they do well in whatever they put their minds to – with proper planning and motivation. The good thing is that they often try as much as they can to stay away from trouble and making erratic decisions. However, the problem arises when plans don't fall into place as anticipated or fail to meet their set high standards.

On the contrary, those who have low conscientiousness can delay their gratifications. This makes them more prone to adhering to their emotions. While this are so much fun during parties and they have something people find valuable when situations arise, the problem is that they prove to be complicated. This explains the reason why they often get in trouble with people in authority.

That said, you may be wondering whether these big five traits are universal. According to a research study that looked into different people from over 50 cultural backgrounds, there is evidence that shows at least five dimensions that can be used to accurately describe personality. This is the reason why several psychologists believe that the five personality dimensions are not just universal but also have a genetic link. According to David Buss, a psychologist, personality traits are a representation of the key characteristics that shape our social landscapes.

But what factors influence these big five personality traits?

According to research, it is evident that both environmental and biological factors go a long way in influencing and shaping our personality traits. Two studies suggest that both nurture and nature have a central role to play in personality development. One of the studies examined 123 pairs of identical twins and 127 of fraternal twins. What was interesting was that 53% of the heritability pointed at extraversion, 44% to conscientiousness, 41% each to neuroticism and agreeableness, and finally 61% to openness.

On the other hand, longitudinal studies suggest that these five personality traits tend to stabilize as one goes through from childhood to adulthood. According to one study involving working-age adults, there is evidence that personality traits stabilized over four years and very minimal change brought about by adverse life events.

Studies also show that maturation dramatically impacts the personality traits. As we progress in age, there is a tendency for one to become less extraverted, open, and neurotic. However, features like conscientiousness and agreeableness tend to increase with age.

That said, what is essential to bear in mind is that behavior is something that comes as a result of interaction between one's personality and other situational factors. The situation in which you find yourself in has a role to play in how you respond. However, these kinds of responses are consistent with one's personality traits.

Wrapping It Up

The five personality traits that we have just discussed – extraversion, agreeableness, neuroticism, openness, and conscientiousness – account for the difference between people.

For instance, when researchers have studied the personality traits of such animals like chimpanzees and dogs, the same features are also observed, plus more. Take a minute to think about dogs you know – keep at home or are in your neighborhood. What you will notice is that they are different from each other. Some are more friendly, active, and outgoing than others. Some are emotionally stable, while others are not. Some are friendly and agreeable, while some are vicious.

The chances are that you already know dogs that are very conscientious than others – in other words, they try too hard to do what is required of them just so that their master is happy. On the other hand you probably know other dogs who don't care what their masters want. Dogs also vary in terms of how open they are to new experiences, while others are more explorative and curious.

The sixth personality that we do not have but animals do is the ability to be dominant while others are more submissive. While human beings differ in terms of dominance, humans are more reflective of extraversion than independent.

Several people wonder how possible it is to sum up personality traits in only five features. Well, if you think of all the people you already know, you might realize that they differ much more than the five personality traits. However, take a minute to think of this; if you take one character at a time rather than a collective personality, you will start to appreciate how diverse we all are.

People differ in personality ranging from low to very high on each trait. Even though each of the personality traits involves a large number of possible scores along the spectrum, you can choose to simplify this by thinking of it on a scale of 5. Now, if someone scores from very low, moderately low, average, moderately high to very high, this means that we can give each one a score between 1 and 5.

Now that we have five traits, each one of them has five possible score levels starting from very low to very high. If you do that, then you can get at least 3,125 possible combinations on all five traits. That means 5 x 5 x 5 x 5 x 5. This means that if you were to classify people into all possible unique combinations of the five big traits, you would have to use all the five levels of each trait.

Additionally, it is essential to note that based on one's standing, the traits will manifest in quite diverse ways. A character like neuroticism appears to be different based on where a person stands on that trait. Let us consider another simple example. If one is high in neuroticism and agreeableness, they will have more unpleasant emotions - even so, they are still pleasant to be around. In other words the fact that they are neurotic means that they tend to be clingy, annoying but does not necessarily affect other people much. If that very person is highly neurotic but has low agreeableness, then you had better watch your back!

When someone is highly emotional and is disagreeable, the truth is that they will tend to make their problems your problems too. They will be very difficult to deal with. While neuroticism manifests itself in various ways depending on their level of agreeableness, what you need to note is that such combinations change how our behaviors manifest outwardly.

Chapter 2
Types of difficult people

Perfectionists

When I first started my company, it used to take me at least 12 hours to produce an article that I thought was worthy of being published. My writers would send in their work, and I spent sleepless nights trying to edit and come up with the "perfect" piece. The thing with a perfectionist personality is that nothing will ever be good enough. You will find ways to look for mistakes, even where there aren't any.

One thing that is important to note is that being a perfectionist is something that is crippling. There may be that person in the office that is so passionate about their work that it is bursting with ideas but unfortunately cannot express them with unbridled freedom. It is the same thing with perfectionism – it holds you back because of anxiety, a sense of haunting unfulfillment and depression.

Well, so many people think that being a perfectionist is only about having the desire to be perfect. The truth is that it goes beyond that. You are merely choosing to derive your self-worth from the world around you. That explains why you end up being overly sensitive to criticism or rejection, and you end up believing that you are a stupid worthless failure or worse.

If you are a people-pleaser, then that is a sign of being a perfectionist. The thing is, seeking perfection often causes people anxiety because all they are thinking of is how they can be the best. You desire to control the outcome of your actions just so that you can gain approval, acceptance, praise, and rewards.

But do you think that the perfectionist in your office knows that they are obsessive and cynical in their behaviors? Certainly not! Just like I was, they may not even know that they are perfectionists, let alone putting in efforts to stop.

289

So, how do you deal with them?

Well, the thing with a perfectionist is that they are often detail-oriented, negative towards others, and sticklers for the rules. If your boss, subordinate or colleague is this kind of person, the ways to handle them vary widely.

Dealing With a Perfectionist Subordinate

There are different types of perfectionists based on the personality types that we have discussed in the previous chapter; neurotic perfectionist, narcissistic perfectionist, hyperattentive perfectionist, and the principled perfectionist. The thing that these people have in common is that they all notice details and have very high standards that an average person cannot even breath close. To deal with them, you must:

Avoid Giving Them Large Project Scopes

One thing that is important to note is that most perfectionists have admirable qualities that many people find worthy. However, there are quite a few of them who choose to hone skills on a small component of a project instead of paying attention to the bigger picture. If you work with these kinds of people, it is helpful to assign them select tasks based on their skills.

In other words, you can choose to give them projects that are limited in scope but are detail-oriented. The truth is that most of them are not willing to delegate tasks, and the best thing you can do is allow them to work independently on projects – as long as the project requires a unified vision to complete.

Appeal to Their Sense of Vanity and Empathy

What if your employee is a neurotic or narcissistic perfectionist? Well, these kinds of people have a powerful desire to please others. The most effective way to motivate them is to explain to them how their style of work affects those in the team. Ensure that you phrase it in such a way that they realize you already know they have high standards – and that you appreciate these high standards they hold.

You may say things like, "Mary, you have very high standards, just like me. That is what this company is all about. However, remember that good morale is essential for good productivity." What you are merely telling them is that the best way forward is to give a compliment even where they feel like there is something to criticize.

Appeal to Their Self-interest

What you will note is that several perfectionists want to be so perfect – either because of internal or external motivation. If you find that a subordinate is treating their colleagues poorly in the workplace just because they are perfectionists, remind them that such kind of people struggles hard to climb up the ladder. Remind them that the more they raise the ranks, the more they have to learn how to compromise for the sake of the whole team. Say something like, "I know you have been trying to ensure that the details of the project have been attended to, and the book does everything. That is great because if one is going to get the big things right, they will have to start by getting the little ones right. You are on the right track to the big things. However, what you need to remember as you progress is that the upper rank is about looking at the bigger picture. This means that if you focus too hard on getting 100% success, that will only bog you down. Have a vision for the next phase and not just a tunnel vision that might cost you more than you can pay for."

When you put it like that, they will start to realize that 100% is not all that counts, but achieving the primary goal, however, the approach you take is what counts at the end of the day.

Dealing With a Perfectionist Colleague

Choose Your Battles Wisely

When you are dealing with a perfectionist colleague, it is paramount that you know when to take a stand and when to let go. While this is something difficult to attain, you must take time to think about how important the issue at hand is so that you know when the time is right to take a stand.

The first thing is for you to keep a perspective. Agreeing with what your boss says does not mean that you have to follow their suggestions to the letter. While this seems at first as being passive, simply say yes and move on with your life. This will reduce the chances of stirring up conflict and stress. Saying yes to what they say does not mean that you have given away your power. It is quite the opposite because this will set you free from paying attention to their demands.

Ask Them What It Is They Would Like to Do Differently

Did you know that criticism is one of the best ways perfectionists use to hide their insecurities? While this is upsetting, it always helps to remember that this is their defensive mechanism. They may just be lashing out because they feel insecure about one thing or the other.

When you take time to ask them what their preferred methods of going about something is, you are merely disarming those insecurities. Try telling them that you care about their emotions. When they realize that you understand their feelings, they will start to feel secure – and less critical in the future. Say things like, "I see that you are upset about the outcome of this project. Would you like a chance to talk about it?"

Stick to Your Guns

Think about it, is the problem you and your colleague have relevant? If so, then you are right to stick to your guns. There is a chance that no one at the office knows that your colleague is a perfectionist. If there is something you consider relevant to you and do not agree to that, then realize that it is your right to let than be known.

Don't get me wrong- by disagreeing, I don't mean that you should argue about it. Simply say what it is that you disagree with and then move on. You don't have to let that disagreement define the kind of relationship you both have. Simply say things like, "I understand where you are coming from. I just think that our perspectives are quite different on this one."

If that stirs up an argument, simply walk away. No one will blame you for walking away from a case.

Keep Distance
One of the simplest ways you can stay away from conflict is keeping a safe distance from it. If you have to work together on a project, simply remind them that each one of you has their roles and responsibilities and that you will do yours to your supervisor's satisfaction and not theirs.

You always have the choice of disengaging. If they keep going on and on about inconsequential details, all you have to do is remain noncommittal. Simply make your escape with such statements as "Huh, I didn't know you felt that way."

Dealing With a Perfectionist Supervisor

Manage Your Manager

This is simply what I often refer to as 'managing up.' The main aim of doing this is to help you identify the personality of your boss – their strengths and weaknesses – so that you can effectively tailor your conversation to match theirs.

The problem with a perfectionist boss is that they always desire to be in charge. At first, this may be self-evident, but the truth is that it is not. Ask them what their expectations are. When you do this, you are giving them an enhanced feeling of being in control. This also protects you from providing an arbitrary response. While perfectionism may be unreasonable – inherently – you must try as much as possible not to be. The trick is for you to pay attention to their start points, endpoints, or boundaries to lower the chances of getting them angry.

Push Information Their Way

Once you know what it is that your perfectionist boss is looking for, simply give them – don't wait until they ask for it. The more you offer them a wealth of information they are interested in, even before they can ask for it, the less likely they will think of you as a flawed person. This way, you escape conflict by being in the right place, at the right time doing the right thing. Remember, out of sight, out of mind!

Be at Peace With The Fact That There Is Only So Much You Can Do

The fact that you are a subordinate means that you have very little influence on your superior's personality traits. There are times when they are critical and others overly-critical. But the good news is that you can still earn their trust and respect. The only downside to that is that you might have to endure too many interactions that are draining. Just do what is right and let the rest be decided by fate!

Seek Mentorship and Support Elsewhere

Now, you have a perfectionist boss who is supposed to be your mentor, but the truth is that they have set unreasonable standards you cannot attain. This means that if you take them as mentors, you will strain yourself too much just to earn their praise.

Perfectionists make very poor mentors!

While we all need support at one point or another, you cannot find it from your perfectionist boss. The truth is that such people tend to hurt your self-image even more. The last thing you want is having your self-worth determined by people who already think that everyone but them is worthy.

Jump Ship When You Have to
Consider that dealing with such a boss is something that you have to adapt to and not accept it indefinitely. You must know when to cut the cord. The trick is for you to earn their recommendation and move on. This might mean that you seek employment elsewhere.

Start planning your exit strategy as early as you can.

Control Freaks
Let us consider the following situations;

You want to hang out with a friend you met recently, but then your long-term friend insists that you should not because you have not known them well enough to hang out with. This friend asks that if you are going to hang out, you must tell them where exactly you will be meeting when - date and time.

Does this sound familiar?

Well, the truth is that this has happened to us – whether by partners, friends, or family members.

Such kind of people is referred to as control freaks. Dealing with such types of people is not fun – no matter how much they mean to you. It could be that they are doing it because their heart is in the right place, or they mean you no harm, but this is entirely lethal force you don't want to mess with.

You may be thinking, but who exactly is a control freak? Well, a control freak simply refers to perfectionists who feel vulnerable to anything that seems to them as uncontrollable.

The term "control freak" is a psychology-related slang. It describes a person who wants to dictate what everyone does and how everything is done around them. People who have an extremely high need for control over others are considered as control freaks.

Their main attempt is to hide their vulnerabilities by ensuring that everything within their surroundings is under their control. They try hard to manipulate people and put so much pressure on them just so that they don't have to change themselves. Everywhere you go, you will spot a control freak – whether at home, school, or workplace.

With the right strategies up your sleeve, you can deal with them and live a happy life.

Get Rid of Turf Wars

So many control freaks often feel the need to retain control of each aspect of their work just because they do not want to lose their status. It could be that there was a time when they were the only employee in the office and were used to do all things by themselves. The problem with these kinds of people is the fact that they are very difficult to handle because of their resistance to change – especially growth and expansion.

The real problem is that they feel that the person who has just joined the workplace is out to get "their" job. At first, they did not need any help, and now, they still think that they don't need any help at all. It does not matter how competent the other person is because the control freak will not welcome any ideas or suggestions that are not theirs.

To deal with such a person; what you need to do is get rid of turf wars by ensuring that you engage them fully during role allocation. Allow them to create their projects so that they feel as though they have a sense of tenure. If it is possible, you can separate their duties from those of other employees. Once they see that their roles are highly valuable to the company, they will ease off on their controlling attitude – giving the others ample space and time to go about their duties with minimal interruptions.

Stroke Their Ego

According to research, there is evidence that shows control freaks are often very insecure. The thing with such people is that they often fight just so that they can retain control, considering that they are not sure of themselves. Such people hate trying new things and desperately are afraid of new situations and events. They feel that by retaining control over their work surrounding – something familiar to them – they can keep their insecurities in check.

Well, unfortunately, the approach they use in controlling things and people around them depicts their domineering and overbearing attitudes. This is precisely what stands to undermine their self-esteem and confidence further – especially if they spent the time to evaluate their behaviors honestly.

To deal with such kind of people, you need to find a way to help them regain their control so that they can feel secure. The best way to do this is for you to appeal to their ego. While they may come off as confident people, the truth is that inside they are fragile. They are just hiding under that assertive shell so that they can win others' approval. Before they can offer you any help, go to them and ask them to help you with a difficult task. Even when you feel as though things are not looking up, simply compliment them on anything so that they can relax and make it easier for them to relinquish control over small things.

Stand Your Ground

There are instances when you feel that there is nothing you can do to appease someone who is controlling. This is because they firmly believe that they know best. They will even go as far as throwing tantrums if they don't get their way.

The best way to handle them is to try and assess what it is that you disagree on. If it is something important, you should stand your ground. While this may stir up conflict and friction at the workplace, it will help them know that not everyone can be toyed around. The trick is that you choose your battles with caution. If it is an issue of how the office should be cleaned, ask yourself whether it is something you would want to die for.

Take note of the little Things

Just like stroking their ego, taking note of small things is about paying attention to what their needs are. Whatever it is, ensure that you pay attention to these tendencies. Reassure them that they are doing an incredible job. Tell them that the place would not be as excellent as it is without them. Praise them for their underlying qualities, and before long, you will realize that their controlling attitude reduces significantly as they soak in praise!

Give a Little

Is there someone in your office or home that thinks they know so much more than anyone else? Does it even matter that they believe this? Well, the truth is that in the grand scheme of things, the question that truly matters is if this person is involved in all your daily activities and in your ability to do your job. If they don't stand in the way of your getting your job done, the best way to control them would be to give to their selfish and immature attitude – and simply move on.

Ask Questions

One thing you will note about a control freak is that they often are obnoxious. Several people around them dismiss them because of their bossy attitude and their desire to control every little thing. Well, the truth is that in reality, they just desire to be part of something – and can offer valuable input – if only people would listen.

Therefore, the next time you find yourself with a control freak at home or in the office, and they want to boss you around, ask them pointed questions about how they want this or that to be done. If they insist on installing the lights in a specific manner, ask them why they think it cannot be done differently. It could be that they have a phobia for heights, and that is why they insist that it be done a different way than that avoids falling. This allows you to realize that these control issues do not hurt and have the potential of affecting security in the workplace or at home.

If they are adamant that stationeries go to the right side of their desk and the picture frames on the left, ask for an explanation. There are times when you will realize that they don't have a valid reason for that. If it is not their desk, then that is unacceptable. However, if it is their desk, the best thing is for you to oblige. The point is for you to help them confront their obsessions so that you can know whether there is an actual control issue going on, or there is something else subtler that goes beyond stationeries.

Spending time with them talking about these issues will help both of you to amicably solve the problems so that you can both get back to what matters and be productive at it.

If Necessary, Enlist Help

What if you are not able to reach a point of compromise with someone who is a control freak? In such a case, you can seek advice from your superiors or line manager. You must try to explain to them that your intention is not to cause disharmony in the office. Instead, what you are interested in is creating an atmosphere where each one of you can succeed.

This will also go a long way in helping the boss understand that you are not there to complain, but that you have in mind the company's best interest. You must tell your manager that the other person's tendencies are getting in the way of your working and reaching your goals. Ask them to clarify what your roles and responsibilities are at the office. There is a chance that management has no idea of what the situation is like, and asking them to step in will help a great deal to clear things up.

It is also essential that you are always ready to offer possible solutions to the issue so that your bosses are aware that you are also a team player. While working with someone who is controlling can be difficult, realize that it does not have to be impossible! Just a little effort aimed at understanding their motivations and alleviating their insecurities will go a long way in helping you to work together in harmony.

Narcissists

Narcissists are people who are ready challenging the work mainly because of their big ego and vanity. The problem with them is that they pretend to know it all. If you have such a person at home or at work, you must decide where they are real experts and where they are pretentious.

If they are real experts, then your research should prove that they are knowledgeable in the area because of the validity of their ideas and information. You must not subjugate their ideas or permit any condescension. The trick is for you to be respectful when dealing with them. Where you feel they are wrong, simply correct them without being confrontational or overly aggressive.

Gossips

With the advent of technological devices, gossiping is no longer restricted to the water cooler. Today, people gossip with ease on emails and social media platforms. What is interesting is that in spite of all these technological innovations, chatting today at the office or home can be traced back to one single individual who always knows and shares information – whether true or false.

If you have such a person in your life, the best way to deal with them is to avoid sharing information with them or someone close to them. You must practice remaining cordial when around them. Whenever they try to pry into your life or that of others, gently pull away from the conversation and change the subject into something more productive and useful.

Bullies

These people are a fact of life, and the most unfortunate thing is that by the time they are graduating from high school, if they will not have changed then chances are that they will never change. These are the kind of people who end up taking their insecurities to the workplace, marriages, and friendships. The problem is thinking of others as weak and susceptible and hence use that to be vindictive. They will always try to get other people to gang up against one or more people around them.

When you are dealing with such a person, you must try as much as you can to hide your weaknesses. Stand up to them and don't tolerate them being respectful to you. Don't get me wrong, I don't mean that you get aggressive with them. However, you must not allow them to interfere with your life. If they try to bring their attitude to your place of work or home, simply ask them to leave.

Slackers

These are the kind of people who are not motivated and are unreliable. They are the kind that cannot carry their weight. If you have never worked with one of these, thank you, God! They are the kind of people who will leave all the work to you. When you are asked to partner with them, ensure that the job assigned to them is done to completion. If not, then you should be prepared to take on their portion of work.

Trust me; they are out there to let people down – beware!

Pessimists

Some people view the world through shades of gray. They are the pessimists whose primary agenda is to dismiss every idea someone comes up with, without necessarily offering an alternative. Much of their time is spent complaining about this or that. If you have such a person in your team, the trick is to remain positive. Remind them that you cannot just sit and do nothing; instead, they should give their contributions as well.

Oh, and be prepared to shoulder much of the work!

The Hostile or Bossy

The one thing I have learned when dealing with this kind of people is that strength and tact goes a long way. People who feel as though they have been wronged tend to be violent.

The other trick is for you to try as much as you can to help them meet their needs without necessarily being aggressive or discriminatory about it. Try to stay away from any interaction with them that stirs up intense emotions like violence – as they say, don't hang out with the enemy when they are carrying a weapon or drinking! Check your actions to ensure that they don't stir up anger. In short, try not to be a pushover.

The worst thing you can do is strongly retaliate against an aggressive person. Remember that hostility often begets hostility. The best thing you can do is try to divert their attention to something more meaningful. This way, their anger tends to go down. Try to explain to them more about the situation pointing out common interests so that they are open to calm and rational ways of resolving the issue at hand.

The Chronic Complainer

These are the kind of people who will always find fault in everything you do. They will go to the extent of blaming you. They pretend as though they know all that should be done when, in fact, they are never open to correcting the situation themselves in the first place.

If you want to cope with this kind of people, the first thing is for you to pay attention to all they have to say and then ask questions to seek clarification – even though you have been falsely accused or are guilty. The secret is for you not to complain, apologize, or be overly-defensive. If you do, then you are causing them to restate their concerns in a more heated manner. You must be strict and supportive of it. Accept the facts and get all the complaints in writing. Involve them in the process so that you all actively find the solution. Rather than staying too much on what is wrong, try to get them to think of what should be done.

The Super-Agreeable

Has anyone ever agreed with everything and anything you say to the point that they make you angry? Well, these are the super-agreeable people. While it is a good thing to get along with people at home and the workplace, some people agree with every idea you give, and then when things suddenly go south, they back down.

What you need to note about these people is that they are after approval. We all come from different family backgrounds with diverse upbringings. Some learned that the best way to get love is through pretense. In the same way, those people who are super-agreeable tend to promise heaven on earth but cannot deliver that. They will tell you,

"I will submit the report tomorrow, or I will help you run errands." Don't be fooled; all they are doing is buttering you up.

The best way to handle them is to assure them that it is okay to say "No" when they feel like they will not be able to deliver. It is okay to speak the truth even when it is hard to spit it out. You must take time to ask them to try and be candid so that they can find it easy to come out and be frank about anything. When you support them overcome this habit, they will stop making promises they know they couldn't possibly keep. Show them that you value the relationship you have, and the truth won't hurt. Ensure that you let them know you are ready to compromise, considering that they will be fair and just.

Critics

"It's hard to kiss the lips at night that chew your butt all day long."

- Former Congressman Ed Foreman

Criticism is not all that bad, but the truth is that there are times and places for it. Debates are where the most effective solutions are born. This is where some of the best minds challenge every point of view in the room.

But is that always the case with criticism? Are there demanding critics?

Indeed, there are so many demanding critics whose criticism is destructive. They are not seeking answers. They are not even concerned with the give and take that leads to a strong team and a consensus. They are the people who behave like politicians. I like to think of critics as spectators and not players.

Look around your office; is there is a critic there? Is your spouse or friend a critic?

Often, you will notice that critics are the kind of people who will always be quick to point a finger, and yet when their help is needed, they will not lift one. They are the kind of people who will not cooperate within the project, and it is their negative attitude that makes it hard to work and achieve the set goals in a team.

Liars

"Honesty pays, but it doesn't seem to pay enough for most people."

-   Kim Hubbard

This saying is sad, but it is probably right. Think about it, if you have a project you are working on, and the members of your team don't want to cooperate and are dishonest, will the project mandate be fulfilled?

The chances are that you will not even have a team to work in the first place. Honesty goes a long way in fostering cooperation, teamwork, and productive working relationships. If you lack trust, then you cannot work together peacefully. You cannot be productive.

If you think about lies, the truth is that they come in so many different forms. It could be that little white lie you tell a client to impress them or those you say to your spouse so that they are not upset. They could be the lies you show potential employers when you are trying to get them to hire you. One recruiter once said, the closest anyone comes to perfection is when they are trying to fill out a job application. There are three kinds of lies, according to the former Prime Minister of Great Britain; statistics, lies, and darned lies.

305

Whatever kind of lies you tell, the truth is that it is difficult to deal with a liar. The thing with lying is that it is rarely necessary. It does not matter how distasteful the truth is, the truth is more comfortable to accept than a lie. Once you tell one lie, it spirals and continues for as long as you take it. By the time you realize it, you have caused so much harm than good. The thing with liars is that they will always tell a lie to cover up the first lie.

If there is someone that is always lying, simply talk to them about the value of the truth. Don't try to look down on them. Help them always tell the truth by holding them accountable for their word – bitter or sweet.

Chapter 3
Common Traits of Difficult People

Everything Is About Them

Have you ever noticed that there are people who are masters at spinning things – conversations and situations – so that it is about them? Such people often have a way of doing all it takes to bring the discussion back to them when they realize that it has veered off, and the spotlight is no longer on them.

The truth is, interacting with such people is boring. The reason is that whenever you start discussions with them, you are almost sure that the story will be tied to them – how they spent the weekend, what their thoughts are, what ideas they have, or everything else going on in their lives.

Many people ask themselves why they even do it in the first place. Well, the truth is that difficult people are not necessarily cruel. The thing is that they are experiencing a slight immaturity in their personal growth.

They are so used to unabashed attention such that everything is about them and have no time to think of what others think or have to offer too. In worst-case scenarios, everyone that is around them is only there to boost their ego and make them the center of the universe.

They Are Verbally Toxic

Difficult people always have something nasty to say about almost everything. If they are not gossiping, then they are blaming or whining or busy shouldering off responsibilities to the next person they want to bully or use.

In short, these people don't even know when the right time to shut up is. They will always run their mouths about this or that – a typical master storyteller. If someone at home or the workplace experience something even in private, they want to be the first ones to break the news to the whole world – especially those who might be interested.

However, if the news does not seem so unusual, they choose to stand on it on their own two feet. What is worst is that they try to add in salt and sugar just so that the story is compelling – talk of fiction!

Just like the first trait, this reason why they choose to do this is so that they can be the center of attention. What is funny is that instead of making the whole story about them, they choose to be the traveling poet who is busy distributing the news everywhere. They do this so that they can control everything that people know.

They Paint Themselves As Victims

The other trait you will notice with difficult people is that you cannot tell them anything because they tend to portray themselves as less-than-charming. For instance, if you call them out on something, they will suddenly become emotional and start apologizing profusely. As they do this, they give people a million and one reasons for their actions.

It could be that they are behaving in this manner because they were not brought up in a loving family, or that they are insecure about something from their childhood. It could also be that they have an incredibly rare mental disorder that causes them to act this way.

Their behavior is a prime example of what deflection is all about. While there are some of these people who are consciously unaware of what they are doing, there are instances where some have adopted this kind of defense mechanism from their childhood into adulthood, and everything seems reasonable to them.

Often Oblivious to the Obvious

Whenever you meet someone trying, one thing you need to bear in mind is that you are not the only one that feels that way. Someone difficult to you will always be trying the same with everyone around them.

The lives of difficult people are filled with several people interested in confronting their challenging behavior. You will find their families sighing about it, people looking at them, sneering at them by the roads, or coworkers having angry faces when they meet by the corridors. However, no matter what happens, these signs don't seem enough for them.

They choose to be oblivious about it all so that they can keep behaving in the same way.

The main reason why they do this is that they have an excess of pride or are simply not aware of their behavior.

They Count Everything

The thing about difficult people is that they will never do something and keep quiet about it. They have to go on and on talking about what they have done. Whenever they are asked to do something that goes beyond their usual roles and responsibilities, they will ensure that you pay them for it. Even once you have paid them, they will remind you over and over again that they did you a favor and will use that to get what they want.

The main reason is that they are too self-absorbed – something that causes them to be too self-serving. Each minute they use doing a task that is not directly linked to their interests they live in anguish.

That said, a difficult person is one that will never exemplify all the typical traits we have discussed in this chapter. Instead, they often tend to have a different blend of problematic characteristics that cause them to be complicated.

We all certainly have at least one or two of these traits that make us as demanding in one way or the other. By recognizing these features, we can act on them, work on fixing them – whether in us or on the people around us – so that we can all live a happy and free life.

Chapter 4
Identifying the Complicated Issue

What will get you ready and self-aware whenever tough situations involving difficult people arise is if you choose to turn the situation inward and analyze each trigger and reaction. According to Elizabeth B. Brown, there is a wide range of questions you need to reflect on for you to better understand the root cause of issues, and why the other person involved is driving you crazy. These questions include;

- What are the emotional tornadoes that the problematic person brings to your life?
- What is your reaction to the difficult person?
- How do they respond to your reactions?
- If the other person in your life is the cause of all problems, have you found ways to grow unhealthy actions and responses towards them?
- Is it possible that you are a difficult person driving others crazy?
- If that is the case, how do they choose to respond to your actions and responses?

When you are trying to deal with a difficult person, the last thing you want is to feed into your frustrations. The truth is that when you do this, you are just continuing a vicious cycle that will not end. The problem with most people is that they tend to see or to hear things the way they want to and then interpret them based on assumptions rather than facts and actions.

Unfortunately, we often lack information on why one shows up the way they are. This explains the reason why we often fill in the blanks with our theories and assumptions, because we don't have the facts or do not want to find them in the first place.

Mitigating These Situations
If you are going to objectively deal with the difficult people in your life,

you have to be willing to separate facts from assumptions or theories. It is often beneficial to try and separate ourselves from our negative emotional feelings that we may be experiencing at that very moment. While this may be easier said than done, those who can get to this point can arm themselves with the power of friendly and productive interactions with people who make them cringe.

To achieve this, you must use the three different lenses to have a general outlook of the world. These lenses include:

Realistic Optimism Lens

To use this lens you must start by asking yourself two simple questions when you feel that someone has unfairly treated you. These questions include;

What is the factual information in this case?

Is there a story I am telling myself about these facts? What is it that I anticipate as an outcome?

The Reverse Lens

This kind of glass requires that you look at the world around you through the glass of the person that triggered you. Well, don't get me wrong – I don't mean that you should sacrifice your own opinion just so that you can make others happy. Instead, you must widen your perspective. Using the reverse lens, you need to ask yourself;

- What is the other person feeling? How do their feelings make sense?
- What is my responsibility in all these?

You may see this as counterintuitive at first, but the truth is that this is something compelling in helping you reclaim your value. Whenever you feel threatened, you must find a way to appreciate yourself and the other person, too – this is essentially what we refer to as empathy.

The Long Lens

Did you know that at times the worst fears you have about the other person may turn out to be true? Most difficult people I know often derive satisfaction from unreasonably bullying others. If you choose to see things from their perspective, that might not make sense at all. These are the people that will take credit for your work. When and if this happens to you, the first question you need to ask yourself is, "irrespective of what I feel at this moment, is there a way I can learn and grow from this experience?"

Realize that when you are dealing with difficult people – irrespective of what their personality traits are – there are essential steps that you must take to make the best of the whole situation. You can work hard towards finding a more productive outcome. We will discuss this in detail in the next chapter.

How to Manage Your Reactions

Managing your reactions and emotional feelings are all about taking in deep breathes. According to research, slow and deep breaths go a long way in triggering something below the spine – referred to as the vagus nerve – which transmits neurotransmitters to the brain to calm down.

You must ensure that you take a moment to reflect on how you are feeling. The most important thing is for you to ask yourself how you would like to respond to those emotional feelings. Is it possible for you to create a good outcome from the situation?

Well, this may feel at first as though it is an overkill. However, realize that this will get your brain out of its automatic response. You will not feel that negativity, sharpness, and defensiveness anymore. When you force yourself to think of ways that create positive outcomes, your brain automatically assumes a positive mode of thinking.

Leveraging Self-control

If you are going to handle every difficult situation with a difficult person in an amicable manner, you must know yourself. When you have a clear sense of who you indeed are, what it is that stirs up the tension, and where your limits are, you will be better off socializing with people however difficult they may prove to be. You must learn how to stay calm, develop your awareness and skills in emotional intelligence so that you can effectively manage your reactions to every frustrating situation.

Today, challenge yourself to always start by seeking to understand the situation at hand better. When you have more clarity about the situation – by asking questions – you will not only manage your reactions better but also help you find a mutually satisfactory outcome. Reflect on what it is that you consider a satisfactory result before you can interact with difficult people so that in the first place you rather place to keep your focus on what truly matters.

The other trick is for you to ensure that you stick to the facts and acknowledge your emotions. When you make use of examples rather than interpretations, you will be able to keep your interactions with difficult people in check. Before you can respond to what it is that they said, ensure that you paraphrase and check the accuracy of their words so that you have a good understanding of what they mean rather than choosing to make assumptions by hearing what you want to hear. When you check for the accuracy of the information first before responding, this is an indicator that you want to work with others effectively.

When you respond by stating your emotions or what impact their words have on you, this can be a great nudge that will help the other person realize that what they are doing is wrong and hurtful. If there is something you think is not right, it is better if you seek the help of others.

The truth is that you are not alone in this.

So many people have been through what you are experiencing at the moment. Their experiences may have been productive when dealing, working, or interacting with someone difficult. When you seek their advice or coaching from someone experienced, this can go a long way in helping you overcome. Research shows that when you talk about your feelings, you will be in a better position to reframe the whole situation to a place where you can effectively facilitate a positive result.

Where necessary, ensure that you keep records. There are times when things get a little bit more abrasive to the point where you run the risk of hitting an end-state you never intended in the first place. If the interaction gets to the point where it is toxic, you must start making intentional efforts to document them. This means that when things begin to go south, you will have an excellent map to lead you to a place of restoration and peace.

Chapter 5
Developing Coping and Negotiation Strategies

As you may already have learned, difficult people are everywhere. There is a chance that you, too, are difficult. The truth is that several people struggle to go through periods where they are not in their best behaviors. If you desire to maintain a healthy working relationship with someone difficult, then it is high time you learned some of the most practical and helpful coping and negotiation strategies that will make your life easy.

Here are some;

Method 1 Approach the Problematic Person
Step 1 Choose Your Battles Carefully
When you are butting heads with someone difficult, the most important thing for you is to decide when you think your efforts will yield fruit – that is when you go ahead to discuss the issue at hand. Realize that not every fight that comes your way is worth fighting. The sooner you realize that battles are to be chosen wisely, the better you will be.

In an ideal world, both you and the difficult person would simply set your differences aside and make compromises. While this is often impossible, what you need to ask yourself in such a situation is whether the issue is so distressing that you must address it right there and then. Consider your relationship with this person. If you disagree with your boss or with someone in authority, the sooner you accept the things that you cannot change, the happier you will be. If the issue arises between you and a member of your family, then you have to choose between saving your time, efforts, and grief, or if you prefer to allow a bad behavior.

Take a step back and think whether by fighting the battle, you stand to win. You can only take on someone that displeases you once you have assessed the whole situation and consider whether there is a possible resolution to it. If the timing is not right, then take time to formulate a plan, seek help, wait for the right time or find another practical option.

Step 2 Take a Pause
Before you respond to any situation, the first thing is for you to take in a deep breath. This will allow you to recollect all your thoughts, calm your mind, and your emotional feelings. If you are dealing with a problematic person via a mobile text message or email or other digital means, try as much as you can not to send anything that might stir up the war further. Allow your stress levels to come down first before you can approach the other person and reason together.

Try also to have a neutral meeting place where you both can discuss the issue. For instance, you could talk over the issue while taking a walk or doing something else. The importance of this is to try and limit one-on-one negative interaction.

Step 3 Clearly State Your Needs With Assertive Communications
The thing with difficult people is that when you try to communicate with them and have a reasonable discussion, they will try to manipulate you or twist your words around. The best way you can avoid that is by using the 'I' statement instead of 'you' that may sound accusative.

Let us consider an instance where someone has been consistently late to work the whole week. Now, if their boss is the difficult one, simply say, "I understand that you are mad at me for being late this week. That is precisely how I would feel. Unfortunately, our subway line is under construction, hence the constant delays at the station. My apologies for making you wait every morning this week. "

This is different from saying something like: "You are such an unreasonable person for expecting me to get to work on time when the subway is under construction. You don't care about anything but your work. If you did, you could have already paid attention to the news and known that the line had issues."

The first response is the best one. It shows your remorse for being late, your respect for the boss, and your plan to resume routine once the subway has been completed. You must try as much as possible to sandwich your response while talking to someone difficult. Always start with a positive comment to show how much you value the relationship between the two of you. Then head right into the tough part of the conversation. Finally, complete it with a positive remark like thanking them for lending you a listening ear.

Step 4 Keep Being Polite

My grandmother always said that being polite is something that will not cost you anything but will earn you every good thing. The same applies when dealing with someone difficult. It does not matter what the difficult person's response is because what truly counts is how you respond to it. If you keep your cool, things will always not escalate out of control.

Several people get in the trap of name-calling and abusive behaviors. The trick is for you to take a step back, take in a deep breath, and then give your response politely. Try as much as you can to not allow yourself to sink into the other person's level. The calmer you remain, the higher the likelihood of the other person noticing and trying to mirror your behavior.

It all starts with how you respond!

Ensure that you do it right.

Step 5 Stick to the Facts

Have you ever tried arguing with someone whose speech is all over the place – throws around claims and accusations – without really taking the time to substantiate their claims? This can be annoying!

When dealing with a difficult person, the trick is to keep your conversation short, clear, and to the point. It does not add any value to fill everything down with too many unnecessary details that will only stir up negative emotions. Chances are that you will not successfully get to them enough for them to see your point of view. There is no need to convince them. Just say what took place and don't try to explain yourself.

You must avoid all forms of triggers. If you always fight about holidays with your brothers, stay away from the whole topic. Instead, allow someone neutral to mediate. Don't try to be defensive. Yes, you might want to argue your point, but if it is with a difficult person, you better skip the whole argument. It does not add any value trying to prove you are right. Let the situation stay as neutral as you possibly can.

Step 6 Minimize Your Interactions

It is one thing to be hopeful about dealing with the issues you have with the difficult person and get the desired outcome. However, the best advice you can give yourself is to try and avoid spending too much time with them. If you must interact, then keep it short. You can excuse yourself from all conversations or even bring on a third-party. Throughout the interview ensure yourself that you stay positive and always try to calm down afterward. Just accept that this problematic person might never be the colleague, neighbor, friend, or sibling you ever wanted to have – and that is okay.

Step 7 Talk to Allies

If you are not getting along with someone and you think that you should, then it helps to find a potential mediator to help bring the two of you together. If you are colleagues, then perhaps your boss can help make the situation better. If the conflict is within your family, then you can reach out to a mutual neutral party to help you negotiate. The point is for you to always seek to share complaints only with those you trust.

Method 2 Change Your Mindset
Step 1 Realize that there will always be difficult people anyway

As we have already mentioned, you will always find difficult people everywhere you go. There will always be people out there who are looking for someone to hurt. The key here is for you to learn how you can deal with such people. While they may be impossible to avoid, you must take time to study their personality traits so that you better know how to deal with them.

For instance, if the person is a hostile type, you may notice that they are cynical, think that they are always right, and are argumentative. These are mostly people who do well in authority or power roles. If it is someone that is emotionally sensitive, they will always look for insults – are easily offended, hence choose to use textual approaches when expressing their disappointments and anger. Egotists, on the other hand, are concerned with their selfish interests without really caring much about what others want – often dislike compromise, and are ungrateful and insensitive. Finally, neurotic types are those who are anxious, overly critical, and pessimistic.

Step 2 Increase of Frustration Tolerance
You can control a bird from building a nest on your head, but you cannot prevent them from crossing over your head. In other words, the other person's behavior is something that is beyond your control, but your reaction to them is within your control. You are the one to choose whether or not to engage them. To achieve this, you must be ready to build your frustration tolerance – which involves you taking the lead at challenging irrational beliefs that might contribute to stress, anger, and outbursts.

When you are interacting with a difficult person, you may think that you are unable to deal with them. Those are just irrational thoughts trying to scare you off. The best approach is for you to take in a deep breath and then question the validity of that thought.

In reality, you can deal with anything you put your mind to. If your mother-in-law is trying to micromanage you in your own house, you will not go crazy because you can deal with that. You are stronger than you give yourself credit. The trick is for you to fine-tune your mind to handle it. Instead of stressing over it and causing yourself harm, take in a deep breath and hand her some work to do so that she is occupied. Watch the words you use and ensure that they are rational.

Step 3 Examine Your Behavior

If you find that people continuously attack you, then chances are that you are attracting the wrong crowd. If you are overly negative, the chances are that you will attract a group of pessimistic people who will gather around you.

To deal with fire, you have to arm yourself with fire. To attract positivity, you have to engage in positive behaviors. Think back to all the negative experiences that you might have gone through and ask yourself what your role was in them. How did you respond to the other person's behavior? At the office, there may be someone that always picks on you – how you talk, dress, work, or do things at work – how do you respond to them? Do you have the power to stand up for yourself? Take time to recognize all your strengths and weaknesses so that you are better placed to confront the difficult person in a way that puts them in their place.

Step 4 Beware of Your Perceptions of Others

Have you ever thought that maybe the reason why your friend is acting up is that they are going through a rough patch in their lives? While that is no excuse for their behavior, you must not be quick to judge others behavior. Take time to practice empathy. Simply take a step behind and reflect on how you would respond if you were in a similar situation. Your sensitivity to differences in personality might just be the reason why you hand a wide range of conflicts.

The trick is for you to learn how to practice acceptance. Take in a deep breath and look at them with such compassion. Talk to them with so much calm and tell them that you see that they are suffering and in pain. Let them know that you accept the fact that they are scared and anxious, even if you don't understand the reason behind their situation. Let them also know that their situation is making you anxious.

The truth is, when you accept the situation just the way it is, you let go of so much tension that might have stirred up resistance and conflict between the two of you. Yes, you may not understand why your client blew up at you as they did. Rather than becoming angry and snapping back at them, consider the possibility that they may be hurting inside. Whether the reason is valid or not, it will help you stay calm and not yield into the power of negativity.

Chapter 6
Steps on how to deal with a Difficult Person

If you ask any manager or coach, they will tell you that there is always that one employee that is not so great to work with. As it turns out, management is still there to ensure that they are there to oversee the performance of all other employees within their department. This does not mean that being a manager or parent or in a leadership position means that you are not a difficult person to work with. Even those in authority can prove very difficult to deal with, whether at the workplace or at home.

The last thing you want is to be held hostage, spend lots of time and emotional energy thinking of how you are going to get your work done without someone standing in the way or trying to make your life a living hell. There are times when you are left debating whether or not to let them go, but you never get around to pulling the trigger.

So, if you are this kind of person that has been pulled by difficult people into the endless vortex of frustration and ineffectiveness, these are the steps you can deal with them gracefully;

Step 1: Listen
Often, when someone is difficult, the truth is that we stop paying attention to what it is going on. We get irritated and lose hope in them. We decide what we think of them just so that our focus shifts to something else – because we want to avoid them and protect ourselves from them.

However, if you want to be effective at dealing with them, then you have to be very attentive when they are not doing well or are being hard headed. Your best shot at making things better is to seek to have a clear understanding of the issue – including knowing the other person's viewpoint. In most cases, the first thing that you need to do is simply listen. Listening alone can save the day.

When you listen, you set yourself up to hear what the real problem is, and you may even note that it is not the other person's fault. The truth is that the problematic person might just start acting differently once they know that their concerns have been heard. Not everyone difficult becomes that way just for fun – it could be that there are real issues they are airing, and they need them to be addressed.

Step 2: Offer Clear Behavioral Feedback

If you look around you, you will notice that most people spend weeks, months, or even years complaining about someone in their lives, which is annoying. What they don't do is give actual feedback on what it is that they need to change or do differently. You cannot keep doing the same things over and over again, expecting a change each time.

While giving harsh feedback is something that can be uncomfortable for many people, you can choose to do it responsibly. When you change your ways, you will realize that the other person will also change. The approach that you can use to give transparent and honest feedback is first to lower the other person's defensiveness so that you can offer them with the information they need to be better. Whatever approach you choose to use, they must do these two things – and you will be on the right track.

But why do we hate giving feedback, and how can we make it easier?

Well, over the past three decades, my friends and I have worked to train and coach thousands of people to become better managers and leaders, whether at home or in the office. When we asked them what they consider is the toughest part of their daily job, they said giving others corrective feedback – almost without exception.

So many of them said that at work, they find it hard to fire someone – painful or not. But then this is something that they still have to do, however hard it may be. However, this is not to say that everyone is afraid of giving feedback. There are a handful of other people I know

323

who are not afraid to give people harsh feedback.

But really, the question is, why is it hard for you to give your employees, friends, or spouse difficult feedback to tell them that they are doing something wrong and they need to change?

Well, the truth is that we are often afraid of how these people will react. We think to ourselves, they are already complicated, what if they explode in anger? What if they break down? What if they respond by telling me that I am an idiot? What if they become defensive and start blaming me. There are times when we want to tell someone that their attitude is terrible, but we stop and think of what it is that they might say; "you don't even have respect for me. You don't care about what I am going through," - all of which worsen the situation.

With all these myriads of thoughts racing through our minds, we convince ourselves that it is not a big deal at all. We tell ourselves that it will all go away soon. We tell ourselves that if they are the right person, they will realize that what they are doing is wrong, and they will just let it all go away. While this will make you feel justified and self-righteous, the truth is that you are causing more harm than good. There are people I have seen lose their jobs just because their bosses or the people in their lives chickened out and did not tell them what they are doing is not alright. They needed your corrective feedback, but you did not give them. Some people cannot magically know that they are difficult and that they need to change. They need you to be their eyes!

Here are the tips you can use;

Pay Attention First

While this might seem counterintuitive at first when you know that you have screwed your courage, you just need to stand up and get it over with. The first thing is for you to listen to what the other person has to say. Walk up to them and tell them that you would like to talk to them about something. Invite them to share with you what their view is about the whole situation.

For instance, you could say something like, "Hey Mary, I'd like to have a word with you about the ABC project. What time are you available for a chat?" Once you meet, you can ask them, "what do you think has been working well, and what has not been working well on the ABC project?"

When you do this, you are merely offering the other person a heads-up on what you would like to discuss. You are telling them that you would love to have a balanced picture of the whole project – not just focusing on the good news but the bad news as well.

Then give them ample time to share with you their opinion. Try not to interrupt – whether in agreement or disagreement - when they are talking to you. This way, you will be able to gather what it is that the other person thinks so that you have all the information you need to give a more objective response. You may realize that the other person will say so much of what you were going to say too. This way, the conversation turns into a coaching session!

Often, you will notice that the other person will see part of the problem and that allows you to pick it up from there and clarify what they have said. Now, if the other person is entirely oblivious to the whole situation, listening first to what they have to say makes the entire conversation less confrontational. This allows them to listen to you better when you start giving them your take on the issue.

Camera Check

The other useful tip you must consider is what I refer to as the camera check. This is mainly feedback on people's behaviors rather than on their mental state. Let us go back to the example that we have already used in the previous point where you think that the employee has a bad attitude.

Now, at this point, you know that if you just say it plainly, that will not help, and the chances are that it will make the situation worse than it is. Such a comment is guaranteed to make the other person feel defensive because it mentions that they have a flawed character. You also are giving the other person no indication of what it is that you want them to do differently, which they don't have an idea how. How does the right attitude look like?

Rather than jumping in and making these comments without basis, simply do a camera check. In other words, what you need to do is take a mental video of what you consider a bad attitude and the other person doing it. What is it that you see in your mental tape? You might see them coming to work late, turning in their assignments late, saying negative things about their colleagues or the company, consistently not offering support to clients, among others.

These are some of the things that you can tell them. "Hey Mary, I notice that you have been turning in your assignments late, coming to work late this month, and saying negative things about your colleagues – Mark and Jane." When you frame it this way, you make it a hell LOT more comfortable for the other person to hear, rather than just saying that they have a bad attitude.

The point is, if someone is difficult, you can camera check what you consider to be an evil character or attitude and frame it in that manner. This is reasonably comfortable and skillful when trying to offer corrective feedback. When you let them know what it is they need to do differently for improvement and success, you are not only helping them be better but also yourself and the organization as a whole.

Step 3: Document

I cannot stress this enough, but whenever you have significant issues with someone, you must jot down all the key points. There are several times when I have had people in top management levels tell me that they couldn't let go of a difficult employee because they did not have a record of them having bad behavior. It is this lack of documentation that comes as a result of misplaced hopelessness. The manager either thought that they did not want to be too negative about the employee or believed that it would soon go away.

If you are smart enough, then you know the value of documentation. You are keeping a record of each employee or person in your life, and what good and evil they do is nothing negative. If anything, it is something very prudent. What you need to note is that you can solve problems. All you need to do is take in a deep breath, follow it with a sigh of relief and write down everything you like or do not like about the other person – everything they are doing that qualifies as bad or good behavior.

You will thank yourself for it when "enough is enough!"

Step 4: Maintain Consistency

If there is a behavior that you consider not okay with, then there should not be a time when you all of a sudden are okay with it. Remember that where you are, people are watching you. The last thing you want has everyone thinking that you are inconsistent or mistreating others. If it is at the employee, what you must remember is that employees are always looking to see what it is that you do more than you say.

For instance, if you tell everyone that they must turn in their end month reports by Friday midnight and then there are times when you are upset about it and in other times you are not, the truth is that they will not take you seriously. Those employees that are difficult won't do it at all.

You must learn to pick your shots. Set standards that you are willing to hold to – then hold tightly to them.

Step 5: Establish Consequences For When Things Don't Change

If at this point you still feel that there is no improvement, then it is high time you start getting specific. There is a saying, "I believe you can still turn this around," and this is where you apply that. Turning things around simply means that if you don't see behavioral change by a specific date, then something will happen – letting them go, initiate corrective actions, disciplinary committee discussion, or lose their eligibility for promotion.

The consequences have to be substantively negative for them to see the seriousness of the whole issue. If difficult people don't believe that their actions have serious consequences, then what makes you think that they will even change in the first place?

Step 6: Work Through the Company's Processes

What you need to note is that when you are a good manager or leader, you will hold out hope for improvement to the point where you cannot see any more hope and decide that you are letting go. You ensure that you have dotted all the i's and crossed every t so that you have a clear conscience when you finally make go of the other person. Maybe this is the point where you are in your marriage, parenting, or at work. If this is the case, then what I would advise you to do is to have a clear conversation with your spouse, boss, or child on what exactly you need to do to clear the whole path to termination – if necessary.

Step 7: Don't Poison the Well

If there is something I have learned over the years I have worked for my company is the value of not poisoning the well. There are times when junior and senior managers alike come to the office and lousy mouth a problematic employee in their department to all and others. This is not the right way to address an issue like this. Instead, you must follow all the steps that we have pointed out here.

It does not matter how difficult the person is, how crazy they drive you, or how hurtful their actions are. What matters the most is that you don't talk trash about them – you will only be adding salt to injury. Remember that the people you are telling are the same people that will go out there to talk – with distorted information. This will only create an environment of distrust. You will be choosing to back-stab them, something that pollutes the other person's perception. You will also be opening yourself up for the rest of the people to look at you as weak and unprofessional.

Trust me; this is no way to resolve an issue.

Just don't do it – however tempting it may be!

Step 8: Manage Your Self-talk

There are instances when someone frustrates you to the point where you end up having an inner conversation about the whole issue. While the internal dialogue is calming, it never should be unhelpfully negative or unhelpfully positive.

You may think to yourself, "what an idiot, Mary will never change" or "I will not worry too much about this. I am certain that things will turn out to be fine. Mary is such a great employee or wife or child, and there is nothing to worry about." These two thoughts are not helpful at all.

You must be willing to take a fair witness stance so that everything you say to yourself on the inside is not only accurate but also possible. You could say something like, "Mary's behavior is stirring up problems for the entire family. As I do everything I can to support them to change, I have to monitor their behavior closely. If she changes, that will be great. If not, then I will have to do what I promised to do."

Now, that is helpful because you are taking the facts and using them to make informed decisions that are not only going to make you look good but are aimed at helping the other individual.

Step 9: Have the Courage

By this time, you know that firing someone is the hardest decision most managers have to make. If the difficult person you are dealing with is your spouse, then you know that the toughest decision you are going to make is to seek marriage counseling or divorce. Whatever your situation may be like, the most important thing is that you do it right.

Instead of making excuses, putting things off, or making someone else do it, just brace yourself, gather your courage, and do it yourself. Realize that you are the manager of your life, and if you are as good as you think you are, then you are going to make the tough decision impeccably well. If – Hallelujah – things change against what you hoped for, dare to accept them. Realize that sometimes being proved wrong when we have lost hope in someone is as tough as being proved right.

If you learn to use these steps when dealing with a difficult spouse, colleague, employee, or friend, then it does not matter how things turn out because, in the end, you will know that you did the best you could to salvage a tough situation. That alone is enough to reduce your stress levels!

Chapter 7
What Do You Do When All These Do Not Work?

This is one of the questions that so many people ask. There are times when we feel that we have done all there was to be done, and we still cannot see any improvement. While we may be tempted to think that there is nothing more we could do, the truth is that there is always something new we can do. If you have reached this point while dealing with someone challenging in your life, here is a message for you – there is still more you can do!

Here are some of the things you can do;

Be Calm

Sometimes, you may be tempted to lose your temper and snap at other people. Well, I will tell you that this is not the best way to handle a difficult person. If you go around snapping at other people, don't you think that you are difficult for other innocent people yourself? What makes you think that you are any different from a difficult person? You are not going to get the other person to collaborate with you if this is the attitude you choose to have.

One thing that is important to note is that you cannot trigger the other person – unless you are silently using it as a strategy – it is best if you keep your cool.

One thing you will note about someone calm is that they often appear as though they are in control – even when that is not the case. Keeping your cool tends to help you stay centered and respectable. If you are always on edge, no one would be willing to reason with you. If you keep your cool, you will start noticing that the other difficult person gets all your attention.

Understand the Other Person's Intentions

I believe that no one chooses to be difficult just for the sake of being tough. While there are times when the other person seems as though they intend to get you, you have to realize that there are always underlying reasons why they are acting up the way they do.

Well, this kind of motivation is not always something apparent. The most important thing is for you to identify what triggered their actions. Is there something that is making them act the way they are doing? Are they willing to cooperate with you? If not, what is stopping them from working with you? Is there something you can do to help them amicably resolve the issue?

Get Some Perspective

There is a chance that people around you have experienced exactly what you are going through now. The truth is that while this may be happening to you for the very first time, some can help you see things from a different perspective and offer you a different take on the whole situation.

The challenge is for you to try and seek them out, share with them your experience, and then pay attention to what they have to say to you. The chances are that they will offer you valuable advice amid your conversation, and you will have overcome what seemed impossible at first.

Let Them Know Where You Are Coming From

If anything has worked perfectly for me, it is letting the other person know what my intentions are. I always come clear on why I am doing what I do. While there are times when my words face resistance for thinking that it is just being tough on them, the truth is that it works. When you let other people in on the reason underlying your actions and what is happening on the ground, they will not only empathize with the situation but will also change their behaviors. This is how you can get difficult people on board!

Do it today.

Establish a Rapport

Today, the use of a computer system in messaging and communication has simply turned work into a mechanical process. The best way you can re-instill that human touch when interacting with others is always set aside time to connect with them at a personal level. You can choose to go out with your friends, family, or colleagues for drinks, lunches, or dinners. When you do, don't just concentrate on what you are eating or drinking, always spend time knowing each other – hobbies, families, life in general. Fostering a valuable connection with others goes a long way in helping you appreciate the beauty in diversity and know how best you can deal with situations that might arise between the two of you.

So, how do you establish rapport?

One important thing that you must note is that building rapport is not just about mirroring, matching, or leading the other person's behavior and actions. When dealing with a difficult person, think of it as a therapy session or sales. If you want your relationship to be productive, then you want to pay attention to the building blocks of good rapport. The general idea here is for you to mirror their posture – such that if they cross their arms while talking to you, you do the same shortly after. You can also speak in the same tone, pace, and language they speak in – adding in a couple of unique phrases and words they use while communicating with you.

When the other person starts to notice these similarities in their unconscious mind, the truth is that they will begin to feel that they are on the same level as you are, like you, and tune in to what you have to say. Little by little, you will start to lead them towards the direction you want them to go. You will begin to make them feel relaxed. If the rapport you develop is sufficient enough, then you will start noticing on your end that the other person is slowly matching your behavior without even realizing it. They may lean back, integrate your ideas, and echo their enthusiasm in all the skills you are trying to bring to life.

Does it all happen in one go? No. Just like every other good thing, establishing rapport with a difficult person is something that takes time and effort. You have to be persistent and patient enough to see this through. Remember, you are dealing with someone difficult, which means that they are not just going to all of a sudden take up your ideas and support you. The truth is that you will experience moments of resistance, reluctance, and lack of focus on what you are saying. The sooner you make the other person feel heard and understood, the sooner you will be able to connect and integrate therapeutic interventions.

But how can you do that? How is it possible for you to instantly connect with a difficult person, build rapport with them, and make them get where you are coming from?

The Power of Utilization

Each time you want to have a connection with someone, you will need to use the principle of utilization to build rapport. One of the most straightforward approaches is for you to discuss your experiences and interests as you talk to them, even though you don't share them.

My friend Lance serves in the military. He told me that their former commando was such a difficult person to deal with. He wanted for them to get along, and he just knew the right way how – going into a trance. He said that hypnotic trance simply takes advantage of the narrow focus of attention and the passing of time. He simply re-evoke part of his military exercise to his commando and boom – it was all there in his mind. Now, it made it very easy to lead him one step at a time to where he desired to go – leveraging that alert and focused state of mind. This way, the commando started becoming receptive – by integrating his perspective, ideas, and ability to control pain. By the end of the session, they both were getting along like never before.

Effective Communication Through the Utilization

The other trick is for you to utilize the other person's interests when talking to them. This is one of the most straightforward and powerful tools you can use to capture their attention and get them interested in what you have to say. Once you have them hooked, you can then bring up topics that you find interesting – but do it gradually just so that they don't feel overwhelmed and lose interest. While flirting is something that is not recommended in professional settings, you can bring on the game instinctively!

Realize that even the stand-up comedians don't always bring their comedy to people that love it but to those who think that they are not funny too. How do they get them hooked? By employing the power of utilization. The thing that seems to get people to laugh at their jokes if recognizing that what they are saying is true, but the chances are that they have never tried to put them in words. They also seem to exaggerate things to an entirely absurd level. Why is that? They can utilize what the target audience already understands.

Even though the examples I share here are from a therapeutic field of hypnosis, the principle of utilization goes a long way in communications as well as teaching. If you become too professional, you might just lose them.

Flirt instinctively!

Stop the Psych-jargon

Occasionally, meeting someone for the very first time I can tell whether they are difficult or not, and the ideology that is ingrained in them. While there are people who speak like they have swallowed a self-improvement book, every word they say is plainly but psych-jargon.

With the principle of utilization, all this goes out of the window. If you are going to have any influence on them, you must learn to see things from their perspective, learn their language, and understanding instead of dragging them into your thinking.

If you talk to any hypnotherapist, they will simply hand you ready-made scripts. This is not what you want to do. You cannot just dish out ways the other person should get along with you as though to tell them you don't have the slightest regard for their uniqueness. When you understand and practice the power of utilization, they will start to feel respected. You cannot just force your interests or ideas on the other person.

Instead of trying to change the other person from the outside, why not try changing them from the inside? This means that every action and the word you use must appeal to their unique personality traits and interests. This way, you offer them a chance to grow through progression quite naturally while at the same time facilitating a deeper level of rapport with them.

Let us consider a smoker who is always prone to outbursts. Where do you channel that anger? Well, you can make them direct that anger towards the cigarettes. In doing so, they don't dismiss the reality of their passion but then helps a long way in constructively managing their anger until they know the best way how. You could also argue that when anger is directed towards something potentially harmful, this is completely helpful.

Utilizing the Gaping Problem

According to Milton Erickson, you can use the difficult person's issues as a way of helping them make progress in life. He narrates a time when he treated a suicidal patient that was convinced life had no meaning because she believed that she was unattractive and could never find a partner. But what did she think was making her unattractive? A gap between her teeth!

Now, you don't just tell that person that they are attractive and ignore all their worries and concerns. What Erickson did was to utilize the very things she worried about just so that she could change her thinking. The girl squirted water through her supposedly "ugly" gap on her teeth during a break at the office. The young man thought of this as a provocative act and asked her out on a date! That completely changed her thought process.

In the same way, you can utilize the power of gaping problems when dealing with a difficult person, and you will be amazed at how fast they begin to change their minds and perspective.

It works!

Treat the Other With Respect

Do you like being treated as though you are incompetent, stupid, or incapable? Well, no one does, and neither do you. The thing with treatment is that it is a two-way traffic. You have to do to others exactly how you would like them to do to you. You cannot possibly expect others to respect you when all the time you interact with them, you are disrespectful.

Today, ask yourself how you love others to treat you. Then use exactly those requirements when interacting with others. Respect is earned – so earn it!

So, how do you even treat a difficult person with respect, in the first place?

Well, if you want to lay the groundwork for respect, here are some of the things that you need to do;

Stop to See Where They Are Coming From

As we have already established, people do not just choose to be difficult for no reason at all. It is not like this is a default setting – even though there are times when it seems like it when trying to manage and work with them. Think about it, if you have a difficult coworker, do you think that they just found themselves in that job? Someone somewhere must have selected them as a candidate out of all others vying for the same position.

Why is that?

Because they brought on the job skills and personality that would get things done. If you think about it, they probably fit in well with the rest of the team at the beginning. However, if they no longer embody these traits and skills, the only honest thing to do is stop and find the reason why. Is there something in the job description that has changed? Are they having trouble finding the right balance with their work and private life? Is there someone on the job that keeps irritating them every other day?

When you set aside time to have an honest and open discussion with them concerning all the challenges they may be facing, this could help. While this is a necessary step in addressing the problem, it is something tricky to do. Therefore, rather than getting frustrated, open yourself up for a candid conversation with them.

Trust Them First

If you want to build respect with a difficult person, you have to start by building trust. This is one of the most critical steps, especially in an instance where the other person does not trust you. A difficult person that does not trust you at all with always challenge you at every level. To give the benefit of the doubt, choose to believe them first.

While you may have the authority to manage their actions, the truth is that you cannot change their attitude. It does not matter what position you hold in the company; the truth is that the only way out is to try and influence them. Whenever you make promises, ensure that you live up to them. Do everything that you said you would do – and this will earn you trust. Soon enough, everyone around you will take your word for it and know that you expect nothing less from them. When you trust them to do the same, you are opening doors for higher results and respect.

Pay Attention to the Positive

As you work hard to establish trust and respect with the difficult person in your life, the one thing you must not forget is to offer positive feedback. You can do this by way of appreciation. Are there areas that the difficult person is trying hard to improve? If there are, recognize them in front of the whole team. To make it even better, you can take a step further to ask them what it is that they think is the best trait they possess at work and then recognize it too.

In so doing, you are demonstrating to them that they truly matter, and their contributions are much appreciated. You can understand them vocally whenever they do something commendable. Soon enough, they will realize that they are an essential part of the team. To earn your employees respect or anyone for that matter, you have to show them that you value them.

It all starts with you!

Have a New Perspective

What is the bottom line of respect? Well, the truth is that you have to earn it. In other words, you have to give it for you to receive it – it is reciprocal. When you treat someone with respect, however hard headed they were when interacting with you, their opinion of you will begin to improve.

Rather than trying to label difficult people as being impossible, try to change your perspective of them. Always perceive them as an essential component of your team – one that the team cannot do without. It could be that they like challenging every idea, protocol, or project you initiate. When you make that shift in your mentality and perception of them, they will start to change how they talk about you. The point is for you to listen keenly to their feedback and then act accordingly.

Focus on What Can Be Actioned

There are times when your awkward friends, colleagues, or family

339

colleagues put you into a hot soup. For instance, you may have some work to be turned in, but then they fail to do it, or they may do something, and then you are held responsible for it when you don't even deserve that kind of unfair treatment. Whatever it is that the difficult people in your life do to you, the first step towards resolving the matter is for you to accept that it has already happened. Instead of crying over spilled milk, simply focus on what the next steps should be like.

What are some of the necessary steps to take in resolving the situation?

Create the change you want to see.

Ignore

If you have already tried all you could and still thought that nothing works, the other trick is for you to ignore everything. The best way you can treat someone difficult is to ignore them. You cannot possibly argue with yourself, right? They may try as much as they can to trigger you into being angry or acting up. However, when you ignore them, you simply cause them to stop because they are not getting the kind of reaction they are looking for. When you act up, you are giving them the satisfaction that they won, and they will keep on poking until you break.

Think about it, have you done everything you could within your means to handle the situation responsibly? If so, then you have nothing else to give them. Simply get on with your life and try as much as you can not to interface with them unless necessary. If they play a central role in your daily work and it is standing in the way of your productivity, then you can choose to escalate this to the higher authorities to help you resolve the issue. This is often referred to as a trump card. You should not use this unless you have exhausted all other possible options.

In most cases, if you want to get to someone moving you can do it by employing the top-down approach. You must exercise caution when using this option. Try not to use it every often lest your bosses begin to think that you cannot handle small issues independently. While this works, it is only to be used when all else is depleted. Trust me, I have used it, and it works like magic.

Employ Kindness

I get it, when you are dealing with a difficult person in your life your gut feeling is usually to be difficult as well. When someone is attacking you, the first thought you have is often to try and defend yourself. I have been there, done that. The problem is that when you do this, you get sucked up into a vacuum such that you don't even take a moment to slow down and just breath.

In almost every difficult situation, I have found myself in is that showing kindness goes a long way in helping one calm the case down. When two difficult people are hard on each other, the chances are that the whole situation tends to escalate to the extent that nothing can be accomplished.

However, when you choose to be kind, you will diffuse the whole situation so that you can get all that you want. This is one of the techniques that should be at the top of your list whenever you encounter a difficult person in your life.

Show Compassion

If you have been in a problem before then you know that you must deal with your issues. The truth is we all have issues, and we tend to think that what we are going through is so harsh that no one can bear. However, if you sat down to listen to what other people are going through, you will simply take your baggage with you and shove it back into your backpack.

Well, I love that!

My point is, no one knows what it feels like to have another's problems. When you are dealing with someone difficult, this should be your principle – it could be that they are experiencing a very tough ordeal or an enormous problem that you wouldn't even be able to bear in part.

Often, when you choose to show a problematic person a little bit of compassion they tend to respond positively. Several of us get stuck in our heads and lives that we don't even open our eyes to what the people around us might be experiencing. Your friend might just be looking for a little kindness. The next time you encounter someone difficult – whether at work, home, or elsewhere – show them some kindness, and you will be amazed at how that works magic.

Find Something in Common

When you are talking to someone for the very first time, what you will note is that sharing something in common with them often makes your connection stronger. Each one of us has been made in such a way that we desire to belong to a group. We are natural beings that want to have a strong sense of belonging.

When you meet someone it always feels nice to know that you both went to the same college, even if during different years. Having something in common creates a form of kinship. My children are in high school now, and each time I met a parent that has children the age of mine or that our children attend the same schools, I feel like we have a parental connection.

Today, if you have someone difficult in your office, at home or elsewhere, try to establish something that you both share in common. This will go a long way in helping you get along with each other afterward.

Control What You Can

There are things in life that we can control, and others out of our control. One thing that is important to note is that we must focus our attention on the things that we can control.

When you are trying to handle a difficult situation with a difficult person, you must start by thinking about what it is in that situation that is within your control. It could be that there is someone else you can deal with instead of that difficult person. That is the person that might just pave the way for you to do things right.

A few months ago, I was trying to work with the sales department on a novel initiative I was trying to bring to life in our company. One of the team members suggested that I should speak to a specific person to seek their help because that has been the tradition. When I first contacted the person I did not get a response. I kept sending them emails after emails, left several voicemails, but still did not get a response. I finally got frustrated and resorted to speaking to other people in the department.

Several people in the sales department were willing to help with the project with so much joy. That was a difficult person that I managed to work around. Today, you can do the same – control all that you can!

Look At Yourself

The scripture in James 1:23-24 states, "For anyone who hears the word but does not carry it out, is like a man who looks at his face in a mirror, and after observing himself goes away and immediately forgets what he looks like...."

If you are going to deal with a difficult person, then you will have to know who you are first. Your focus should be on what you hold inside you. Is there something that you are doing or not doing that is standing in your way of dealing with a difficult person?

There are so many of us who know precisely what kind of people we are. We know that we are always in a good mood and are sociable. Every single day is a smooth one. There are instances where you may have lots of things racing through your mind – solving one problem after the other.

Even when you are having a conversation with a friend, your mind is probably elsewhere. You may come off as though you are condescending, abrupt, and short. It is this kind of attitude that can make someone that is already irritated to get upset quickly. How you choose to respond will determine whether you are adding salt to injury or quenching the fire.

Therefore, spend some time to reflect on how you interact with other people – especially the difficult ones – to ensure that you are not making the situation worse than it already may be.

Overcome Your Fear of Conflict

If there is a technique that I like the most when dealing with someone difficult is overcoming my fear of conflict. You cannot deal with a difficult person if all you do is run away from them. So many people are scared of stirring up strife and conflict with a difficult person, but what you need to realize is that the more you try to run, the more you are giving that person the power to walk all over you.

While the process of dealing with someone difficult in itself is challenging enough, the truth is that if you do not stand up to them and set boundaries, the situation will only get worse than it already is. Each one of us deserves to be treated with respect. Therefore, do not allow them to manage you less than that.

Don't get me wrong; I am not saying that you should intentionally stir up conflict. What is merely asking you to do is that in the event a difficult person treats you less than you deserve to be treated, stand up to them and confront them about the whole situation. Conflict does not mean that it has to be something terrible. In so many cases, it is a good thing – especially when it leads to a resolution of issues and brings to fruition what you desire most.

The bottom line is, if you look around you, you will not miss at least one difficult person. You cannot run away from them. The key is for you to communicate with them gracefully and peacefully so that you can both reach a consensus. It is better to "agree to disagree" so that you can both move past your selfish interests and live a happier life.

Chapter 8
Expert Techniques to Handle Difficult People

Practice Reflective Listening

Have you ever been upset, and then someone comes in and tells you, "I understand," Did that ever make you feel better?

I didn't think so!

Well, one thing that is important to note is that using such kind of statements will not help you accomplish anything. Let us consider an instance where you have a client in your company. They tell you that they are frustrated because of the budget cuts and the fact that you are not willing to offer them discounts even though they have been your loyal clients for several years. How do you respond to that? Do you just tell them that you understand what they are going through?

The truth is that if you did tell them you understand, that conversation is probably never going to have a good ending.

If you are in such a tight spot with a difficult client, the first thing you should tell yourself is to practice reflective listening. In other words, try to put yourself in the other person's shoes. Understand what it is that they are saying by simply interpreting their body language and words. This will help you to respond by reflecting their thoughts and emotional feelings back to them.

Instead of telling them plainly that you understand, try something like - "So, if I get you correctly, you are saying that our pricing is too high that is becoming a barrier to your business, right? – and because of the tight budget you are working with and the fact that we are not offering discounts. Is that right?"

If you have understood what they are telling you, simply move on with your conversation. However, if you have not yet understood what they are going through, ask them to give you more information so that you can understand their situation better. The trick here is for you to make them feel that you get where they are coming from and that you are concerned. They want to feel your empathy.

Try as much as you can to avoid making promises you know you might not be able to meet. The goal is to make the difficult person feel that they have been heard and that they are greatly valued.

Consider Their Affect Heuristic

This simply refers to a mental shortcut. This plays a significant role in helping you make a quick and efficient decision based on your emotional feelings towards the other person, situation, and the place you are at. In simple terms, our choices are greatly influenced by our experiences and general outlook of the world around us. It is merely because of our bias.

The leading cause of the problem is that we are not objective in such situations, and facts do not matter that much. We choose to run every decision we make based on our mental software and then develop strong opinions based on that.

If the difficult person keeps having a different opinion and keeps asking you what you think is the catch, try not to respond rubbish them off by saying that we have to move on because of ABCD's. There is a chance that this person may be trapped in another information source, contract, or agreement with the previous vendor who failed to deliver what they had promised they would. Based on that very experience, they may be looking at you through the same lenses.

What you need to do is ask questions so that you fully understand what the root cause of the problem is. Some of the questions you can ask them so that they can relax and offer you insight as to why they are resistant include;

- I really would like to understand why you are a little skeptical about this. Would you tell me more?
- Is there anything we can do to relieve your fears?
- What can we do to help you feel comfortable enough so that we can all move forward?

When you ask such questions, you are allowing them to simply redirect their thoughts from thinking that you are not trustworthy in considering what is needed for the team to move forward and make progress.

Tap Into the Beginner's Mind

The beginner's mind is often referred to like the Zen mind, and it serves as a strategy of approaching each situation as though you have no prior experience in it. Whenever you adopt this kind of thinking when dealing with a difficult person, every conversation you engage in is made with the "I don't know" mindset. This allows you to try as much as you cannot judge the other person or the situation.

This also goes a long way in helping you not to live with the 'should' kind of thinking. "You should have thought of the budget before the year started. You should have read my email concerning the discount expirations. You should have known that I am a busy person and available only once in a week for consultations."

When you are addressing a difficult person, try not to use 'should' statements. They only set your mind on the defensive and get in the way of your productivity and conversation before it can even start.

The good thing with adopting the Zen mindset is that it allows you to let go of an expert mindset. While you may be an expert in your field or in what you do, you have to realize that you are not an expert when it comes to a difficult person or situation.

For instance, instead of saying things like "You said that you wanted to increase your sales by 30% by the end of the month and the kind of delays am seeing will not make this possible," choose to approach the conversation in a beginner's mindset. Try not to prejudge the other person. Forget what it is that they should have done and perceive the conversation you are both having as a puzzle that needs to be solved.

You can choose to say something like this instead "It seems to me like with these delays, we will not be able to reach our sales goals. But, let's explore strategies that will help us achieve the results that we are aiming for." If you keenly study this statement, you will realize that you are acknowledging the fact that there is a problem, but immediately starts moving in the direction of a possible solution.

Let Go of Fear

Again, you cannot be afraid of negative results to the point that you allow that to drive your reactions. It is because of doubt that we tend to feel the need to control things and the people around us. If a colleague is difficult, you may feel afraid of challenging them because that might just put your relationship at risk. If a client expresses displeasure in your services, timelines, or pricing structure, you may be afraid because you think that you might not be able to fix the whole situation.

The first thing is to let go of the idea that there is something that needs fixing. When you are having a conversation with a difficult person – whether a friend, child, client, or coworker – remember that your role is to listen, understand what they are saying and then discern what the next steps forward should be. I don't mean that you start dishing out solutions immediately. Take time to go over what they have told you and then think through the possible solutions to find the best way forward.

For instance, rather than trying to validate emotional feelings, slap together common fixes, or apologizing, what you can do is express how unfortunate it is that the situation happened once again. Assure the other person that you get how the whole situation is affecting the business or your relationship and then appreciate them for being patient enough to allow you to work towards resolving the issue.

"Chunk" the Problem

You may be wondering what 'chunking' is all about. Well, this simply refers to the process of taking a huge problem and then breaking it down into smaller manageable portions that you can address one at a time. When you break problems into smaller portions, this allows you to handle them. They also make people more willing to start dealing with all the issues at hand.

What I have learned from my mentor over the years is the importance of chunking things and then organizing them into tasks that you can handle every other day. This is the same way you can choose to deal with a tough situation with a difficult person.

Does your employee always find a reason not to turn in their work on time because they cannot get started using the new software?

What you can do is to ask them to help you break down each of the steps into smaller bite-size pieces that you can work on to come up with an easy to follow protocol. The point is for you not to apportion blame or say that they are lazy, but to find the best way forward. When each task is chunked, it becomes easier for the other person to digest what is left to be done.

Remember, Anger Is Natural

We have all encountered difficult people – clients, friends, and colleagues alike – that we get so furious. It could also be that you have been on the other side of things. For instance, if you are a customer at a store and you have paid for a new product upgrade, and then you realize that it is not what they offered you and that makes you angry.

The recalibration theory of anger states that anger is a natural emotion that is wired into human beings. In other words, you have to realize that anger is the best way we have been made to get into the bargain. We press our lips together, bite our tongue, furrow our brows, or flare our nostrils just so that we can drive the other person to a place of higher value based on what we have to give.

If you are dealing with a difficult person, the point is for you to try and avoid justifying your actions or position. Realize that the reason why they could be feeling that way is that they think that their opinion is being undervalued or that they want to control the situation. It is advisable that you take the other person's frustrations seriously and not personally. Once you have understood the frustrations and arguments of the other person, thank them for bringing that to your attention. Also, let them know that you will think through everything and get back to them with a solution or a way forward.

When the other person is already furious, the chances are that they will not take any solution you offer at that time. However right the answer might be, they will not feel like it is the best way to go about the whole situation. Therefore, you must allow them some time to calm down before you can pick up the discussions where you left them – this time, with practicality and reason.

But what if the difficult person is already raging with anger, how can you deal with the situation?

Well, there are so many ways you can try to calm the whole situation down;

Keep Your Calm

This is probably a point you will see everywhere in this book – because it is essential and easy to get wrong. If someone sends you an angry text or email or starts shouting at you on the phone, the truth is that it is hard not to get personal. There is a chance that you will get angry, and defensive thoughts will begin to pop into your mind of how wrong you think the other person is. You will start to think about how ungrateful they are for all the hard work you give the company, and before you know it, you are exploding with fury.

The best thing to do is to take in a deep breath. Try to take in what it is that the other person is trying to say. In between those lines, you might note that the other person is in a struggle or is frustrated with the whole process, product or service to the point that they took it out on you or the team. We are all human, and there are times when we are caught in our moments of weakness. If you try to understand this fact, you will not see the reason why you should take their difficulty, comments, or arguments personally or hold it against them.

If the other person is being abusive, rude, or aggressive in their language or intonation, don't tolerate their behavior. If at some point during the conversation, you feel like they are belittling you, simply feel free to escalate the situation to a third-party that can help you resolve without killing the other.

Let us consider an instance where a client calls the support team in your company expressing how upset they are about the delay in the delivery of their products. They may be agitated and are shouting at the top of their lungs on the phone call. This is where your support team or you should remain calm and try to ask the three what's; what is the problem, what are their goals, needs or desires, and what are the available options. If you are the one on the other side of the phone, keep your cool and find out more details about their issue. That alone will work to de-escalate an angry person.

Practice Active Listening

Try as much as you can to focus on what they are saying - rather than the anger behind their words and voice. When your attention is on what they are really saying, you will be better placed to determine what it is that is agitating them. This will also help you resolve the issue rather than trying only to de-escalate it to comfort them. When you know what the problem is, you can find a solution, and you will have a satisfied colleague, friend, or client at the end of the day.

Let us consider an instance where a client walks into your store and tells you that the product you sold them stopped working for them a few days after they bought it. They continue to tell you how surprised and disappointed that you could offer such a poorly designed product.

What will you do? What will your response be like?

Well, the simplest way to go is to pay attention to the words they use – surprised, disappointed. Those are the words they used to express their emotional feelings. The point is that they are not angry but surprised by how your product behaved.

In such an instance, you may be tempted to respond with the words "I understand that you are frustrated…" while that is a response, it is not only going to escalate the other person's feelings but will now make them angry. By saying that, you are only giving them a reason to go from disappointment and surprise to anger.

However, if you demonstrate that you are actively listening to what they have to say, you will calm the situation down. You can say things like "that is certainly surprising and disappointing. Let me take a look to know why the product stopped working unexpectedly." With this response, you are acknowledging the client's feelings without necessarily escalating them.

Repeat Back What Your Customers Say
One of the key components of active listening is ensuring that your client and you are on the same page. Once you know the root cause of their anger, you can simply repeat what you heard from them so that you are sure you understand what is making them angry. In so doing, you are also letting the other person know that you have heard their concerns are and are working on a resolution or response.

Let us consider an instance where someone badges into your office ranting about the product you sold them not working. You can simply start your response with such words as "What am hearing you say is…" this will simply get the ball rolling. Try to highlight how the issue is standing in the way of them achieving their goals. This will show them that you did not just listen but understood their needs and are going to help them.

Thank Them For Bringing the Issue to Your Attention

When the other person you are conversing with is angry and is sending negative vibes about the whole situation, you can thank them for speaking out their concerns. This will go a long way in helping you establish a good rapport with them. With just a simple 'thank you,' acknowledging their time and contributions, you will sufficiently calm the situation down.

One of the best ways you can deal with someone who is continuously difficult and angry is to ensure that you thank them each time. When a difficult member of your team starts an inquiry, simply acknowledge their efforts for reaching out. If you have held onto a case file for extended durations of time, thank your team for being patient while you were troubleshooting. When that difficult person shares their negative views about the project, thank them for being bold enough to share their perspective and making the whole team better.

Explain the Steps You'll Take to Solve the Problem

When that difficult person at your office raises an issue, you must make it clear to them that you will get started on addressing their concerns. It does not matter whether or not it is a simple issue that you can finish up over the phone or something that requires a whole process that might take days, weeks or even months – the trick is for you to plainly spell out your intentions and next moves to them so that they feel valued, heard and at ease.

One of the best ways you can achieve this is if you set timelines for their issue to be sorted out. Spell out every single step you intend to take, and when each one of the steps is expected to be complete. This way, you are communicating to the other person that you know exactly what it is that you are doing and the time when you expect to have a resolution ready.

Set a Time to Follow-up With Them, If Needed

There are instances when a simple phone conversation cannot solve the problems that arise between you and another person. Some will require you to sync up with the manager or fill up a request form for the resolution process to be initiated. If that is the case in your instance, then you will need to explain this to the other person. Try to give them timelines of when you expect to have a response for them.

The benefit of talking directly to the other person is so that your client, coworker, or friend has ample time to calm down. At the same time, this will give you sufficient time to seek guidance and feedback from your superiors on how best to proceed. If at all, you will need to follow up with the other person, explain clearly why that break would greatly benefit them.

For instance, it could be that you will need to speak to the product expert for troubleshooting purposes. The point is that you are as transparent with them as possible. Let them stay aware that they cannot take any further action, at least until you can seek clarification with those concerned as well.

If they keep being uneasy about what you propose to them, you can also choose to offer them a contingency plan. Tell them exactly when they expect you to reach out to them and the kind of information you will have for them. This will justify the follow up you will be taking up with them.

Be Sincere
The same way remaining calm when dealing with a difficult person is essential, so is sincerity. Trust me, people know when they are being spoken to in a somewhat condescending way or even an angry manner. Choose the right set of words to use and the intonation to employ when communicating with a difficult person. Ensure that your tonal voice is not only intentional but also respectful. No one likes being talked to with an angry tone. Simply take the high road and make the other person feel like what they are saying is being taken seriously.

There are times when that difficult person in your office will call you at midnight with an "issue," but then after reading through or troubleshooting, you realize that it was an error on their part. You may be tempted to poke fun on the other person who did not pay attention enough to pick the error out, costing you your good night's sleep.

What you need to understand is that this other person could very well be you. It is through them that you know whether the services you render are quality enough or not. Even though they may be at fault, it is their contribution that makes the whole product quality. Therefore, ensure that you are politely explaining the reason why an issue arose in the first place and the best ways to prevent them from happening in the future again.

Highlight the Case's Priority

One of the common frustrations for people who conflict is feeling like their support case is not as crucial to the business as the other person's. This is especially the case when dealing with a company or a situation that has a broader client coverage. The other person might feel as though their case is expendable while the rest of the team is busy providing poor experiences.

To get this feeling out of the way, you must highlight how critical the situation is to everyone involved - whether directly or indirectly. Let the other person know that you are putting in efforts to notify essential stakeholders in the company so that the issue they are concerned about is solved as fast as possible. This way, they will feel as though the whole company is on their case even if it's only one support team that is working on it.

One Last Word

Indeed, dealing with difficult people is one of the toughest tasks in life. They are the kind of people who will ruin your perfect day before it can even begin. It could be a colleague, family member, partner, or friend. It could also be anyone random you run into at the street. Whoever that may be, the trick is to ensure that you have armed yourself with the above methods, steps, and approaches to deal with them appropriately.

Realize that difficult people exist all around us, and if you don't do something about them, then you risk letting them hurt others.

The truth is that there is no easy way to deal with these people – after all, they are different combinations of personality traits. They all have different ways to make others' life difficult.

As the saying goes, "It takes two to tango." Realize that these difficult people may not even notice that they are difficult. To most of them, this is their usual way of life. In fact, to a difficult person, everyone else around them is difficult. They don't have your perspective of things.

So, have you been continually dealing with difficult people yourself? If so, it might be time for you to take a look at your behavior. Ask yourself whether you are the one being difficult. Look for such indicators as;

- Lack of close connections at home, school or the workplace
- You lack a sense of self-worth in what you do
- You find yourself being misunderstood too often or complaining about this or that
- You always think that people are talking ill of you
- You still are an emotional person
- You feel like people don't even care or remember you

You might just be the difficult person we have been discussing here. If that is the case, then it is high time you use the strategies above to deal with your behavior. If these traits are what you see in someone around

358

you, then you can also use the techniques we have discussed to help them become a better person.

Remember, a little self-reflection goes a long way in helping us be a better person to the people working and interacting with us daily.

You can help yourself and the difficult person around you to see what they are doing so that they can change for the long-term.

It is a win for all of us!

So, what are you waiting for? Start identifying them around you and help them BECOME!

© **Written by:** Katerina Griffith

Milton Keynes UK
Ingram Content Group UK Ltd.
UKHW051031160823
426904UK00024B/824